THE PREPPER'S CANNING & PRESERVING BIBLE

7 in 1. The Ultimate Guide to Water Bath & Pressure Canning, Dehydrating, Fermenting, Freezing, and Pickling to Stockpiling Food. Prepare for The Worst!

Jonathan Henry

ISBN: 979-8848034622

10 9 8 7 6 5 4 3 2 1

The **PREPPERS' PANTRY** SERIE
by Jonathan Henry

THIS BOOK INCLUDES A
FREE BONUS

**SURVIVAL FOOD
TO STOCKPILE**

BUILD YOUR PERFECT PANTRY
TO SURVIVE 365 DAYS
WITHOUT A SUPER MARKET

**MEDICAL HERBALISM
FOR BEGINNERS**

101 EASY HOME REMEDIES
WITH HERBS FOR COMMON
AILMENTS AND PAINS

The **"Survival food to stockpile"** is **100% free**, with no strings attached.
You don't need to enter any details except your name and email address.

TO DOWNLOAD THE BONUS SCAN THE QR CODE BELOW OR GO TO

https://jonathanhenry.me/bonus-pc

3

Table of Contents

Book 1

THE PREPPER'S WATER SURVIVAL GUIDE

The Ultimate Guide to Life-Saving Techniques for Surviving in Any Emergency. Learn How to Find, Collect, Purify, Filter, and Store Water for Off-Grid Survival

Jonathan Henry

Introduction

Water and food are two of the basic needs of all human beings. Have you ever been in a situation when you have been unable to get one of these essential things? How did it feel? For instance, have you tried holding your breath for a minute or so? It's not a good feeling. Think of a situation when you were thirsty or even dehydrated. Would you be capable of surviving without a plan? Probably not. Planning and preparing are vital. This book will lead you through everything you need to do to guarantee you have all the emergency supplies you need.

Natural calamities like earthquakes, volcanic eruptions, landslides, flash floods, severe storms, hurricanes, and power shortages are only some of the possible emergencies we may encounter at any time. Imagine the authorities telling you that you need to evacuate in ten minutes. Picture what would happen if the stores were all closed because of the difficult situation in your community, and there was no way for you to get food or water for your family. What would you do? Would you be able to gather enough resources to help you and your entire family during these emergencies?

Most of us seem to prepare for emergencies only when it is time to face one. We never recognize the importance of being prepared at all times. Being adequately prepared will make it easier for you to react quickly and do the necessary things to keep your family safe in an emergency.

This book will provide essential tips on how to store food and water to prepare for future emergencies. Continue reading this book to learn everything you need to do!

Alternative Methods to Locate and Collect Water To Survive

Water is one of the fundamental items required for survival. Man can survive without food for almost 3 weeks (nearly 21 days) but cannot go without water for up to 7 days. During an emergency period, there is a possibility that there will be a shortage of water supply. That is why there is a need to provide water storage in an emergency; this will help you survive until help comes your way.

The first step toward water storage is to source the water. Whether you are dealing with an emergency at home or a survival situation out in the desert, there are many ways to source water for storage. These are some of the common means to source water:

1. Rain Water

This is the most accessible source of water during an emergency. You can get as much water as you want from this source, especially during the rainy season. All you need do is to get containers and probably improvise a large surface for collecting water (the roof of a house, a large polythene paper r sheet metal is sufficient for this) very fast. All you have to do is to fold the polythene paper or sheet metal on the ends to make it easy to collect all the water and direct it towards one direction, i.e., where you've placed the collection/storage containers. The only disadvantage of rainwater is that it is usually contaminated by dust, bird droppings and radioactive remains in the air. Therefore, there is always a need to decontaminate the water before drinking or using it for any other household chores.

2. Hot Water

This is another source of water for home emergencies. Hot water can be gotten from the water heater in your home. You may not be able to depend on this water source for long since the supply is limited, meaning you may have to look for other alternative sources.

3. Tap Water

You can also source water for storage from your tap water. Like rainwater, you will need to decontaminate your tap water before use. This is because tap water often contains many chemicals and contaminants such as atrazine, chromium, fluoride, radon, hexavalent, and many more. when taken into the body,these chemicals can lead to health complications. That is why there is a need to purify the water before storage.

The three sources of water mentioned above are for home emergencies (except rain water- it rains in the wild too!). From this point, I will discuss other water sources if you are outside your home. For instance, if you are lost in a desert or a bush, you can source water from these means until help comes your way.

4. River Water

The first is to look for a river or stream. But how do you know there is a stream nearby when you cannot see one? Well, there are several signs of a stream/river nearby.

- You may hear the sound of rushing waters- simply stand still in the open space (where you won't hear anything else except birds chirping), then listen keenly. You should be able to hear a stream of water from a mile away.

- If there is water nearby, the temperature of the location will be cooler than that of other places.
- Also, you can be on the lookout for croaking frogs- especially in the evening or at night. Frogs are known to live on riverbanks or streambeds.
- You can also follow animal tracks to lead you to a nearby stream or any other source of water.
- Finally, look out for mosquitoes because the mosquito is one insect known to live in puddles of water.

If you cannot find a stream or find mosquitoes or hear frogs croaking only to discover that the river has no flowing water, you can dig up.

5. Dig Up Water

If you find that the riverbed has dried up or there is no flowing water, don't be discouraged. You can still get some water from the surface of the dry riverbed. So how do you go about it?

How To Dig Up Water
- Locate the lowest point of the streambed or outside edges of the bend of the stream because this is the deepest part of the stream and usually the last to dry up.
- Use a shovel or hoe to dig some inches into the ground. You are probably going to see some muddy water. Scoop out the mud and continue to dig into the hole until you notice a trickle of clean water.
- Allow the trickle to fill up the hole you dug, then scoop as much as you want with a bowl and transfer into a bigger container.

But if you cannot find a nearby stream with water or that's drying up, don't give up still; you can collect enough water to drink from dew! All you have to do is wake up early before it dries up!

6. Collect Dew Drops

Another way to source water in the wild is to collect dewdrops. If you are in a location with many trees, you can keep containers under the trees to collect dewdrops at night. The dew always condenses in the morning to form water droplets. But how do you collect dew drops?

How To Collect Dew Drops As Water:
- To set up a dew collector, you need three long sticks, two short sticks, a large nylon cloth, and a gallon to collect the water. Dig a little hole in the ground and drive the three long sticks as wide as your nylon cloth can allow. Drive the two short sticks in front. Tie the sticks to the cloth in such a way that the drops slide towards the two smaller sticks into the container.
- Keep a container in front of the smaller sticks, then keep the collector outside at night. A small dew collector can gather as much as 3 litres of water overnight.

After you have sourced a sufficient amount of water, the next step is to purify the water to make it ready for storage.

Methods Of Purifying Water

1. Filtering Water

One of the methods for water purification is filtration. It is the simplest of all. It helps to remove large particles and dirt from water. Some filters can also filter out bacteria and viruses from water.

2. Filter Water: How, Why, and What

From a survey, it has been proved that clean drinking water is one of the most important things needed when outdoors. Therefore, survivalists suggest that water filters are important to keep with you. They don't need to be expensive. A mini, portable, cheap filter could do the job and get you going.

There are a lot of different filters available for purification, depending on the quantity of water you want to filter and what you want to be filtered. There are a lot of unwanted things in water from water bodies. These include viruses, bacteria, dirt, and other unwanted particles. Therefore we need water filters to have clean drinking water at all times.

Another reason we need water filters is that half of the countries in the world face the problem of water shortage. More so, the shortage of clean drinking water. It is affecting the hygiene of the people. It is causing various diseases. Therefore, it is important to develop ways to provide clean drinking water to these communities. Filtering water is one of the ways. Most industries and companies are working on it and trying to develop something cheaper, effective, and feasible for all to solve the problem.

3. Why You Need to Use Water Filters

With the rapid increase of population and development of industrialization, environmental problems such as pollution and global warming have increased greatly. It has affected our water resources as they become more polluted day by day. Also, natural sources of water such as rain are being affected. Thus clean drinking water is becoming scarce day by day. The level of underground water is decreasing, and even the developed nations face the problem of water shortage. Also, in emergencies such as floods or war, the water sources are immediately cut down; thus, access to clean drinking water in such circumstances becomes limited. Therefore, we might have to use water that is not clean and purified, which may cause problems such as diarrhea, skin diseases, and stomach diseases. So to purify it, we might need to filter it ourselves. For this purpose, we need water filters. They are readily available, cost-effective, and extremely easy to use. A layman can also use them easily. A simple filter such as a sawyer filter or the life straw costs about $20.

The DIY Alternative

It is a do-it-yourself water filter. It is a technique mostly taught to scouts. It is not as effective as the other filters but can come in handy. For this, you need a filter and some activated carbon. These are some simple steps that you can take to make a water filter by yourself.

- Arrange a nail, a water bottle, a paper filter or cloth, a paper clip, and some activated carbon.
- Take the nail, heat it on a flame and make some holes in the water bottle but not too many. If there are many holes, the filtration will be less.

- Add the activated carbon to the bottle. Don't fill the bottle.
- Now take the paper filter or cloth and fold it into a cone shape. You can use the paper clip to fix the end.
- Now pass the water through this cone. It will filter out the dirt and particles from the filter.
- The water will then pass through the activated carbon, which will filter the rest.
- You will get clean filtered water from the holes in the bottle.

The process is quite slow. You can speed it up by blowing into the water. It will create pressure, and the water will move fast.

4. Other Purification Methods

There are a lot of ways of purifying water other than filtering. They are also quite easy to use. A method depends on the type of water you are purifying. These methods help kill microorganisms while others remove large particles such as dirt. Let us have a look at some of these methods.

1.1.1 Boiling

This is a technique that most people know, but sometimes some of the most straightforward techniques are the best! To purify the water, you can boil it, but boiling water will not filter anything out of it, so make sure to pass the water through some straining material before boiling it (using a clean cloth or a coffee filter, etc.).

Follow these steps to boil water to kill bacteria and other nasty stuff (such as pathogenic bacteria and viruses):

1. As mentioned before, the first essential step is to filter the water through some material. You could use some clean cloth, a coffee filter, or even a specific paper boiling water towel. This step is crucial if the water is visually cloudy or has sediment floating. Let the water settle so the sediment collects, then pass it through the filter slowly into another container.

2. Once filtered, put the water over high heat and bring it to a boil. The water should remain on a rolling boil for at least a minute. If you're at a higher altitude (above 5000 feet or 1000 meters), boil the water for at least 3 minutes. Some experts recommend keeping the water boiling for at least 20 minutes to be safe.

3. Once boiled, remove the water from the heat and leave it to cool naturally.

4. Once completely cooled, store the water in clean containers (preferably ones that can be covered).

5. EXTRA: If you want to improve the taste of the water, add a little slat! Add a pinch of salt to each quart and pour the water from one container to another to help mix the salt into the liquid.

1.1.2 Bleach

If you don't have access to a reliable heat source or any energy source whatsoever, one alternative is to use some household bleach. Bleach is a simple solution, but it's not the best one if you need water quickly, as the bleach needs to be left to treat the water for an extended period, a minimum of 30 minutes (some sources recommend at least a few hours). It's also not the best solution regarding taste unless you like water that tastes a little like chlorine.

NOTE: You need to ensure that the bleach you use for this is a regular unscented bleach product that includes chlorine. Suppose bleach is suitable for sanitation or disinfection. It should be indicated on the label of the product. DO NOT use bleach that is color safe, scented or bleach products with added cleaners.

To disinfect water using bleach, follow these steps!

1. You first need to filter the water through straining material, cheesecloth, coffee filters, paper towels, etc.

2. Make sure you have a sterilized (or at least clean) dropper you can use to put the bleach into the liquid.

3. Make sure the bleach you want to use to purify the water is liquid chlorine bleach that is less than a year old and has been stored at room temperature.

4. The amount of bleach you should add depends on how much water you want to disinfect and the strength of your bleach (6% or 8.25% of sodium hypochlorite). See the table below at the end of these steps for the amounts of bleach you need to add.

5. *Double the amount of bleach you add if your water is cloudy (even after being filtered), colored, or extremely cold.*

6. Stir the water and allow it to sit for a minimum of 30 minutes. The odor of the water should be slightly like chlorine. If this odor is not present, repeat the exact dosage and let it stand another 15 minutes before consumption.

7. If the chlorine taste is too much, pour the water from one container to another and leave it to stand for a few hours before consumption.

Water Volume	How Much Bleach to Add: *6% Bleach*	How Much Bleach to Add: *8.25% Bleach*
1 quart	2 drops	2 drops
1 gallon	8 drops	6 drops
2 gallons	16 drops/ ¼ tsp	12 drops (⅛ tsp)
4 gallons	⅓ tsp	¼ tsp
8 gallons	⅔ tsp	½ tsp

1.1.3 Solar Stills

A solar still is a device that distills water using heat from the sun and evaporation. Solar stills are an excellent solution for water purification in tropical and poverty-stricken countries, as they're an easy contraption to put together with limited materials. Therefore, they're perfect for a makeshift purification system if you're prepping in a hot place and have several hours to spare.

There are many benefits to solar stills - their simplistic design and straightforward installation are a few. But actually, the best advantage is the fact that the water collected via this method will be immediately safe to drink, without any further treatment, and will taste a lot better than water that has been boiled or had chlorine bleach added to it. When you boil water, it often has a "flatter" taste, and the reason for this is that boiling brings down the PH level of the water, which changes the flavor. Water collected in a solar still will have a more balanced PH level and should taste a little more similar to tap water or even commercial water.

The only downside to solar is the time it takes to set it up and collect the water. But if you pre-plan and set up the still when you know your water supplies are nearly used up, you'll be fine.

If you don't want to waste time making your own and still have access to online shopping resources, you can easily purchase your solar still on amazon. Some types of solar stills you can buy are designed to be used on bodies of water, so they are inflatable. If you're living near a body of water, this is a convenient choice, as these solar stills can easily be deflated and transported from one place to another. The one by Aquamate is a popular choice and can yield between 0.5 and 2 liters of drinkable water per day. It can be purchased on Amazon for around $200.

If you want to make your own solar still, which is much cheaper and easier than you may imagine it to be, you'll need the following items:

- A container – Preferably one with a wide opening that will be able to catch droplets (a small cooking pot or plastic washing basin would work well. This container will be sat at the bottom of your solar still, so if you're making a smaller sized one, then a cup or a plastic bottle with the top cut off would also work well)
- Several stones or rocks
- A 6 by 6 ft sheet of clear plastic or tarp if you're making smaller solar, this sheet can be smaller as long as it can cover the entire top of the hole.
- Some leaves from plants (Any vegetation will suffice).
- A plastic tube (If you want to reuse the solar still).
- Shovel
- Tape (Optional but makes life a little easier).

Follow these steps to make your own make-shift solar still:

1. Dig a hole that is around 4 ft wide and 3 ft deep (the size can vary, but this is the size we recommend)

2. Dig a second hole in the center of your hole to hold the container and position the container in it.

3. If you're using some plastic tubing (if you want to reuse the solar still, this tubing will act as a straw so you can access the water without removing the sheet), put one end of the tube in the container and run the other to the outside of the hole.

4. If you have access to some vegetation, position some leaves inside the pit around the container (being careful not to obstruct it). Doing this will encourage more moisture to collect and help the distillation process.

5. Cover the entire hole with the plastic sheet or tarp, ensuring that the sheet doesn't drop onto the pit floor. Secure the position of the sheet using rocks and some tape if available (and depending on the terrain).

6. Once the sheet is anchored, put a small rock directly in the center of the sheet on top to be just over where the container is located. This rock should be heavy enough that the sides of the sheet/tarp are pushed down to a 45-degree angle.

7. Secure the edges of the sheet/tape more with rocks and dirt once the sheet is in the correct position - it should be secured enough that moisture won't be able to escape out of the sides.

8. Tying the end of your plastic tubing if you're using it so moisture can't get out of it.

9. To get the most out of your solar, wait at least 12 hours. The longer, the better. It will be far more effective if you leave your solar overnight, as much condensation can be collected from morning dew.

10. Before collecting the water (via the "straw" tubing or opening up the solar still), make sure to gently tap around the sloping edges of the tarp/sheet to encourage all the liquid collected there to trickle down to the container in the middle.

11. As the water has undergone a natural purification process, the water is ready and safe to be consumed immediately. Ensure that no loose sediment from the dirt has gotten into the water. If it has, simply filter the water with some cloth or a coffee filter before consumption.

Note: If you make a solar still without vegetation, it will collect between a few hundred ml to 1 liter of water within 24 hours. Of course, the amount of water collected depends on the weather conditions, the still's size, and how moist the soil is. If you want to maximize the water collected, add a lot of vegetation and create a larger still.

1.1.4 *Granular Calcium Hypochlorite*

If you don't have access to bleach, it is possible to make a DIY chlorine solution to disinfect your water using granular calcium hypochlorite (HTH). To protect yourself, make sure to make this solution in a well-ventilated area while wearing eye protection.

To make the solution, follow these steps:

1. NOTE: Granular calcium hypochlorite is a powerful oxidant, so it must be handled and stored with care.

2. To make the chlorine solution add a heaped teaspoon or ¼ an ounce of high-test granular calcium hypochlorite for every 2 gallons of water and stir until the particles have completely dissolved.

3. This will give you a chlorine solution that contains around 500 milligrams per liter.

4. To disinfect your water, add one part of your previously-made chlorine solution to every 100 parts of the water you're disinfecting, around 1 pint of chlorine solution to every 12.5 gallons of water. This will require a little bit of calculation but will be worth it.

5. If the water tastes too much like chlorine, carefully pour it into another clean container and let it stand for a few hours before consuming it.

1.1.5 Household Iodine/Tincture of Iodine

If you happen to have a tincture of iodine lying around in your medical cabinet or even stored in your first aid kit, you can use this to purify water. This method is pretty simple.

1. Add five drops of 2% tincture of iodine to every quart/liter of water you're disinfecting.

2. If the water is quite cloudy or colored, it's recommended to add about ten drops per quart/liter.

3. Stir the water well and let it stand for 30 minutes before consumption.

1.1.6 Charcoal

This is a purification AND filtering method that many preppers swear by. Some even call it the best method after boiling! Given that you can buy a water thermos that has built-in charcoal filters, it's no surprise that this method is a well-loved one.

The method we're going to discuss here is a bit of a 2-in-1 filter and purification method (A.K.A. a purification filter).

To follow this method, you need the following: an empty plastic bottle, a canteen, a knife, some pebbles, some sand, charcoal, and a container to hold the purified water (a cup or mug would do the job), some clean cloth or bandaging.

1. Using the knife, cut off the bottom of your plastic bottle.

2. Holding the bottle upside down (with the cap at the bottom) and keeping the cap of your bottle sealed, put a layer of cloth at the bottom and top it with a couple of pebbles and use the end of your knife to stuff the pebbles down as much as you can.

3. Add a layer of sand on top of your pebbles and use the end of your knife again to flatten the sand down into a clean layer.

4. Lay your piece of cloth/bandage over the sand.

5. Throw in your charcoal on top of the cloth layer; you may have to crush it to make it fit.

6. Add another layer of cloth on top of the charcoal.

7. Add another sand layer and top that with pebbles.

8. There isn't much importance in the order of layers, so if you have a big enough bottle, you could even add another layer of charcoal somewhere within the layers.

9. Remove the cap from the bottle. The cloth you put in the beginning should prevent anything from falling out.

10. Put your bottle into a cup or mug facing the cap end.

11. Slowly pour the water you wish to filter through the cut-off end and let it trickle into the mug/cup at the bottom.

12. Make sure to do it bit-by-bit to ensure the layers have enough time to filter the water properly.

13. It's recommended to filter the water at least twice to ensure sufficiently purified.

Get Ready to Build Your Water Supply

It's time we start building the water supply, one that corresponds with the number of members that will be sheltered whilst things improve outside. The idea is that you do the calculations well so that there is no shortage, so be accurate when calculating your needs.

5. How Much Water Do You Need to Store?

For a temporary emergency, you should have at least a 3-day supply of water: Plan to have at least 1 gallon of water per person per day for drinking and sanitation, although those of us who are preppers should have water for even more time.

If possible, try to provide a 2-week supply of water for problems like a major earthquake or other tragedies that could affect supplies for this period.

It is also essential to store more water for pregnant women and the sick as well for when it's hot.

If you use store-bought water, be aware of the expiration date. This is because the packaging it comes in, especially the thin plastics in disposable bottles, can start to leak unhealthy chemicals. But generally, still, water is safe for up to 2 years and sparkling water for 1 year.

Replace non-store-bought water every 6 months.

Prepare a bottle of odorless liquid household chlorine bleach (labeled to contain 5–9% sodium hypochlorite) for water disinfection, general cleaning and disinfection, if needed.

The amount of water necessary to maintain life and health in an emergency varies with the type of disaster, the climate and the general health of household members. Of equal importance is to decide how much water is required by the bunker members based on the amount of water they used to use before a disaster.

Poor rural communities may have much lower expectations about the amount of water they need to live than people living in wealthier urban areas. Therefore, consumption is generally lower in poorer neighborhoods.

How much water do people actually need? People use water for a wide variety of activities. Some of them are more important than others. For example, drinking enough water in a day is more important than having water for personal hygiene or laundry. However, these are still necessary to perform to prevent skin diseases.

Women and men differ greatly in their use of water. Women are generally concerned about the essential use of domestic water and water for personal hygiene during menstruation. In contrast, men may be concerned with the availability of water to drink and for animals that provide food. In the assessment, waste and water loss are taken into account.

In emergencies, as the demand for water increases, the quality can be reduced in accordance with its purpose. Water used to clean floors does not have to be of the same quality as drinking water; water used for subsistence farming may be of lower quality.

The type of sanitation (excreta disposal) will always greatly impact water demand. Sanitary systems with hydraulic flushes, such as toilets, require large amounts of water (up to 7 liters per person, per use). Much lower water requirements are needed for simple flush toilets.

Water is essential for many other humanitarian services provided in emergencies, such as that of health, food, and education. The affected communities also require water for agricultural, commercial, and/or religious activities. The user, not the provider, ultimately decides how to use scarce water resources in an emergency. If people think their livestock is more important than laundry, they will allocate water based on their personal priorities. You must ensure that there is enough water to meet people's needs and priorities and enough water to meet priorities related to effective emergency management.

After a catastrophe happens and if you don't have water at home, you must ensure that you have access to water suitable for your purpose.

Remember this information to decide how much water to store for use in an emergency.

- Enough quantity is at least 1 gallon of water per person for each day, half of which is for drinking, the other half for cooking and general cleaning.
- The amount will vary according to age, activity, physical condition, and diet.
- In case of heat, you need more water—double the usual amount if the heat is very intense.
- People with medical conditions, nursing mothers and children will need more water.
- An additional amount of water must be kept available for medical emergencies.

There are many ways to make sure your emergency water supply stays fresh:

- If you buy bottled water, you have to keep it sealed and replace it after 2 years.
- Purchase a food and water storage container at a camping supply store, clean and rinse well, and then fill with water following the manufacturer's instructions.
- Proceed to store the water in dry and fresh environments. If you are not using commercial water, you should replace it every 6 months.

6. Build Your Own Water Container

Household containers and water storage containers can be made from different materials, such as plastic, metal, and ceramic. They can be new and/or the same material that will serve you in an emergency. Homes/households must have a sufficient number of containers to meet the quality requirements for adequate storage and supply of water.

In emergencies, people need containers; households should buy these directly from local markets and use them to keep water safe.

Find plastic containers that you can use to store the water, but when you have them, you have to put them through a process:

Cleaning

Since the purpose of storing water in the home is to ensure its quality and purity, the handling and use of containers require care. The household members must keep the water stored in these containers clean and drinkable.

Before using a water storage container, all types of containers must be cleaned and disinfected regardless of the material, origin, state (new/used), type, or shape. To clean the container, use a mixture of detergent and hot water (laundry soap) to scrub and clean all its internal surfaces.

For this task, the container has a wide mouth to facilitate this cleaning. This can be done with a stiff brush or a high-pressure water jet. After cleaning, rinse the container thoroughly with water, removing all water and detergent used in the cleaning process.

Disinfection

After the initial cleaning of the container, it must be disinfected with a bleach solution. The amount of chlorine used to sanitize a container will depend on the concentration of chlorine used and the capacity of the container (liters per gallon). Fill the container with the prepared bleach solution, let it sit for 24 hours, and then rinse the container well before use.

Characteristics of the Container and Basic Recommendations

- The container should preferably have a lid and a wide mouth to facilitate cleaning and filling.
- Water storage containers must be covered at all times.
- If the container doesn't have a tap, use a clean spoon or cup to remove the water.
- Position containers in a cool place and, if possible high up, away from animals and rubbish.
- Clean water storage containers periodically with water and chlorine.

The Process to Disinfect Water in Containers

While it is recommended that water distributed to households in an emergency be chlorinated, a variety of situations can occur where each household is advised to disinfect the water they receive.

For small capacity domestic tanks, disinfect with 15 drops of sodium hypochlorite in 1 liter of water.

Preparation of the Chlorine Solution

- When using calcium hypochlorite, in a 20-liter container (5-gallon bucket), place 1 tsp of bleach powder, mix well and let stand for 10 minutes before applying. Solutions prepared in this way will produce concentrations of 150–200 mg/l (ppm).
- When using 5.25% sodium hypochlorite, dissolve 15 drops of chlorine in 1 liter of water. It is mainly used in the case of residential deposits. Apply the solution inside the container, let it sit for 5 minutes, and then rinse with clean water. Also, disinfect the inside of the lid.

For this task, it will be easier if the container has a wide mouth for cleaning.

The tank must be clearly labeled as a potable water reservoir to avoid contamination or confusion with other types of tanks.

The lid must remain closed and inaccessible to people not involved in your operation.

7. When You Need to Rotate Your Water Stocks

Most commercial bottled water has an expiration date. However, the shelf life should be around 2 years. The tap water comes from a municipal water source and needs to be stored in plastic containers that must be changed every 6 months so that it will last for a long time after the catastrophe happens.

Storage Containers

The storage container is one factor in determining the amount of time the stored water will remain in good condition. Food-grade plastic containers or specially designed packages are useful for water storage. Most containers will have "HDPE" or "PP" printed somewhere on the outside or a recycling triangle labeled "1" or "2" inside. But not all "HDPE" with a triangle "2" is food-grade, so it's best to use a container that has previously held water or food, such as a soda bottle, milk bottle, or specially designed container to contain water. Ideally, a 2-liter soda bottle will hold more water and is safer than a reusable milk bottle, as the plastic in a milk bottle degrades over time, mixing the plastic with the water.

Chlorine Must Be Used

If you fill a bottle with municipal water, it usually has enough chlorine to keep it safe for 6 months or more. If you are actually filling bottles with water from a well, add 1 or 2 drops of unscented, regular bleach to each bottle.

Storage

Storing water at temperatures between 35 and 50°F (1.67 and 10°C) will extend its shelf life, while freezing will help keep it almost indefinitely. Be sure to leave about 2-inch (5 cm) of space at the top of the bottle because the water expands as it freezes. Even if the water is stored longer than recommended, it is safer when it is kept out of direct sunlight to prevent algae growth, resulting in water not fit for consumption.

8. Different Ways to Preserve Water

You can store water using different methods and techniques, but the important thing is that you have it in suitable containers; it can even be in a tank that you have at home. Although if it is made of concrete and a catastrophe such as an earthquake occurs, it could break and empty. Plastic tanks can be easily maintained, and you can also move them.

You can also store water in a glass, fiberglass, or plastic containers.

Never use metal containers because these can corrode very quickly. If you leave it uncovered, you invite a fungus, and they can multiply, and the mosquitoes will set up a home there and lay their larvae, and you'll lose all that water, or you'll become sick if you inadvertently consume it.

9. Clean and Prepare Your Storage Container

The water you have stored must be subjected to disinfection and avoid the appearance of bacteria that can cause diseases. It can be done in just 6 steps.

14. Start by closing the tank's water inlet valve. Then, close the valve of the inner distribution tube and open the wash or drain valve to get about 15 cm of water at the bottom. Do not shake this stand or the dirt it contains.

15. Clean the bottom, walls, and top of the tank with the help of a plastic brush or broom. Use only water, never metal brushes, detergents, soap, or cleaning powders. Although before use, rinse them carefully.

16. Empty the tank and rinse several times. Eliminate waste through the drain valve, never through the distribution pipe.

17. Fill the tank halfway with water. Add 1 liter of concentrated chlorine for every 1,000 liters of water.

18. When the tank is completely full, let it sit for at least 1 hour. Drain the water through the distribution pipe and open all the faucets in the house. Fill and empty the tank again until the excess chlorine is removed.

19. Fill the tank and it is ready for use.

How To Test Water Pollution-Home Made Methods

1. The Most Effective Ways to Check Colors and Odors in Your Water

The color is one of the sensory parameters that indicate the quality of drinking water for people and is related to the dissolved substances and suspended particles within it. Color measurement is important for understanding the amount of natural organic matter in water, as its presence is a risk factor for the production of harmful by-products of water disinfection, such as trihalomethanes.

So, the color, the turbidity, the smell and the taste are characteristics that show the quality of the water. Therefore, color is one of the sensory parameters, which establishes a healthy standard for water quality for human consumption and is mandatory in the analysis, control, running, and complete assessment of drinking water.

The color of the water is because of the presence of dissolved or suspended natural organic matter such as certain metals like iron, manganese, or copper.

It is essential to distinguish between dissolved substances and suspended particles, as this affects the "true color" and "apparent color" values of the water. The correct color is only determined by the color of the water and the substances dissolved in it, while the apparent color also includes the suspended particles. The latter is what causes the turbidity of the water.

Water turbidity is often a major interfering factor in color measurements of the water and should be eliminated as it can affect measurement accuracy and/or cause light scattering and increase values of apparent color. The sample must be centrifuged to remove suspended particles to eliminate this interference.

Thus, the apparent color will be the sample's color, while the proper color will be the sample' once filtered or centrifuged, leaving only the dissolved material.

It should also be noted that watercolor formation includes, among other factors, pH, temperature, available substances and solubility of coloring compounds.

Organic Matter and By-Products to Disinfect

Humic substance accounts for 50–75% of the dissolved organic carbon in surface waters and provides color to the water. Most of them are fulvic acid and humic acid, which are harmless to the human body under natural conditions. But these substances undergo chemical changes during the oxidation and disinfection of water with chlorine, forming potentially health-threatening byproducts such as chloroform, dibromochloromethane, bromoform, and bromodichloromethane, collectively known as trihalomethanes.

In this sense, the color measurement of the water will provide you with valuable information since it allows you to evaluate and manage the presence of said humic and fulvic acids, which are the main precursors of the formation of disinfection by-products (DBP) in chlorinated water.

To eliminate the presence of this organic matter during the disinfection stage and, thus, limit the risk of disinfection by-products, I recommend some additional treatment before chlorination to reduce the presence of humic substances in the water. For example, it can be treated with activated carbon, ozone, UV radiation, or by being treated with chlorine oxide.

How Is the Color of Water Measured?

The maximum value of the parameter for watercolor for human consumption has been determined to be 15 mg/l Pt/Co (platinum cobalt), but how is the color of water measured?

There are 2 ways to determine watercolor: visual comparison and spectrophotometry.

The first is based on comparing the sample with a colored solution or a previously calibrated colored glass disc. You visually compare the color of the water with a series of color standards that simulate—in units of measurement—the color produced by the addition of 1 ppm of platinum (in the form of chloroplatinate) to a certain amount of cobalt, which is used to match the color of colored water. Results are expressed in platinum cobalt units (PCU).

In the second case, the color is determined using a spectrophotometer, an instrument capable of projecting a light beam of a single wavelength or multiple specific wavelengths through a sample and measuring the amount of light absorbed or transmitted through the sample. Compare the results obtained with the established standard colors.

2. What Water-Related Diseases Lurk in Your Well

Now we will discuss the diseases you can get if you drink contaminated well water.

Hepatitis A

It is a liver disease that is very contagious, and although it may not be dangerous, it could be fatal if it progresses. Hepatitis A is spread through feces and by drinking contaminated water and microbes from the gut.

The main symptoms are pale stools, dark urine, yellowing of the skin and whites of the eyes, chills, fever, weakness, nausea, fatigue and loss of appetite.

Giardiasis

It is an infection of the digestive system that is caused by the parasite *Giardia intestinalis*. It is transmitted when you consume food or water contaminated with feces that have parasite cysts; it is also an infectious disease.

The symptoms are abdominal pain, fever, diarrhea, weakness, nausea and weight loss.

Amebiasis or Amoebic Dysentery

Amebiasis, or amoebic dysentery, is an infection caused by the protozoan *Entamoeba histolytica*, which settles in the intestine and prevents the body from absorbing vital nutrients. It is transmitted by ingesting food or water contaminated with feces containing mature amoebic cysts.

The symptoms usually include abdominal pain, diarrhea, fever, and chills. Sometimes the stool may contain blood, mucus, or pus. In more severe cases, the disease becomes aggressive when other organs such as the liver, respiratory tract, and even the brain become infected.

Typhoid Fever

It is an infectious disease that is caused by *Salmonella typhi* and is transmitted when you ingest water or food contaminated by the parasite.

The symptoms are vomiting, high fever, constipation, abdominal pain, headache, diarrhea, weight loss, skin rash, or loss of appetite.

Cholera

The digestive system is greatly affected by cholera, specifically the intestines. It is caused by bacteria that may be present in contaminated food or water, producing toxins that cause the symptoms of the disease.

Its main symptoms are severe diarrhea and vomiting—which can lead to severe dehydration.

Ascariasis or Ascaris Lumbricoides

It is mainly caused by the parasite *Ascaris Lumbricoides*, which lives, develops, and reproduces in the intestine. The disease is spread by ingesting water or food contaminated with parasite eggs.

Its major symptoms are abdominal pain, dizziness, or difficulty in evacuating;

Treatment: This is done by using antiparasitic drugs such as albendazole.

Leptospirosis

The origin of this disease is the bacteria that live in the rat's urine or other infected animals such as dogs and cats in sewers. The bacterium enters the human body through wounds in the skin or through body mucous membranes such as the eyes, nose, saliva, etc., that come into contact with contaminated water.

Its main symptoms are headache, high fever, vomiting, loss of appetite, chills, or diarrhea.

Contaminated sewerage, or poor sewage treatment, affects the entire population, especially sensitive children between 1 and 6 years of age and also increases the chances of stillbirth in pregnant women.

Common Problems and How To Solve Them

1. Not Considering the Materials

The wrong material could mean contamination or leakage, and neither does anyone good. You must have the right material to store your water based on your needs and location. Not all materials are created the same.

There are several materials that could be considered for your water storage. Plastics are often the first choice because the containers are lighter to carry. But plastics can be dangerous if they are not the right kind- you can't just grab the first thing you find and fill it with water and hope for the best.

For instance, milk jugs are almost impossible to clean out and can be contaminated with milk proteins even after they have been rinsed countless times.

Other materials can break on the road or break because of temperature changes. Some can be too heavy to carry on long journeys. You must know your materials to make the safest choice for your water storage.

Plastics

All plastics for food and water must be listed as food grade safe. Look on the bottom or the side of the container. You will see a triangle of arrows indicating that it is or could be recycled. Inside the triangle will be a number- for the container to be considered safe for food or water, it should have a number between one and seven.

The best plastic container will be the number two container which is made of a plastic called high-density polyethylene or HDPE.

The others considered safe for food or water storage are number one (PETE), number four (LDPE), and number five.

Glass

Again, not all glass containers are created equally. The best glass for food and water storage is borosilicate glass which is most commonly known as Pyrex.

This type of glass can handle temperature changes and is fairly resistant to breakage. Be warned. There is a form of glass that calls itself the Pyrex name but is made of the lesser quality soda-lime glass and does not handle temperature changes or extremes as well.

An example of this glass is Mason jars, as well as the home canning jars that are meant to look like Mason jars but do not perform like them.

Make sure that the jars you choose can handle canning situations, including pressure cooking or they are not the real deal.

Any glass subjected to extreme conditions can break or crack, leading to leaking or more obvious flaws. This glass could also have small flaws inside the container, which can become breeding grounds for contaminants.

Stainless Steel Tanks

A stainless-steel tank may seem expensive at first, but it will more than pay for itself over its lifetime. Most well-made tanks will last roughly forty years or more depending on circumstances and location.

These tanks are the best for collecting rainwater and storing it for filtering and use when fresh water has been used up.

2. Not Preserving Your Water

Water must be stored correctly so that it does not become contaminated. For longer-term storage, it must be preserved or small microbes can breed and cause illnesses that can lead to even more serious medical conditions. If you are storing tap water, you may not need to add anything to it because most cities add chlorine as part of their system anyway.

If you use any other type of water for longer-term storage, you will need to add bleach or iodine. Use bleach for stored water and iodine for possibly contaminated drinking water at the point of use.

DO NOT DRINK THIS SOLUTION!

Be sure to carefully label the solution with the proper warnings and instructions for usage. The solution will be one teaspoon of the shock to every two gallons of water. When you store the water, you use the solution in a ratio of 1 to 100 – one part of the solution to every 100 parts of the water you are storing.

Again, do not drink the storage solution. Used in this way, a single pound of pool shock will effectively treat as much as ten thousand gallons of water.

3. Not Storing Water in Proper Place

What you store your water in and how you store it is important but where you put it is equally important. All stored water must be kept away from temperature extremes and should also be kept out of direct sunlight.

A dark closet might be a good choice if you do not have an underground shelter to keep it in but you have to consider the possible hazards that you might face.

Will the area be protected from things like earthquakes, fires or floods?

4. Not Considering the Shelf Life

Even with proper storage, in the perfect location and the right storage material, your water has a shelf life and must be rotated and replaced.

The typical shelf life for water is about six months or so- all of your materials that you are prepping, water, food, medications and more, should be clearly labeled so that you know when they were put into your storage and when they are set to expire. Rotate your stock so that items near their expiration date are brought to the front to be used up so they do not go to waste.

5. Not Thinking Beyond What You Drink

Remember, you will need water beyond just what you drink each day.

You will still need water for bathing, cleaning your dishes and utensils and the food preparation surfaces.

To get an idea of how much water you might need to realistically store, keep track of your daily water use for a few days and average the amount out.

Conclusion

There are several justifications for why water storage is a wise move. It is essential for survival first and foremost. Water on hand can make a life or death difference in the event of a natural disaster or other forms of emergency. It's always a good idea to have some water on hand in case there is an unplanned interruption, even if you live in a region where the water supply is typically dependable. A simple approach to being ready for any emergency is to keep a few gallons of water on hand. Gallons of water kept in reserve?

Water storage has another benefit because it may be utilized for various activities like bathing, cooking, and cleaning. In essence, water is a tool for survival and should be used as such. It can ensure you have the supplies you need to survive and keep you hydrated. Additionally, keeping a supply of water on hand will help you stay hydrated and cool if you live in a hot climate.

Depending on your demands, you'll need to store a different amount of water. It's a good idea to keep at least one gallon of water on hand per person every day. However, you might want to raise that quantity if you have young children or live in a hot area. Additionally, stockpile more water than you anticipate needing if you have the space to do so is never a bad idea.

If you've ever waited in a long line at the grocery store, you know that when people fear running out of water, they can become rather agitated. Keeping at least one gallon of water on hand is a good idea. Although it can seem like a lot, it's not as much as you might expect. Since a gallon of water weighs eight pounds, a family of four would require 32 pounds of water to be stored. Of course, you'll want to boost your supply if you live where power outages are often. The same is true whether you have young children or pets, live in a hot area, or are under any of these circumstances. However, it's always better to be safe than sorry even if you don't believe you need all that water. Therefore, stock up now; your future self will appreciate it.

Book 2

SURVIVAL FOOD TO STOCKPILE

The Ultimate Guide to Stockpile Food for You and Your Family to Survive Any Crisis in the Safety of Your Own

Jonathan Henry

Introduction

What should you include in your food storage, whether it's for winter or survival? That is a really good query.

Because you can't predict the exact nature of the emergency, you must prepare ahead of time if you want the food to be healthy and feed your family. If you haven't planned ahead, you might not have access to running water, electricity, or a way to cook and prepare food in a situation where you need to survive for a medium or long period of time.

Preparing for anything is essential for a successful homestead, whether preparing for a harsh winter or a sudden epidemic.

It's crucial to determine just how much you need to store and how much room you have for it. The Department of Homeland Security advises that each home should have at least 72 hours worth of food and water for every family member. The foods you choose for your stockpile should be ones that will last for a long time, which brings up the second crucial point.

Many foods can be kept for up to 20 years when stored properly and yet preserve their nutritional value and flavor. It's also vital to remember that not all food with the designation "Survival Food" will be suitable for your specific circumstance.

You can store a variety of food items in your stockpile. These consist of dried foods like beans, pasta, or rice, dehydrated foods, freeze-dried foods, powdered foods that are reconstituted with water or other liquids, canned fruits and vegetables, canned meats, and condiments.

Most people decide to include all of those mentioned above in their stockpiles and various foods.

Essential Food to Stock for Survival

When choosing foods for your prepper's pantry, you should choose those that are easy to prepare and store well. It is important to remember that, in case of an emergency, you may need to rely on your resources since local stores will likely find their shelves depleted by people panic buying, and the arrival of new supplies may be delayed. How much food you should store depends on where you live and how you think the area will be impacted in case of a disaster. FEMA recommends at least three days, but you might want to put aside enough to last at least a week or even more. Some prepper groups even suggest that you store enough food to last a month or more to prepare you for the worst.

Here is a list of foods that should be part of your prepper's pantry:

- Rice. This is an important staple food used as a base for filling meals when mixed with other food. When considering how much rice to buy, consider the UN World Food Program recommendation of 400 grams per day per person, which is good for two meals including other ingredients and provides 2,100 kilocalories daily. You can buy several rice varieties to avoid boring your families, such as jasmine rice, wild rice, short grain Asian rice and basmati rice. If you want a rice option that can be prepared quickly, you can stock up on instant rice, which is not as nutritious as regular rice with minimal processing.
- Oatmeal. This is another essential staple for providing healthy and filling breakfasts since it is rich in fiber and low in saturated fat. One person will consume around a half-cup of oatmeal per day. In addition, you should also store ingredients to mix with the oatmeal, such as dried fruit, to add flavor and variety.
- Dry cereals. You should keep some of these foods, both for variety and to prepare for the possibility that the water and power will go out and you will need to have foods that you can eat without cooking or other preparation. One recommended cereal is shredded wheat since it provides a rich source of energy. However, you should choose the cereal that your family eats.
- Pasta. This inexpensive food product is easy to prepare and can be easily made into various meals when mixed with meat and other foods. Get a variety of pasta including the typical spaghetti and macaroni, egg noodles, soba pasta made with buckwheat, and bean curd pasta.
- Beans. These is another food you should stockpile since they are a rich source of fiber and energy, as they have some 1,250 calories per pound. In addition, you can use dried beans to sprout beans in a pot or backyard garden in as little as five days. Two cups of dried beans equivalent to one lb will give you six cups of cooked beans. However, you should also consider that beans take an extensive preparation time - from 40 minutes to over an hour - depending on the bean you are making. You will also need water to soak them in preparation for cooking.
- Canned meat. Canned foods are an important part of any prepper's pantry since they store well and can be eaten straight from the can or with minimum preparation if necessary. Focus on canned fish such as tuna, salmon and sardines since they are rich in healthy Omega-3 fats. If you anticipate that refrigeration won't be a problem, you can stock prepared meat products such as hot dogs and sausages in the freezer since you can store them for a long time.
- Canned fruits. These are another essential staple since they are a rich source of fiber and other nutrients such as vitamin C. For example, a can of fruit cocktail will give you some 300 to 400 calories per pound, which is double the number of calories per pound

compared with canned vegetables. One recommended fruit is canned peaches, which are rich in calories, while canned juice provides a valuable source of hydration. To get a regular source of vitamin C, get canned citrus fruits such as mandarin oranges and pineapples. Look for the biggest cans since these will save you money while giving you the maximum number of servings.

- Dried fruits. These can supplement canned fruits by providing healthy snacks and an easy way to meet your daily fruit requirement. A handful of raisins, for instance, can give you one full serving of fruit. In addition to raisins, you can also consider dried mangoes, dates and apricots.

- Canned vegetables. Make sure you get a variety of veggies to ensure that your family will get important nutrients. Recommended canned vegetables are sweet potatoes and other root crops since they are filling and rich in vitamin A. You can also include canned peas and carrots since they are an ingredient in stews, and artichoke hearts and asparagus that can be used in pasta dishes.

- Nuts. If you anticipate that you won't have to store them for long, you can add nuts to your prepper's pantry, since they are rich in protein. However, you should avoid giving them to children below five since they are a known allergen. Get dried nuts such as cashews, raw almonds, walnuts, and mixed roasted nuts. For added variety, you can also get peanut butter. But make sure that you avoid those which contain hydrogenated oils and sugars, and buy peanut butter whose ingredients are simply peanuts, salt, and oil (these are the ones that have oils on top, which are the peanut butter).

- Honey. Although this may be expensive, it is well worth the investment since it is a versatile food that does not spoil. You can use it as a flavoring for oatmeal, teas, and other breakfast cereals and grains. In addition, it is also an ingredient in many recipes such as bread and has medicinal uses. For instance, you can put it on wounds to act as an antibiotic and can also be used to soothe a sore throat.

- Salt. This is one of the most important things you can have in a prepper's pantry since it has a variety of uses. Apart from flavoring foods, you can use it to preserve food by salting it. For health reasons, make sure to get rock salt in addition to iodized salt.

- Spices, herbs and condiments. These are an essential part of your pantry since they will help make your staple foods such as rice taste better so you won't get bored eating them every day during an emergency. Basic spices include dried mustard, red pepper, ginger, dill, rosemary and chili. Condiments include mayonnaise, ketchup, Worcestershire sauce and Tabasco sauce. Also, consider sweeteners such as maple syrup, cocoa powder and vanilla.

- Oils. These are used in cooking. The healthiest oil is olive oil but can easily spoil, although it potentially has a shelf life of as long as two years. A more affordable alternative is coconut oil, which does not spoil easily and is a quick energy source. You should also store some lard as it is also good for cooking. However, make sure you buy your oil in small containers since once the package is opened, it can deteriorate quickly due to oxidization.

- Vitamins. Since you may not be able to get all the nutrients you require only from food, you should also include a variety of multi-vitamins in your pantry. To help fight off infections, store some Calcium vitamins fortified with vitamin D, and for stress management, buy some magnesium.

The foods and supplements listed above are the minimum basic ones you will need to help you get through an emergency. If you anticipate a prolonged period where food will not be available, however, you might also consider storing basic ingredients that you can make into food. Some of these ingredients include:

- Potato flour. Made from the whole dehydrated potato, including the skin, this healthy flour can be used to make pancakes, waffles, bread, and soups. In addition, you can also use it as a thickener in place of cornstarch, and it is also gluten-free.
- Whole wheat flour. This basic food product is rich in nutrients such as selenium and other minerals, fiber, and protein.
- Dried corn. This is a versatile food that can be made into various dishes. For example, if you choose popcorn, but you can not only pop it to make a healthy snack but also grind it in an emergency to make flour. You can get Hasa Marina flour made from finely-ground maize and used to make corn tortillas if you reconstitute it with salt and water, or use it as the base to make dough for tamales and empanadas. Corn grits are a versatile dried corn product that can be eaten for breakfast with honey and milk.
- Dry yeast. This is an important ingredient in baking bread since it is a leavening agent. However, it does not keep indefinitely and you will have to replace it after several months since it loses its potency.
- Baking powder and baking soda. These are a pair of leavening agents you should have in your pantry. Unlike yeast, baking soda and baking powder can last for more than a year when stored properly.

To ensure that you maintain your strength in an emergency, make sure that you get at least one balanced meal per day, and drink enough water and other liquids (at least two quarts a day).

Stockpile Food Methods. Starting From Scratch

Discovering how to stockpile your food in case of an emergency, such as a worldwide epidemic or natural disaster, might save you money as well as your life. To begin the emergency food stockpile, follow the given steps to ensure that you are prepared yet not wasteful.

Step One: Evaluate Your Food Storage Potential

Shelf-stable non - perishable food should be maintained at room temperature, far from excessive temperature swings for safety reasons. They must be kept free of pests as well as dry.

Where Should You Keep Your Food Stockpile?

Food shouldn't be stored in unfinished basements & attics, especially in spaces with unregulated temperatures. Look for a location a little out of sight but yet fits all of the food storage requirements.

- Are there any cabinet shelves or cupboards in your kitchen or closet that you don't use?
- Do you have a large enough storage container to keep your stockpile?
- Do you have enough room to keep the food off the ground but out of the real way?
- Is there a place inside your living room where you could store the food?

Select Your Storage Area

After you've examined issues such as water, temperature, and accessibility, you'll need to choose a location for your stockpile. Take measurements, then write them down, so you'll always remember how much space will be there to work with. Snap a picture of the area and save it to your phone so that you can refer to it when shopping.

Step Two: Estimate How Much Food You'll Need To Stockpile

Food stockpiling for emergency scenarios necessitates careful and rational preparation. It'll be a waste of resources and money if you stockpile foods you'll never eat.

Gather information about your family's eating habits

Before calculating how much food you'll require, you must first determine how much food everybody consumes on a routine day. You must also keep track of the kind of meals your family consumes daily.

- Create a list of every member of the family's customary meals, snacks, desserts, and beverages for one day. Make a checklist of the quantities and particular objects.
- Create a list of any dietary limitations.
- When others, such as grandparents, might utilize your home as a haven in an emergency, you regard their requirements as well.
- Replace perishable foods within your lists with non-perishable alternatives, such as boxed milk rather than cold milk.
- Mark that item off your list if there isn't a suitable non-perishable equivalent.

Make the calculations

At Ready.gov, the US Division of Homeland Security provides information on food stocks. They recommend keeping a three-day stock of non-perishable foods on hand to serve one entire family or home. The FEMA and Red Cross recommend a two-week stockpile.

- Generate a checklist of the precise foods and beverages that each family member consumes throughout the day, as well as appropriate non-perishable equivalents.
- About each item in your checklist, enter the number of times a serving is consumed per day.
- Multiply every serving number with 3 for the 3-day supply, then write down the number. That's how many servings of each item an individual requires for a three-day supply.
- Instead of multiplying by 3, multiply by 14 for the 2-week supply.
- Repeat the process for each member of the family.
- Create a new master food list. Many family members take the same food in a day, but their serving totals together to determine the total serving size they'll require.
- Look there at the serving size information above the can, package, or jar to see how many servings seem to be inside one container of any specific product.
- Remember that your data indicates the number of servings required, not the number of cans or jars. You'll have to perform the math to determine how many containers you'll need to obtain the number of servings you want.

How to Increase Your Stockpile

Divide the master list totals by three to get the number of servings the entire family needs each day if you prefer to stockpile food now for a longer period. Multiply this quantity by the number of days you are planning to stockpile. When you're preparing a one-month stockpile and notice your family requires three servings of peanut butter a day, multiply 30 by three to get 90, the total amount of servings of your peanut butter your family requires for 30 days.

Step Three: Choose Which Foods To Keep.

You will now have your master inventory of what your house members consume in a day to three days, but you don't have to store everything.

Determine which items your family requires

Examine your shopping list to see which things are the most nutritious and which are actual requirements. If you have the room, you should hoard these products.

- Anything with a lot of salt isn't a good idea since it will make you thirsty, and you won't have much to drink.
- To increase morale amid an emergency, choose one "desire" item for each family member.
- Only keep non-perishable foods in jars, cans, sealed cartons or bottles on hand.
- The American Public Health Association suggests that each drink at least a gallon of water every day.

The Foods You Should Have in Your Stockpile

Most foods don't require cooking, and they may be stored for one to two years. Meats and vegetables survive the longest in cans, which are the finest packaging alternatives for preserved items.

- Bottled water
- Canned meat
- Canned/boxed milk
- Granola bars
- Protein bars

- Jelly
- Peanut butter
- Canned pasta
- Dried fruit
- Unsalted nuts
- Dry cereal
- White rice

Foods You Might Want to Have in Your Stockpile

Having just a few "luxury" food products in your stockpile might help families cope with stress & maintain a good outlook during a disaster.

- Cookies
- Instant coffee mix
- Powdered drink mixes
- Instant cocoa mix
- Fruit juice
- Instant tea mix
- Fruit snacks
- Hard candy
- Specialty crackers

Step Four: Buy A Few Things At A Time

Putting together your emergency food stockpile doesn't have to be a one-stop shop. Many businesses restrict how many critical things you may buy in a single trip, especially if a pandemic has already begun in adjacent places. That's why it's crucial to begin stockpiling even if there isn't an emergency. Buying two or three products on each regular supermarket trip is an easy method to store food on a budget and also in a socially good manner.

Step Five: Arrange Your Food Reserves

As you accumulate stockpile items, arrange them in a designated storage place in an orderly manner. Items with the earliest expiration dates must be placed at the front/ top of the pile to ensure that they are utilized first. The easiest approach to arranging products is to keep them all together in a sequence of "use by" dates, from the earliest to the latest.

Why Should You Build an Emergency Food Reserve?

Quarantines and global pandemics, state of emergency, natural disasters, or shelter in place orders are not common, yet they could occur at any time. You might not be ready to go to stores; retailers might not be ready to purchase enough supplies, or your electricity may be down, leaving your refrigerator unusable. Though you won't be given previous notice of these catastrophes, having a strategy in place before they occur will assist you.

Success in Stockpiling

Keeping an emergency food supply is a continuous process. Creating a stockpile might take weeks, days, or even months. You'll have to check here every six months once it's been made to ensure that foods aren't ready to expire or have been spoiled. Make sure your food stash includes one manual can opener as well as some dining utensils, so you have everything you require for emergency meals inside one spot.

Stockpiling don't

- **Purchase foods you wouldn't eat** - Ground chicken is two for the one deal! Score! Isn't it better to purchase a full bunch? Maybe. Perhaps not. Is ground chicken a part of your family's diet? A good offer does not always imply that it is the best deal for you. Save space (plus money) for the items your family will need and utilize.
- **Go Into Debt** – While we're on the subject of saving money, don't forget about those budgets. Overeager shoppers might often go down a risky path of overpaying in haste to stock up on great offers. Make your shopping checklist before you go to the store to help you be a more conscious shopper!
- **Purchase What You Couldn't Store** - Notice how much room you have available when you make your weekly inventory. If your pantry seems overflowing, it could be a good idea to take a break from stocking and use up some of your supplies before replenishing them! It's important to remember that stockpiling is about being prepared, not hoarding.

How To Manage Food Supplies Efficiently

Prepping is not easy. It's an investment of emotional energy, mental energy, time, and money. In this chapter, we're going to talk about how to budget for prepping, where to find your food, and how to find space in your home. Everyone's lifestyle is a little different, so take what you learn here and adjust it as needed.

How To Budget

When you start prepping, you'll write a list of essential things you believe. First on the list: water and food. These are not negotiable. Also, unlike most other supplies, this is not an area where you want to try and scale back too much cost-wise. With water, you don't want to scale back at all. You should never plan on rationing water. If anything, you want to get more than you think you'll need.

You do have a little flexibility with things like brands (we'll talk about how to save money soon), but overall, the majority of your budget should be dedicated to food and water. Before you start spending big bucks on other supplies, make sure you have the food and water stockpile you need. What if even the essentials break your budget? Life is expensive, and you may not have a ton of money in the bank to set aside for prepping. The solution is to stockpile slowly. Meet the needs of a short-term emergency first where you can't get to the store for, say, two weeks. Focus on buying all the water you'll need and essential food items like rice, canned beans, and canned vegetables. You don't need to buy a year's worth of food and water in one swoop to be a good prepper. Even getting just one thing from your stockpile list each time you go to the store is great.

Where To Shop

Being smart about how you shop can save you money. Your budget and how you shop are closely linked. One popular way is buying in bulk if your budget allows for it. While you need a bigger chunk of money upfront, you end up saving money on the amount of food you get. There are several places where it's easy to buy in bulk:

- **Costco/Sam's Club**

These are very well-known stores that sell in large amounts. You do need to pay for a membership, but you can save a lot of money on food. You also get access to some surprising benefits like lower gas prices, discounts on pharmacy prescriptions, car part discounts, and so on.

- **Online**

If you're a big online shopper, you'll love that you can get a food stockpile entirely on the web if you want. Amazon is a very popular site, especially if you have a Prime account because the shipping is free. There's also Boxed, which offers lower prices than even Amazon on some items. Membership is free.

- **Restaurant supply stores**

Restaurants have to get their food supplies from somewhere, and most aren't going to the regular grocery store. Restaurant supply stores offer bulk items for a variety of eateries, so you can get essentials like flour, rice, and more for good prices. Keep in mind that not all these stores are open to the public.

- **Ethnic grocery stores**

Grocery stores dedicated to specific ethnic cuisines (Asian, Mexican, Indian, etc.) often sell essentials like rice, beans, spices, and more in bulk. You can find more unique food items for your stockpile, too. Oftentimes, the same products would be considered "special" in a regular grocery store and most likely cost a lot more.

- **Survival food companies**

Some companies sell food specifically designed for long-term storage. That includes freeze-dried meals and individual ingredients, like vegetables. Legacy Food Storage sells a huge variety of freeze-dried food with a shelf life of up to 25 years. Choose from just about any size and food type. Mountain House is another popular brand. Buckets are sold in 29-32 serving sizes. These commercial survival brands can be pricey, but they do make it easy to stock up on nutrient-dense meals and ingredients that last a long time.

How To Save Money

You don't want to build a stockpile that's too small, but big ones can be expensive. How do you save money on the items you need? There are four methods:

- **Generic brands**

One of the easiest ways to save a little money is to avoid big-name brands. These are nearly always more expensive than the generic versions. These are also known as private label or store brands. The concept of store brands started in the 1970s and continues to save consumers lots of money each year. These brands are growing as well, so odds are, you can find just about any item you want. Taste and nutritional content may vary a bit, so try it before committing it to your stockpile.

- **Coupons**

Coupons have been around forever and for a good reason. Some people get really into couponing and save significantly, but you don't need to get intense to make it worthwhile. The amount you save may seem small per trip, but it can add up over time. Grocery stores also send coupons through the mail. Brands sometimes offer deals on their websites. As soon as you get a new coupon, look at the end date. Use the ones that expire earliest first. Some people put their coupons in a booklet, but whatever works for you is fine.

- **Sales**

Grocery stores have sales all the time, so you always want to be on the lookout. That doesn't mean you buy anything that goes on sale because you can end up spending more than you want that way. The secret is to mainly buy items you already planned on buying for your stockpile. If there's a really good sale on an item, you didn't think of—but it's something essential like a canned vegetable, meat, etc.—go ahead and get it. Less popular items frequently have significant sales and items near their expiration date. With prepping, you obviously don't want to get something that's about to expire, so make sure that's not the reason something is cheap.

- **Receipt-scanning apps**

There are lots of phone apps that give you points every time you scan a receipt. Many apps take receipts from gas stations, convenience stores, clothing stores, and so on. Some popular apps include ReceiptPal, Fetch, and Ibotta.

Finding Space in Your Home

Where do you put all the food and water you stockpile? Most people don't have a lot of space where they can easily accumulate a year's worth or more of items. The answer is to find space wherever you can and spread things out. Here are some ideas:

Kitchen Pantry

This is the most obvious place to keep your food stockpile. Set aside a section of this area for your stockpile items and another for your everyday food. You don't want to accidentally start chipping away at your stockpile without knowing it.

Broom closets

Put boxes of items like canned and dry goods in broom closets. If you use the broom closets for other everyday items, just put them on top of the stockpile so you can easily access them.

Bedroom closets

Bedroom closets often have space on the floor. Take advantage and store some of your stockpiles there.

Basement

If your home has a basement, it's usually a great place for food items because it's cool and dark. Make sure dampness isn't an issue before moving your stockpile there.

Garage

A well-organized garage is another popular place for food and water. Just make sure you aren't storing your food near gasoline. Before moving your items there, think about how hot or cold the garage gets since garages aren't always well-insulated. If the temperature shifts too much, it isn't the best food place.

Attic

If your house has an attic, it could work for storing some food items. Attics can get very hot or cold depending on the time of year, so it shouldn't be your first choice for a stockpile location. If you do want to use your attic, you can improve it slightly by making sure it's insulated. Installing a thermostatic heater and air conditioning to fight against temperature changes is also a good idea. All food should be properly sealed in Mylar bags and buckets. My recommendation is to use attic space for non-food prepping supplies.

Laundry room

A laundry room seems like a decent place to keep a food stockpile. However, that area is often humid, so it's not great for long-term storage. If you keep your food well-sealed in Mylar bags and food buckets, it should be all right as long as you're rotating the food. =

Outdoor sheds/buildings

If you have a shed or other outdoor buildings on your property, it can work for food storage. Like garages, a shed is more vulnerable to extreme temperature changes. It can quickly get too hot or too cold for your items. Before stockpiling there, you'll need to make some adjustments to make it work. Proper insulation, airflow, a thermostat, and more are important.

Unique storage ideas

You'll most likely find yourself running out of space as you build up your stockpile. You might also live in a small place where it's hard to find storage even when you're just starting. Here are some more unique storage ideas:

Under beds and furniture

Most people don't think about these areas as real storage potential. Depending on how tall the furniture is, you may have to get creative about what fits. Cans turned on their side will probably work. Be sure to clean thoroughly before moving your stockpile under there.

Shelving

Even in the smallest places, you can use the walls to your advantage. Installing some good shelving in a few rooms gives you more options for canned goods. You can also put-up shelves in your closets and on the backs of doors. Make sure the shelves are strong enough to hold the weight of your items.

Decorative storage bins

Most people want to keep their stockpiles out of sight, which makes sense. However, in small spaces, there just aren't that many options. That's why decorative storage bins are so convenient because they let you keep your stockpile out in the open but are not obvious. These bins can go in guest rooms, bedrooms, and even the living room. No one needs to know the bins are filled with canned and dry goods instead of board games or blankets.

What To Know About Food Storage Locations

No matter how much or how little space you have for food storage, be aware that you will most likely need to move your supplies around at certain times. The garage might work as a storage space for some months out of the year, but then it gets really hot in the summer. Same with the attic and an outdoor shed. While your supplies are in one area, think about where they could go next. Prepare ahead by building shelves, getting storage bins, and so on. Reorganize your other supplies - ones that aren't affected by temperatures—and make room for water and food.

As always, staying organized is important. You don't want to forget where you've put some food supplies and then discover them later in a sorry state. If you have food in areas that become unsuitable based on the season, monitor the temperature and humidity level so you know when to move them. Don't be tempted to get lazy when it comes to proper storage locations. It takes time and energy to get it right, but if you don't think about it, you'll lose supplies, which is a waste of time, energy, and money.

6. Maintaining and Rotating the Pantry

Building a stockpile doesn't consist of just buying a bunch of stuff, putting it somewhere, and never touching it again. A good prepper knows the importance of maintaining and rotating their supplies. This includes staying organized with a list of expiration dates, using food as it gets closer to that date, and replacing it.

1.1.7 How Long Should You Keep Food?

While you can get food that's meant to last 25 years, most of your stockpile will likely consist of canned and dry goods that don't last that long. If you're just buying food and sticking it in your pantry, here's how long you can expect stuff to last:

Water

Water doesn't expire, so it's the only supply you don't really need to worry about if the water is properly sealed and stored.

Canned food (fruit, vegetables, beans, meat)

Low-acid foods and canned meats usually last 2-5 years. Acidic foods expire sooner than other types of canned goods. During these last 12-18 months. Should you pay attention to the package dates? With canned (and dry) food, you'll often see a few types of dates. There is a "best by" and "use by." If a can is past its "best by" date, it's still safe to eat. It just means that its nutritional content will go down as time passes. Even "use by" canned foods can usually be eaten a bit after their date.

Canned soups

Generally, the same canned fruit/vegetables/beans rules apply to canned soups. Plan on keeping these for 2-5 years at max.

Rice

Rice lasts a long time, so it's an ideal stockpile item. Uncooked white rice, wild rice, jasmine, Arborio, and basmati rice last for years. You don't need to worry about expiration dates in terms of safety. The nutritional value decreases over time, so write down the "best by" date. Regardless of age, if the rice looks normal and is completely dry, it's safe for consumption.

Brown rice, however, doesn't last long before it goes rancid. That's because it has more oil in it. In the pantry, it lasts 3-6 months. Put it in the fridge (6-12 months) or freezer (12-18 months) to extend its life.

Pasta

Like rice, dry pasta lasts a long time. It can be eaten 1-2 years past its expiration date. If it looks dry, looks normal, and smells normal, it's safe to eat. It won't contain the same amount of nutrients, though.

Dried beans

Dried beans last for years when stored properly. Nutritionally, they do start losing nutrients 2-3 years after their "best by" date. Dried beans will be safe to eat if you don't notice any bugs, mold, or odd smells.

Jarred sauce

Unopened, a jar of tomato/marinara sauce is at its best for 18-24 months. It will be safe to eat for around a year afterward. Always make sure it looks and smells normal before eating.

Oats

Stored in their original container, rolled oats keep all their nutrients for 18-24 months. They'll be safe for longer after that. As long as the oats are dry, you don't see any mold, and they smell normal, they're most likely safe.

Flour, baking soda, and baking powder

Unopened all-purpose flour stays fresh for 6-8 months. You can keep it at its best for up to a year in the fridge or for 2 years in the freezer. You'll know flour has gone bad when it smells rancid, sour, and musty. If you see any bugs or other contaminants in it, throw it out.

Baking soda and baking powder don't spoil, but they start to lose their effectiveness after their package date. Like flour, they can also become contaminated, so keep their lids sealed. They're at their best for about a year.

Canned milk

Unopened evaporated milk is at its best for about 6-12 months. It shouldn't be frozen. Condensed milk usually has a "best by" date of about 18-24 months, but it's safe for a long time afterward if stored properly. Canned coconut milk's shelf life is between 2 and 5 years. Unopened coconut milk in a carton should last 3-4 weeks after its package date. No matter what type of milk you're using, signs of spoilage include an odd color, smell, and/or flavor.

Honey

Honey is one of the few foods that last forever. As long as it's protected from outside contaminants and kept away from direct sunlight, it will be safe to eat for the future. Over time, it can crystallize, but it's still safe.

Peanut butter

Peanut butter contains lots of oil which eventually goes rancid. The unopened peanut butter will be okay for about one year past its expiration date. Keeping it in the fridge or pantry doesn't make a difference. Once the regular peanut butter is open, it lasts for 3-4 months in the pantry and 6-8 months in the fridge. Remember that the timeline doesn't include natural peanut butter, which goes bad quickly in only 2-3 months. I don't recommend natural peanut butter for stockpiling for this reason.

Sugar, salt, and dried spices

Sugar, salt, and dried spices don't go bad in the traditional sense. The quality just goes down. Spices will start losing their flavor and nutrition after 3-4 years of storage.

Cooking oils

Oils go rancid. Some last longer than others. Canned olive oil will last longer than regular olive oil. Unopened sunflower seed oil and coconut oil last around 2 years, while unopened peanut oil lasts 3 years. You can extend the life of most oils by keeping them in the fridge.

1.1.8 Rotating Your Stockpile

Rotating your stockpile isn't difficult, but it does require good organizational skills. You want to eat the closest food or just past its package date and replace it. Why? Your stockpile will always be its best in terms of nutrition. While most foods technically last past their "best by" date, they lose nutrients as time passes. You don't want to have a stockpile with no nutritional value. You also don't want a stockpile that's so old, and you're not 100% sure something is safe to eat. Getting sick is the last thing you want during a crisis.

Digging into your stockpile regularly allows you to catch any storage problems before they ruin all your supplies. This saves you money in the long run. You'll also get to eat some of the foods you don't normally use, so you can be sure you like them.

What about water? As you know, water doesn't expire, but, if possible, you always want your water to be fresh. Some preppers recommend rotating your water supply every year or so. You can use it for drinking, washing, or cooking and then replace it. This also lets you check on your water to ensure you've been storing it properly. If you forget to rotate a supply but know it's sealed and safe, you don't have to stress about it too much. It is more about its freshness than anything else.

1.1.9 Tracking the Pantry

The key to maintaining and rotating your pantry is staying organized. Keep a list of all your items and write down their package dates. Some preppers write the package date in large letters directly on the item as well, so they don't need to refer to their master list every time. You can also set reminders in a digital calendar, so you'll be notified when a date is coming up.

As soon as you use an item, write it on a list so you know you need to replace it. Do you need to replace it right away? You don't need to make a special trip to the store to get a single can of tomatoes, but don't wait too long. You want your stockpile as complete as possible because you don't know when an emergency might arise.

Conclusion

Do you have what it takes to protect your family from dehydration and starvation in a survival situation? This guide has given you the knowledge you need to create an entire survival pantry. The most important thing to remember, however, is that you can't start your survival pantry when an emergency occurs – you need to start it now.

So, start stockpiling food and water because the truth is that we never really know when these food supplies will be necessary, It could be tomorrow, it could be five years from now but rest assured that using the techniques we have discussed you will be prepared no matter what happens.

Book 3

FERMENTING AND PICKLING COOKBOOK FOR PREPPERS

The Essential Guide to Master the Art of Fermentation and Pickling For Food Preservation. Learn The Benefits, Methods, Tools Needed and Different Homemade Recipes To Start With

Jonathan Henry

Introduction

Gut health is an essential aspect of your overall health and well-being. However, given the modern diet and lifestyle, most people have compromised their gut health and suffer from its side effects. This is the book for you to get your gut biome back to its healthiest state and improve your health,. You might have heard about fermentation and the benefits of eating fermented foods. If not, you will soon discover the wonders of fermentation. People have been consuming fermented foods for a long time, but people have only recently started paying more attention to this type of food. Your beer, bread, salami, etc., are all fermented foods. They all have unique smells and textures and are a great addition to your diet.

Probiotics are good for your body, and making your own at home is invaluable. You will learn about fermentation, the process, benefits, and how to ferment various foods. This book provides simple recipes to help you make the best-fermented foods as you read. There are variations for each recipe that should suit every taste.

Pickling has been another valued method of preserving foods for thousands and thousands of years. Historical research leads us to believe that the process of pickling has been used for at least three thousand years, and potentially longer, first appearing in ancient Greece and Egypt. Even that long ago, pickling was not only viewed as a method of preservation, but also highly regarded for nutritional value and for increasing the physical beauty of those that consumed pickled foods. Through the years that led to modern times, the pickle has evolved into a craft with flavors ranging from simple to sophisticated, producing a treasured food that today is valued for its culinary greatness and health-boosting properties.

When it comes to pickling today, we first need to shed the misconception that the word pickle applies mostly to cucumbers. There are few limits to the imagination when it comes to pickling and the process applies to an incredible range of vegetables, fruits and even meats or eggs. This book, supplies you with some of the most delicious and simple pickling recipes for an incredible variety of foods. You will also find that different methods of pickling. The method you choose will depend greatly upon your intended use and the time you wish to devote to your pickles.

Regardless of your pickling method, you are about to discover how incredibly easy, enjoyable and satisfying making your own pickles can be. All you need is a basic understanding of benefits, tools and ingredients, all provided for you in this book. A bounty of freshly pickled crisp vegetables and luscious fruits to enjoy and share with your family and friends awaits you.

Fermenting

Fermentation is the natural conversion of carbohydrates (such as starch and sugar) to alcohol or acids by bacteria and yeast. The alcohol or acids produced in the food during fermentation act as a natural preservative and give such a food a distinct sour flavor and acidity. Fermentation also promotes the growth of beneficial microorganisms known as probiotics. Probiotics have been known to help with immunological function, digestion, and cardiovascular health. That is why having fermented foods in your diet may improve your general health.

Different Types of Fermentation

Fermentation is the working of living organisms that mingle with the molecules in our food. While doing so, they end up turning that food even healthier. Here is how different living organisms carry out the same process in their unique way:

Fermentation Through Yeast

Sugars present in food are broken down into carbon dioxide and alcohol by yeast. CO_2 is what causes beer to bubble and bread to rise. While yeast is found in various symbiotic cultures, it is solely used to make alcohol ferments and yeast-risen bread. In the past, wild yeasts were used to make beer, wine, cider, and other alcohol ferments. Homebrewers nowadays employ yeast strains that are tailored for vigor and flavor. To prepare quick and easy yeasted bread, you can use instant or fresh yeast.

Fermentation Through Bacteria

When most people think of fermented products, they think of bacteria. Sugars are converted to acids by bacterial cultures. Bacterial fermentation is also responsible for the sour flavor of sauerkraut and yoghurt. Although there are many different types of bacterial cultures, the two most common ones are lactic bacteria and acetic acid bacteria. Lactic cultures are used in the majority of fermented dairy products. Yogurt, sour cream, buttermilk, and cheese are all examples of this. Most vegetables have lactic bacterial cultures on their skin when they come in from the garden. It's why sauerkraut, kimchi, and other fermented veggies are so simple to create.

Fermentation Through Symbiotic Cultures

Many types of fermentation begin with a yeast and bacteria symbiotic culture. Sugar is converted to acids, alcohol, and CO_2 in these cultures. This imparts a distinct flavor to the fermented products. Sourdough bread is created from a wild yeast and bacterium culture. It's easy to catch simply by leaving a flour and water mixture on your counter for a few days.

Kombucha SCOBYs thrive on sugar and steeped black tea. Your grocery store's sealed bottled beverages are nothing like truly fermented kombucha tea. Kombucha is a fermented tea with sweet, tart, effervescent, and probiotics. Jun is similar to Kombucha; it is made from green tea and honey.

Sucrose and molasses are consumed by water kefir grains. The result is a fizzy beverage that tastes more like soda than Kombucha. Kefir grains are used to make milk kefir. It transforms milk into a thick, acidic, and slightly sparkling drink. Again, homemade kefir differs from store-bought kefir, which often consists solely of bacterial cultures. The mother of real apple cider vinegar is a symbiotic culture of acetic acid bacteria and yeast.

Fermentation Through Mold

Koji kin is a rice or barley fermenting mold. Many Japanese ferments, such as sake and miso, have their origins in this culture. Tempeh is a mushroom-flavored cake made from soybeans fermented by an Indonesian mold culture. Other beans and seeds can also be fermented with it.

Foods That Are Commonly Fermented

Fermented foods are consumed in many different ways around the world, including:

- Beer
- Bread made with sourdough starter
- Cheese
- Kefir
- Kimchi
- Kombucha
- Miso
- Olives
- Salami
- Sauerkraut
- Tempeh
- Wine
- Yogurt

1. Benefits

Initially, fermentation was used as a harmless food preservation technique that allowed people to consume a number of fresh produces long after they were fermented. With the advancement of science, we have learned that fermented food is really good for human health and some of the proven benefits include:

Improves Digestive Health

Probiotics are bacteria that are formed during fermentation and can assist in restoring the balance of friendly bacteria in your stomach as well as relieve some digestive problems. Probiotics help with irritable bowel syndrome (IBS), a common digestive illness. According to a one-week study conducted in 2007 and published in Alimentary pharmacology and therapeutics in the article named "Effect of a fermented milk containing Bifidobacterium animalis" the 274 participants with IBS, consuming 4.4 ounces (125 grams) of yogurt-like fermented milk daily for six weeks showed reduced IBS symptoms, like bloating and stool frequency. Fermented foods may also aid in the relief of diarrhea, bloating, gas, and constipation. If you have gastrointestinal issues on a regular basis, adding fermented foods to your diet could help.

Boosts Your Immune System

Your immune system is influenced by the bacteria that live in your gut. Fermented foods can boost our immune system, and they also lower your risk of ailments like the common cold due to their rich probiotic content. When you're unwell, eating probiotic-rich foods can also help you heal faster. Furthermore, many fermented foods are high in vitamin C, iron, and zinc, all of which support a healthy immune system.

Easier to Digest

Fermentation breakdown of nutrients present in the foods, which makes them easier to digest than foods that have not been fermented. Take the example of Lactose, the natural sugar in milk, which is broken down into simpler sugars like glucose and galactose during fermentation. That is why Lactose-intolerant people can consume dairy products like kefir and yogurt. Antinutrients, such as lectins and phytates, which are substances found in seeds, nuts, grains, and legumes that interfere with nutrient absorption, are also broken down by fermentation. Consumption of fermented beans or legumes, such as tempeh, improves the absorption of essential nutrients, making them more nutritious than non-fermented alternatives.

Reduces Depression

Probiotic strains L. helveticus and B. longum have been associated with a reduction in anxiety and depression symptoms in a few studies. Fermented foods include both probiotics.

Weight loss

While further research is needed, several studies have discovered associations between particular probiotic strains, such as Lactobacillus gasseri and Lactobacillus rhamnosus, and weight loss and belly fat reduction.

Lower risk of cardiovascular disease

Probiotics may also help in the reduction of total and "bad" LDL cholesterol, as well as the reduction of blood pressure. Fermented foods have been linked to a number of positive health outcomes, including enhanced digestive health, increased immunity, and greater nutrient availability.

Despite all the benefits, if the fermentation is not carried out properly, it may prove to be harmful to health. If you're fermenting food at home, make sure you follow the instructions carefully to ensure your safety. food can rot due to improper temperatures, long fermentation durations, or unsterile equipment. Negative effects of fermented meals include flatulence and bloating. To minimize spoilage while fermenting at home, always follow the recipes and check the nutrition labels on store-bought items.

2. Tools

Getting the equipment and tools right is the first step toward homemade delicious fermented food. Most of these tools are readily available, which makes it easier for you to begin.

Here is a list of equipment and tools that are absolutely necessary to ferment vegetables and herbs at home.

1. Preservation Jars

Jars are used for the storage and preservation of fermented food. If you have any glass jars lying around, you can wash and reuse them for preservation. Just make sure that these jars have complementary airtight lids. Also, the jars should have wider mouths to hold and pack all ingredients without being spilled. To test the width, slide your hand inside and try to reach the bottom of the jar. If your hand slides in easily, you are good to go. To begin with, you can use 500 ml jars to prepare and store your ingredients for fermentation.

2. Weights

Weights keep your vegetables submerged in the brine which allows faster and adequate fermentation and prevents the formation of mold. If your budget doesn't allow you to buy professional weights, you can choose small rocks that are heavy enough to keep the veggies submerged. Make sure that the rocks are smooth and non-porous. You might want to take a trip to your nearby river or lake to find some rocks. Check the size by putting them inside the jars; it should be easy for you to insert and remove the rocks.

Needless to say, you need to wash and sterilize the rocks to remove dirt, dust, and harmful microbes. Use lukewarm water and soap to scrub off the additional dirt and germs. Next, place them in boiling water and let them boil for around 15 to 20 minutes to kill harmful bacteria and sterilize the rocks. Pat them dry with a clean towel and place them in the jar. Boil them to kill bacteria before and after each use.

3. Fermentation Seal

As the name suggests, a fermentation seal covers the preservation jars and prevents oxygen from entering. Since sealing the preservation containers determines the effectiveness of the fermentation process, this tool is another crucial element. If you are using the glass jars that were recommended above, you will most likely get an airtight lid with each mason container. If not, you should go for a Fido style bail wire jar that comes with tight lids. These lids are equipped with rubber seals that sit firmly on the jar and seal adequately to prevent oxygen from entering. This process (absence of oxygen) allows anaerobic fermentation, which is key to tasty and tangy fermented food. This is why sealants are absolutely necessary.

4. Water Filter

Water is one of the main ingredients in the fermentation process, which can make or break the fermentation results. However, most people tend to ignore this point and stick to the water that they have access to. You must know that veggies need filtered water for optimum fermentation, which makes tap water a poor choice. The water you use should be free of antibacterial chemicals and chlorine. By using the water that contains these chemicals, you are killing the good bacteria that are present on the surface of most plants and vegetables, which will eventually prevent fermentation from occurring. So, it is essential to pay attention to the water you are using.

With the right type of water, you are providing an optimum environment for the good bacteria to colonize and decompose the food. Ultimately, this preserves the lactic acid ferment.

The best choice is filtered water that is either extracted from a Brita filter or any good water filter. Brita water removes chlorine and other impurities that are usually present in tap water. These are unhealthy and destroy the fermentation process.

5. Other Tools

Apart from these essential tools, you will also require some necessary equipment that is readily available at home, such as...

- **Pots and pans:** You need these to boil water or hold your veggies.
- **Colander, sieve, or muslin cloth:** You need a colander or a big sieve to drain excess water after washing your veggies.
- **A ladle:** It is needed to stir the mixture and push down the veggies to keep them submerged in the brine.
- **Measuring cups and spoons:** To have the correct amount of salt or other ingredients required in specific recipes
- **Tongs:** Tongs are useful for serving fermented vegetables, especially if they are prepared in large batches.
- **A thermometer:** It is essential to determine the temperature at which the veggies need to be fermented. Keep it beside the fermenting container to ensure the temperature of its environment. If it is too hot or too cold than the ideal temperature, move it to an apt environment. Or, you can also stop the fermentation a bit early in a hot environment to avoid the veggies from getting too sour. During cold weather, you can move the fermentation jar outside and leave it to mature for a longer period. The ideal temperature to ferment veggies is between a range of 18 to 21 C or 65 to 70 F. You can also tweak the temperature and duration of your ferments if the recipes call for it.
- **Vegetable shredder:** This is an optional tool that will make the process easier for you. Shredding vegetables is easier than cutting them evenly with a knife. Also, if you don't have experience in working with large knives, a shredder is a safer option. Dicing vegetables is a time-consuming process, which adds to the overall duration. If you need to fill a 1-gallon container with vegetables, it can take you around one hour to dice up the veggies. However, with a shredder, you can achieve this in less than 20 minutes. Also, shredded veggies are easier to bite into and retain more flavor.
- **A set of knives and chopping board:** If you are skilled with cutting and dicing veggies, you can avoid buying a vegetable shredder. Also, it is advised to stick to cutting and dicing veggies during your first fermentation attempt. Once you master it, you can then move on to shredding your veggies.

- **Grater:** For veggies like carrots and beetroots.
- **Blender:** Recipes like fermented tomato salsa and ketchup need a blender to blend the veggies and turn them into consistent purees.
- **Garlic crusher:** Some recipes also need a garlic crusher to obtain minced garlic.

These are some necessary tools and equipment that are required for fermenting veggies and herbs. Make sure that you get them right as they can heavily manipulate the results.

3. Methods/Process

Because we are dealing with living organisms to preserve food, and there are so many foods you can ferment, all with their own unique properties, specific steps are discussed in detail in the recipes. There are some universal rules applicable to fermentation, however, which are described here. Keep in mind that cultures need to be treated as live and specific to ingredients.

1. Choose the best produce.

Always use the best products available because these items carry the bacteria that will start your fermentation project. Inspect all produce for blemishes, soft spots, and areas of decay. The skins must be firm, not tough, which would make them less able to interact with the pickling solution and reactions. Always use unwaxed produce when fermenting.

2. Clean your vessel and produce.

Wash your fermentation vessel well with hot soapy water. Ensure that there is no soap residue remaining after rinsing. Wash any soil from the produce but don't scrub it senselessly or use a vegetable cleaner because you need the lactic acid bacteria on the produce to start the fermentation process. Pack your items tightly into the clean container.

3. Make the brine.

The salt brine you need to start the fermentation process can be created in two ways, depending on the size of the pieces you want to ferment. Items with high moisture content and a lot of surface area, like shredded cabbage, will create their own brine when interacting with the salt. For larger pieces, or less water-rich produce, you'll need to create a brine. Follow the recipe for instructions.

4. Submerge your ferment.

Fill your vessel with brine until the items to be fermented are covered. More brine will be created as time passes, so you do not need to overdo it; just fill the vessel so the items are submerged when you press down on them. If you have an airlock, secure your lid, lock it, and fill it with water or brine. If you have a weight, add that to the vessel. If you do not have a weight, create one using a heavy-duty resealable plastic bag filled with brine (if the bag breaks, it will not dilute the ferment). Make sure all items are submerged under the brine. Cover the vessel with a cloth or a few layers of cheesecloth and secure it around the container with a string or rubber band.

5. Store your ferment.

Place the vessel in an area where the temperature is between 70°F and 90°F. The storage temperature will affect your ferment. If it's too hot, the process will happen too quickly and the food will be soft or broken down. If it's too cold, fermentation may not happen at all, or it will happen too slowly and can affect the final product. When the temperature is not ideal, it can lead to other—unwanted—bacteria invading your ferment.

6. Check your ferment.

Scum may form on the surface. Check regularly for scum and remove any immediately. Leaving scum on the ferment will eventually affect your product, so pay attention and maintain a clean surface area on the top of the ferment.

The following will happen under the right conditions. It is important to check your ferment daily and even take notes on your observations. Fermentation begins in just a few days and can last for months in controlled conditions and temperatures. During days 1 to 3, you should see a clear brine with no cloudiness. In 2 to 5 days, you'll have a cloudy brine with gas formation. Gas is forming when you see little bubbles around the items being fermenting that were not there before. In an airlock, you will see the gas pass through. Around day 5 or 6, the brine will be cloudy with no gas formation.

7. Taste your ferment.

After day 6, begin to taste your ferment. Keep tasting and monitoring your ferment until it reaches your desired flavor; the longer it sits, the stronger the flavors. Once your ferment is completed, refrigerate it to slow the process.

Pickling

Pickling is the preservation of food through anaerobic fermentation in brine or vinegar, which can keep perishable items for months. Pickling is most commonly achieved by preserving produce in a vinegar-brine, most commonly using the water bath canning method, or by wild fermentation, which requires fermentation equipment such as a pickling crock or a fermentation kit, such as the Perfect Pickler.

While starting the pickling process at home can be frightening for beginners, with a few simple supplies and tools, we can all be quick-pickling like pros in no time.

Different Types of Pickling

Quick-pickling, salt-brine pickling, and the vinegar brine soak-and-rinse method are the three primary ways for vinegar brine pickling. There are various variants, recipes, and ways to make relishes and chutneys within those procedures. Each pickling method has its own set of advantages, and some foods are better suited to one method than another.

Quick Pickling

While longer-term, shelf-stable pickling necessitates specialized fermentation equipment (such as a pickle crock), the rapid pickling method—ideal for beginners—requires only a pot, a heat source, and a few airtight jars. This approach is not only a simple way to get started with pickling, but it's also a cost-effective and tasty way to preserve your favorite veggies and fruits.

Quick pickles are also referred to as "fresh pickles." The fundamental approach is to pack your fresh vegetables and any extra spices into sterilized canning jars, fill the jars with a vinegar-based pickling brine to completely submerge the fruit, and then use the water bath canning to preserve the jars. Asparagus, for example, are blanched before being pickled. Other vegetables, such as beets, are boiled until soft and then cooled before being pickled. Cucumbers, carrots, cauliflower, peppers, and green beans are all excellent pickled choices. Cherries and apples are other great choices.

Quick-pickles are the most convenient way to enjoy tasty pickles in a few days or fewer. They may lack the depth of taste of fermented pickles and may not be as healthful, but they are the ideal way for first-time and beginner picklers.

Salt-Brined Pickling

The salt-brined pickling method is designed for pickling high-water-content vegetables and produce. You can pull some of the natural water content out of the produce by salting it before packing it into the canning jars. This allows the pickling liquid to penetrate the produce more deeply, improving flavor, texture, and shelf life.

This approach involves sprinkling salt on your produce or soaking it in a salt and vinegar brine solution to remove the water. You'll want to properly rinse and drain your vegetables after they've been adequately salt-brined.

After the product has been rinsed and drained, proceed with the 'quick-pickling' procedure mentioned above. Basically, you place your veggies and any additional spices into canning jars, pour a vinegar-brine pickling solution over them, and then use the water bath canning procedure to preserve the canning jars' texture and shelf life.

Bread-and-butter pickles, kosher-style dill pickles, cabbage, zucchini, eggplant, and other high-water-content vegetables are often pickled using the salt-brined process, and they make for tasty everyday snacks! Salt-brined pickles are the ideal way to make classic-tasting pickles with the taste, crunch, and shelf-life you'd expect from store-bought varieties. This technique is ideal for intermediate picklers.

Soak and Rinse with Vinegar-Brine Pickling

This approach is similar to the salt-brined method above, but it adds a layer of complexity to get the most water out of the produce. This allows the pickling liquid to completely soak the fruit, resulting in a more delicious and well-textured pickle. By soaking, draining, and soaking again with a vinegar solution, this procedure extracts the maximum amount of water from the crop. A salt-water brine and a lot of sugar are sometimes utilized in this technique.

The vinegar-brined method is commonly used in recipes such as 9-day and 12-day pickles, as well as Sweet Gherkins. This procedure is also used to pickle watermelon rind and other soft fruits, albeit there are fewer steps for these fruits than for vegetables. The most conventional of picklers will like vinegar-brined pickles, which have a distinct crunch, texture, and flavor.

Fermentation Pickling

Fermentation pickling is a whole different technique from the vinegar-brine procedures we've examined thus far. To prepare fermented pickles, immerse your food thoroughly in a salt-water brine, usually in a pickling crock or a fermentation kit like the Perfect Pickler. Pickling weights keep your produce submerged at all times, ensuring that it never comes into contact with oxygen or bacteria found in the open air. The vegetables are then buried in the brine and left to ferment for a few days or weeks. Fermentation times differ based on the recipe, the environment, and personal preference.

The salt takes the natural water out of the product as it is fermenting. The carbohydrates are digested by naturally occurring microbes, which produce lactic acid and other helpful bacteria. This technique lowers the pH of the liquid to a level that preserves the product while keeping it safe to eat. To aid the fermenting process, you don't need to add vinegar, sugar, or citrus.

Fermented pickles have a distinct flavor and scent that cannot be replicated using the vinegar-brine procedures described above. Fermented pickles are also the healthiest sort of pickled food because they contain living bacteria and probiotics that are created during the fermenting process.

Sauerkraut is undoubtedly the most well-known fermented pickle recipe, with deli-style dills and barrel-aged pickles coming in second and third, respectively. Pickles that have been fermented are actually quite simple to create. If you have a pickling crock (also known as a fermentation crock), you may use it to make everything from sauerkraut to dill pickles to kimchi and more.

As a budding homesteader, getting into the world of fermentation can be one of the most thrilling things you'll ever accomplish, providing your family with both delicious and nutritious snacks all year!

Pickling Relishes and Chutneys

Pickling your own food at home can be done in a variety of ways. Making relishes, chutneys, and other pickled foods is one of our favorite ways to impress friends and family. Relishes and chutneys are pickled foods made out of finely diced pieces that commonly incorporate a variety of fruits and vegetables for a unique flavor and texture.

Many relish recipes use a salt-brine or vinegar brine to pull the water out of the vegetables before pickling, resulting in a more flavorful result. Although many chutneys are cooked ahead of time to achieve a jam-like consistency, they nevertheless use the same basic ingredients and processes as relishes or other pickle recipes.

These relishes, chutneys, and other unique pickling dishes make excellent gifts or appetizers while entertaining guests. They'll also bring a new dimension of taste and excitement to daily recipes.

4. Benefits

Whether your main concern is improving your health or stretching your pocketbook, there are several reasons why pickling at home can be a good option for you.

Extend Shelf Life

Pickling foods extends their shelf life. Naturally, decomposition would begin in just days at room temperature, but through fermentation, many items can be stored for weeks. And when pickled foods are canned, the shelf life typically extends to one year. By pickling foods, you can take a large harvest from your garden (or bought in bulk at the farmers' market) and prepare a variety of items that will last beyond the growing season.

Provide Probiotics

Pickling foods traditionally through fermentation is a great way to get a healthy dose of probiotics on a daily basis. Probiotics, important for providing your digestive tract with healthy bacteria that improve digestion and promote overall health, are considered beneficial for all people. When you make traditionally pickled products through fermentation, you are growing these healthy bacteria and yeasts yourself that will then colonize your digestive tract and help your body fight infection, improve immunity, and minimize digestive distress. In addition, since fermented foods have already begun the process of breaking down, they are easier for your body to digest than the same foods served raw.

Increase Flavor

Pickling foods increases their flavor and allows you to add hints of additional flavors. For example, cucumbers can taste bland on their own, but when infused with dill, garlic, and other spices, their flavor comes alive and really shines. This is true with so many types of produce and makes pickling a great way to try new foods that may never have seemed appealing before. If you don't like the sourness of pickles, keep in mind that there are also several types of sweet pickles, as well as some varieties that are not as pronouncedly sour as others. It is this wide range of flavors that makes pickles so appealing to so many people.

Increase Fruit And Vegetable Intake

Fermented pickles are arguably a better option regarding advantages for your health, but even quick pickling provides health benefits. If pickling enables you to eat more fruits and vegetables regularly, it can be a convenient way to increase your consumption and, consequently, increase the number of valuable vitamins and minerals you are putting in your body. While quick-pickled foods don't have the probiotic benefits of fermented foods, pickled carrots, beets, asparagus, and other vegetables contain a wealth of nutrients your body needs and add more veggies to your diet in a delicious and unique way.

Save Money

Pickling foods yourself lets you eat a wide variety of gourmet-quality foods at half the price. When produce is at the height of its season, it is at its lowest prices, so this is the best time to snag some deals and get started on a pickling project. You can have pickled vegetables all year long, beyond the growing season, and because you do all of the labor yourself in making the end product, you pay no additional cost—not the case with the myriad artisanal pickled products lining the shelves of supermarkets.

5. Tools

You don't need a bunch of fancy equipment to get started pickling. Sure, you could spend a lot of money on specialized pickling implements, but it is in no way necessary. Starting small and scaling up if you decide that you love the art of pickling is a sensible way to go.

- **Kitchen scale:** For the most precision, a kitchen scale is recommended to ensure that accurate quantity of produce and ingredients are used. Because volume and number equivalents do not always match, this is the best way to ensure your results. You can always measure produce at the market if you do not have a kitchen scale, but it is much more convenient to have one at home. They are reasonably priced (under $20) and make a great addition to your kitchen.
- **Bowls and pots:** Because pickling widely uses both salt and vinegar, which are both quite reactive, it is important that you use non-reactive cookware and bowls when making pickled products from this book. On the range, both stainless steel and hard-anodized aluminum pots and pans work well, while stainless steel, glass, and ceramic are all good options for bowls.
- **Utensils**: A non-reactive spoon and ladle are needed for many of the recipes in this book. Stainless steel, wood, or plastic utensils make the best choices.
- **Fermentation vessel:** You will also need a vessel in which to ferment your pickles. This can either be glass or ceramic. Large quart and 2-quart mason jars are good fermentation vessels, and in some cases, a bowl can be used as well. For smaller batches, there are a few different types of jars available, which are fitted with an airlock to help with the anaerobic process. These are easy to use and are often sold with weights to help keep fermenting foods submerged below the brine.
- **Weights:** The fermentation recipes in this book require that the produce is weighted during fermentation to prevent the food from being exposed to oxygen. For this purpose, a ceramic plate, small jar, or clean rock can be used. If you use wide-mouth canning jars, a regular-mouth jelly jar fits nicely in the mouth of the jar as a weight. In smaller jars, a votive candle holder or a food-safe zip-top bag filled with brine can also be used to hold the produce below the brine. Whichever you choose, the same principles for nonreactive items, such as the bowls and pots, apply here as well.
- **Canning supplies**: If you plan on canning your pickles, at the very least you will need a small canning setup. A large, deep pot with a lid will suffice for a water-bath canner. A drying rack, towel, or canning rack will also be needed to keep the jars off the surface of the pot to prevent breakage. Other necessary tools are a jar filler, a jar lifter, and two-piece canning lids.
- **Jars:** Mason jars in several different sizes are typically all that is needed to store your pickles. If you are canning your pickles, you want to stock up on these in half-pint, pint, and quart sizes. For refrigerator storage, you can also use half-gallon jars. If you are not planning on canning pickles, old repurposed glass jars are fine alternatives to mason jars.

However, these should never be used for canning, as they are designed for single use and are not as sturdy as mason jars, nor do they have the correct lid.

- **Lids:** For pickle storage, it is a good idea to invest in plastic lids that fit onto mason jars. These are available in wide-mouth and narrow-mouth sizes from any retailer that sells canning supplies. These prevent a reaction caused by the acidic nature of pickles in contact with a reactive metal. While canning lids in theory will not react with pickles, if the lid is nicked or damaged, a reaction takes place that will cause the lid to rust. For this reason, you should line a canning lid with a couple of layers of plastic wrap if you are going to use one for storing pickles.

Additional Tools

Additional tools make the prep work in pickling easier. Other tools help specifically when canning or fermenting, so consider them for your wish list.

1. **Kitchen prep tools:** For general food prep, a few other tools can make pickling easier and faster. A food processor can save significant time, particularly when making large batches. An immersion blender makes it easy to puree sauces, particularly hot ones. Consider a zester for citrus, a mandoline for thin slicing, a fine-mesh colander for straining, and finely woven cheesecloth for myriad uses.

2. **Canning tools:** Canning kits often include an array of tools, the most useful of which (besides the must-have jar lifter) is the wide-mouth funnel, because it significantly reduces mess. Bamboo or wooden chopsticks can be used to remove bubbles. You can judge headspace by using the jar's thread: If you run a measuring tape from a canning jar's rim toward its bottom, you'll notice that at ½ inch, you hit the bottom end of the jar's threads on a wide-mouth jar and the collar below the threads on a narrow-mouth jar.

3. **Fermenting tools:** For a fermenting investment, consider a crock, kraut pounder, and pH meter. Modern crocks often come with specially fitted weights and a water-lock rim, making fermentation nearly foolproof. Today's crocks range from the traditional 5 and 10 liters down to 2-liter and smaller vessels. A kraut pounder is particularly useful for cabbage or chile-heavy recipes. A pH meter shows when your fermented pickles have hit pH 4.6 and are ready for storage.

6. Methods/Process

We're going to keep things easy since this is a novice's guide to pickling, so let's do it step by step.

6. Choose Your Vegetables

It is strongly advised you start by visualizing what you would like to see on the plate rather than worrying about pickling.

It's also motivating to think beyond the vegetable box. Consider those pink pearl pickled onions or that bright purple cabbage. Capsicums, Purple cabbage, chilies, green beans, carrots, green tomatoes, and radishes are more options.

7. Clean & Properly Care for Your Glass Jars

Whether you're purchasing new glass containers or recycling old ones, you'll need to thoroughly clean them before sterilizing them. Pickling jars must be sterilized to prevent the pickles from spoiling due to the growth of harmful germs. To sterilize the jars, heat them to the level where no bacteria can live. It's better to disinfect them just before you pickle them.

While the pickling process is enjoyable, the sterilizing step is laborious and time-consuming, yet it is necessary. Before using any spoons, or other utensils, ensure sure they are sterilized.

The Oven Technique is one approach to sterilizing the jars.

As you are pickling in jars that have rubber seals, you'll need to take them off before putting them in the oven. Preheat the oven to 130 degrees Celsius (not higher than this). Wash the lids & jars in super-hot soapy water, wash them (do not dry them), and place them on a baking sheet coated with baking paper. Immerse the lids in boiling water for 5 to 10 minutes while the jars bake for 15 to 20 minutes. Remove the jars off the jar rack and put them on the clean kitchen counter. The jars need to chill to room temperature first. If you're placing hot jams into jars, you should do it while they're still hot. You risk breaking the jars if you put cold components in hot jars.

The Method of the Microwave

Pickling jars may also be sterilized in the microwave, which is really the quickest way. All you have to do is microwave the clean jars for 45 seconds. Start by rinsing them in hot water and leaving them somewhat damp. Clearly, you cannot microwave the jars' metal lids or tops. Pickling requires allowing the jars to cool on the counter,

8. Get The Vegetables Ready

Clean the veggies well in water that is safe to consume. Clean your veggies thoroughly. Some veggies must be blanched, while others must be cooked. You must also choose how to store them: whole veggies, thick coin-shaped pieces cut lengthwise, or thinly sliced matchsticks.

9. Choose Your Aromatic Ingredients

Salt is required, and pure sea salt is required. Experts suggest using 20 to 40g of sea salt on each liter of water, or approximately two teaspoons. But after that, it's entirely up to you what you put in the solution with your veggies. You'll need to follow a recipe for the first few times.

10.   Get the Brine Ready

You will need equal parts vinegar and water for a simple, fast pickle. Boil the water and add the salt to make the brine, then it comes to room temperature.

11. Get The Pickle Jar Ready

Fill the sterilized jar(s) to the brim with the veggies, then add the aromatics, and finally the brine. Place a vine leaf or cabbage leaf on top to prevent your veggies from rising to the surface and being exposed to air, as well as to keep your pickles crisp.

12. Store Your Jars After Sealing Them

Just put a lid on securely and chill the jar for a few days' worth of pickles. They'll be done in an hour, but one can leave them for several days. The longer you keep the pickles sealed in the jar in the fridge, the stronger flavors you'll get. If you want prolonged fresh pickles or fridge pickles, keep an eye on the jars and remove the lids every several days to enable the bacteria to start the fermentation and Carbon dioxide build-up within. When the brine starts to cloud, periodically open the jar, then chill the jar for 1-2 weeks, at which point the pickles will begin to mature fully.

Fermenting Recipes

FRUITS AND VEGETABLES

1. Raw Fermented Beets

Preparation time: 1 week
Cooking time: 0 minutes
Servings: 10
Ingredients:

- 2 pounds beets, peeled & cut into chunks
- 4 cloves gochutgaru garlic, peeled
- 6 peppercorns
- 2 bay leaves
- Brine:
- 3 cups water, boiled and cooled
- 1 tablespoon salt

Directions:

1. Divide chunks of beet in between 2 jars with lids. Place 1 bay leaf, 2 cloves garlic and 3 peppercorns into each jar.
2. In a bowl, mix salt and water to make the brine and stir until the salt is dissolved completely. Add enough brine into jars to cover the beets completely.
3. Close with lids and allow the jars to stand at room temperature for about 1 week until the foam begins to appear at the top. Place the jars in a cool place (10 degrees C, 50 degrees F) for 2 to 3 days once the foam appears. Keep in the fridge.

Per serving: Calories 53Kcal; Fat: 0.2g; Carbohydrates: 11.9g; Protein: 2g

2. Fermented Onions

Preparation time: 1 hour + 3-4 weeks fermenting time
Cooking time: 0 minutes
Servings: 1-2 jars
Ingredients:

- 3 cups onions, peeled
- 2 tbsp salt
- 4 cups water

Directions:

1. Prepare the onions and add them to the jar, leaving 1-inch headspace.
2. Combine salt and water and pour into the jar.
3. Seal jar with lid and store in a dark place. Open once a day to release gas before sealing again.
4. Repeat for 3-4 weeks until there are no more bubbles.
5. Store in fridge.

Per serving: Calories 138Kcal; Fat: 0.4g; Carbohydrates: 32.2g; Protein: 3.8g

3. Bok Choy White Kimchi

Preparation time: 3 hours + 1-2 weeks fermenting time
Cooking time: 0 minutes
Servings: 2 qt.
Ingredients:

- 1 Korean radish
- 3 tbsp. salt
- 1 kg bok choy
- ½ ripe and cored pear
- ½ white onion
- 2 garlic cloves
- 1 fresh ginger piece
- 3 green chilies
- ½ tsp. fish sauce
- 3 green onions
- ½ bunch of cilantro

Directions:

1. Start by slicing or shredding the radish. Cut the bok choy into quarters. Add these cutdown radish and bok choy to a large bowl.
2. Take 3 tablespoons of salt and add to the radish and bok choy. Cover the bowl and let it be for one to 3 hours at room temperature.
3. Take a good-quality chopper. Add chilies, garlic, ginger, onions, puree of pear, and fish sauce only if you want,

and start the blender. Make a smooth paste of all these ingredients.

4. After the required time, wash the Korean radish and the bok choy with water and rinse them thoroughly. Now strain and squeeze them to take out water. Ensure that there is no water in the bok choy.

5. Chop the green onions and cilantro to add them to the veggies. Now add the paste to this mixture.

6. Take the jars and fill them with these spiced radishes and bok choy. Shake the jar and stir it so that there is no air left inside.

7. Make sure the seal is tight but slightly loosened on the 1/8 turn. Store these jars for 2 weeks in the dark. Maintain the room temperature and when these veggies are pickled according to your requirement, store them in the fridge. You can store them for up to a year.

Per serving: Calories 13Kcal; Fat: 0.2g; Carbohydrates: 2.18g; Protein: 1.5g

4. Tomato Ketchup

Preparation time: 10 minutes + 2 to 3 days fermenting time

Cooking Time: 0 minutes

Servings: 1 cup

Ingredients:
- 6 oz of tomato paste
- 1 tbsp. honey or maple syrup
- 2 tbsp. starter liquid (whey, sauerkraut juice, or water kefir)
- 1/4 tsp. salt
- 1 garlic clove
- 1/8 tsp. cinnamon powder
- 1 pinch cayenne
- 1 pinch of ground cloves
- 2 tbsp. apple cider vinegar

Directions:
1. Take a ready-made tomato paste or make it yourself by blending tomatoes.

2. Now, take this paste in a bowl and add starter liquid to it. Mix it well and add salt, cinnamon, garlic, honey, cloves, and cayenne. Mix them thoroughly to make a homogeneous paste.

3. Now, transfer this paste to the jar and shake it well.

4. Take apple cider vinegar and pour it over the ketchup surface. This addition of vinegar prevents the growth of microbes on the surface.

5. Now, you have to store it in a jar at room temperature. Ensure the maintenance of temperature and no entry of light. Keep them in the same conditions for 3 days.

6. When the ketchup is fermented to the required state, stir the whole mixture to mix the vinegar with the rest of the ketchup. You can keep it in your fridge for 2-3 weeks.

7. The consistency of the ketchup depends on the quantity of starter liquid. If you add enough starter liquid, the ketchup will become thinner.

Per serving: Calories 15Kcal; Fat: 0.3g; Carbohydrates: 4.1g; Protein: 0.16g

5. Sauerkraut (Simple Cultured Cabbage)

Preparation time: 20 minutes + 3 days- 2 weeks fermenting time

Cooking Time: 0 minutes

Servings: 1-2 jars

Ingredients:
- 1 to 2 tbsp. of mineral salt
- 1 to 2 heads of cabbage, ~2 pounds

Directions:
1. With a mandolin, shred the cabbage.

2. Add salt (2 tsp.) onto the cabbage and massage it, add more salt (but not too much) to make it salty.

3. Let it rest for half an hour. Add to a jar, push down with clean hands.

4. Leave a 3-inch space from above. Add 2-3 cabbage leaves

5. Check it every day, taste after 3rd day. Let it ferment for 3 days-2 weeks based on the flavor profile you want.

6. Store in the fridge with a lid.

Per serving: Calories 89Kcal; Fat: 0g; Carbohydrates: 1g; Protein: 0g

6. Fermented Lemons

Preparation time: 14 minutes + 2 weeks fermenting time

Cooking Time: 0 minutes

Servings: 1-2 jars

Ingredients:

- 5-6 lemons
- 3 tbsp sea salt

Directions:

1. Clean the lemons and cut them into pieces, either in slices or quarters, as preferred.

2. Sprinkle salt on the lemon and put it into the jar. When full, squish and add more. The salt and juice will combine into the brine.

3. Only stop when the lemons aren't totally submerged in the juice and the jar is completely full. Then, juice another lemon or two on top.

4. Sprinkle a bit more salt, then put plastic wrap over and push lemons down. You want them all submerged in the juice.

5. Throw the lid on and let sit in the open for 2 weeks. Turn over the jar each day to keep salt from settling.

6. After two weeks, put it back into the fridge.

Per serving: Calories 29Kcal; Fat: 0.3g; Carbohydrates: 9g; Protein: 1.1g

7. DAIRY AND BREAD

7. Homemade Greek Yogurt

Preparation time: 50 minutes

Cooking time: 0 minutes

Servings: 1 quart

Ingredients:

- 1 quart (32 ounces) homemade yogurt

Directions:

1. Fold a large piece of cheesecloth over itself (doubling its thickness) and lay it on top of a large bowl.

2. Pour yogurt on your cheesecloth.

3. Take all of the edges of your cheesecloth then bring them together so that you have a bundle of yogurt. Use a rubber band to seal the cheesecloth around the yogurt wholly.

4. After securing your bundle, use one or two more rubber bands to hang it from a shelf or cabinet over the mixing bowl so that the gravity helps drain the whey (liquid) from the yogurt.

5. Allow the yogurt to strain for 45 minutes to an hour.

6. Release the yogurt bundle from its rubber band hold and open up the cheesecloth. The yogurt should look thick and kind of stringy.

Per serving: Calories 215Kcal; Fat: 3.7g; Carbohydrates: 21.2g; Protein: 17.2g

8. Cultured Buttermilk

Preparation time: 24-36 hours

Cooking time: 0 minutes

Servings: 5 cups

Ingredients:

- 1 cup active cultured buttermilk
- 4 cups whole milk

Directions:

1. Purchase a container of active cultured buttermilk. This shouldn't be too hard to find. Most grocery stores carry active cultured buttermilk. Try to find a new container that hasn't been sitting on the shelf for a long time. The closer the buttermilk is to its expiration date, the fewer active cultures it will have.

2. Add 1 cup of active cultured buttermilk to 4 cups of whole milk. Stir the buttermilk into the whole milk and pour the mixture into a glass jar.

3. Place the lid tightly on the jar and let the jar sit at room temperature for 24 hours. Check the buttermilk to see if it has clabbered. If not, let it sit for another 12 hours. If it hasn't clabbered by this point, throw out the batch and try again with new buttermilk.

4. Move the finished buttermilk to the fridge.

5. Once you've made a batch of buttermilk, you can use a cup of buttermilk from your old batch to make the next batch as long as it isn't too old. As long as you stay on top of things, you can continue making new batches using buttermilk from the earlier batch indefinitely.

Per serving: Calories 210Kcal; Fat: 7.7g; Carbohydrates: 20.6g; Protein: 14.5g

9. Sourdough Bread

Preparation time: 3 hours + 12 to 24 hours processing time

Cooking time: 0 minutes

Servings: One Loaf

Ingredients:

- ½ c. sourdough starter
- 1 ¼ bottled water
- 3 ¼ c. all-purpose flour
- 2 tbsp. spices and whole seeds
- 1 tsp. salt

Directions:

1. Take a large bowl for mixing and add a sourdough starter. Now, pour all of the water into the sourdough.

2. Add all-purpose flour or whole grain flour, according to your choice, to the bowl. Mix all of the ingredients already put in the bowl. Keep mixing and kneading the sourdough until it absorbs all the water. The dough will be shaggy, cover it using a towel and leave to rest for 20 minutes.

3. Now add salt to the surface of the sourdough by sprinkling equally. Knead this dough well for 5 to 10 minutes. The dough will not be shaggy anymore but will be consistent.

4. Leave the sourdough covered with a towel for 1 ½ hours. Check the dough every 30 minutes and keep folding it from its corners.

5. You should not disturb this covered dough for another 6 to 7 hours. It will double itself during this time.

6. When 6 hours have passed, uncover the dough, fold it and make a ball, and leave it to rest for almost 20 minutes.

7. After 20 minutes, tightly shape the dough, and transfer it to an olive oil-coated bowl. Leave it undisturbed and covered for another one to 2 hours.

8. Meanwhile, ready your oven by preheating it at 475 F. Score the top of the dough using the bread knife and let it get baked for 10 minutes. After 10 minutes, lower the oven temperature to 400 F. Now, bake the dough for 25 minutes more.

9. After 25 minutes, turn off the oven and transfer the dough to a cooling rack. Wait for it to cool down before slicing it.

Per serving: Calories 174Kcal; Fat: 1.5g; Carbohydrates: 33g; Protein: 6.9g

10. Queso Fresco

Preparation time: 2 hours + 6 hours processing time

Cooking time: 0 minutes

Servings: 450 grams

Ingredients:

- 1 gallon of milk
- 1 packet of mesophilic starter
- 2 tbsp. salt
- ⅛ tsp. rennet diluted with ¼ c. water
- Cheese mold

Directions:

1. Pour one gallon of milk into a large pot and put it on the stove. Keep the flame high then wait till the milk temperature reaches 90 F.
2. Remove the pot when it reaches this temperature. Add the starter to the milk while continuously stirring the milk. Leave this mixture for 40 minutes. Make sure to cover the pot while waiting.
3. Add ⅛ teaspoon of rennet to ¼ cup of water. Stir water and rennet to combine them. Then cover this mixture and let it be for 45 minutes. Check for the visible curd after 45 minutes have passed. This layer will be right below the whey layer. Check the curd using a butter knife. If the pressing with the knife makes the butter break at the surface, the mixture is ready.
4. Wait for the cheese to set into a mass. Then cut this semi-solid cheese into cubes not longer than ¼ inch. Cover the cheese for 5 minutes.
5. Put the pot on the stove to cook the curd. Maintain the temperature at 90 F and keep stirring the curd unless the whey layer separates from it completely.
6. Strain the curd using a sieve and make cheese from this curd using a cheese mold. Press the curd with appropriate weight and add salt to the cheese. Keep the cheese undisturbed for 4-5 hours.
7. When 4 hours have passed, check the cheese. If you are satisfied with the texture, keep it in the fridge for 2 weeks at best.

Per serving: Calories 365Kcal; Fat: 29g; Carbohydrates: 3.6g; Protein: 22g

11. Fermented Kefir

Preparation time: 20 minutes + 2-4 days processing time

Cooking time: 0 minutes
Servings: 1 pint/quart
Ingredients:

- Kefir grains, 1 oz.
- Milk, 7 oz.

Directions:

1. In a glass jar (1 pint), add kefir & milk.
2. Close with a paper towel and place a rubber band around the paper towel.
3. Keep in a darker environment cool environment for 12-48 hours, strain after 12, 48 hours, as to get your desired taste.
4. Do not wash the jars in between straining, replace the jar after 4 days.

Per serving: Calories 87Kcal; Fat: 0g; Carbohydrates: 1g; Protein: 2.1g

8. BEVERAGES

12. Batch-Brewed Kombucha Tea

Preparation time: 15 minutes + 7 days processing time
Cooking time: 5 minutes
Servings: 5 cups
Ingredients:

- 4 bags of your favorite green or black tea
- 1 cup organic cane sugar
- ¼ cup vinegar.
- 8 cups of filtered water

Directions:

1. Wash your hands with apple cider vinegar. Don't use antibacterial hand wash or soap because it can interfere with the bacteria in kombucha.
2. Place the water in a pot over high heat. Bring the water to a boil and let it boil for at least 5 minutes. Turn off the heat and immediately place the tea bags in the water. Add the sugar to the water and stir it in.
3. Wait for the tea to cool to room temperature and pour the tea into a glass jar. Add the vinegar to the tea. If

you have access to kombucha tea that hasn't been pasteurized or otherwise processed, you can use a cup of tea instead. The vinegar (or tea) is necessary to get the pH of the tea low enough to prevent bad bacteria or mold from developing.

4. Add the kombucha starter culture to the tea. Avoid directly touching it if at all possible. Cover the top of the jar with cheesecloth or cloth and band it or tie it down.

5. Place the jar somewhere dark and warm. The ideal temperature range is 80 degrees F to 87 degrees F. Avoid fermenting kombucha at temperatures below 70 degrees F because bad bacteria, mold and pathogens are more likely to form.

6. Let the tea ferment for 7 days. The SCOBY culture may float to the top during the fermentation process. This is fine. Baby SCOBY will typically form at the surface of the kombucha, eventually forming a new SCOBY that acts as a protective barrier. Dip a straw into the tea and block the straw off with your finger to trap tea inside. You can either taste the tea to see if it tastes like vinegar or check the pH to see if it's around 3. More brewing time is needed if it tastes too sweet or the pH is above 3.

7. Remove the mother culture and any smaller SCOBY cultures that may have formed and place them in a clean non-reactive container. Cover them with kombucha to keep them safe.

8. Move the finished kombucha tea to glass containers and place a lid on them. If you're happy with the carbonation level of the kombucha, loosely cap the containers. On the other hand, if you want more carbonation, tightly cap the containers. Let the kombucha ferment for another 3 to 5 days before either drinking it or moving it to the fridge to slow the fermentation process.

9. Periodically open the container to allow gases trapped inside to escape.

Per serving: Calories 86Kcal; Fat: 0g; Carbohydrates: 22.68g; Protein: 0g

13. Ginger Kombucha

Preparation time: 15 minutes + 7 days processing time

Cooking time: 5 minutes

Servings: 10 cups

Ingredients:

- 4 bags of your favorite green or black tea
- 1 cup organic cane sugar
- 1 cup homemade kombucha tea
- 8 cups of filtered water
- 3-4 ginger slices

Directions:

1. Wash your hands with vinegar. Place the water in a pot on the stove and bring it to a boil. Add the tea bags then turn off the stove. Once the water stops boiling, add the cane sugar and stir it in. Let the tea cool to room temperature.

2. Remove the tea bags then place the sweet tea in a glass fermenting container. Add the cup of kombucha tea and place the SCOBY in the container with the tea. Cover the container loosely with a piece of cloth and band it, so it won't come off.

3. Let the tea ferment for 7 days. Remove the SCOBY culture and prepare it for safekeeping or move it to another batch of kombucha. Place the kombucha in bottles with the ginger slices and cap the bottles tightly. Let the bottles sit for another 4 to 5 days. Open the bottle at least once a day to let the gases out or you run the risk of exploding bottles.

4. Once the carbonation has developed to your liking, move the bottles to the

fridge to slow the fermentation process.

Per serving: Calories 95Kcal; Fat: 0g; Carbohydrates: 0g; Protein: 1.2g

14. Cherry Lime Soda

Preparation time: 15 minutes + 2-3 days processing time

Cooking time: 0 minutes

Servings: 11 cups

Ingredients:

- 2 cups 100% cherry juice
- 5 limes, juiced
- 8 cups water kefir

Directions:

1. Add all ingredients to your pitcher or jug and stir together. Pour into sealable bottles and seal.
2. Leave bottles at room temperature for two to three days before consuming or placing them in the refrigerator.

Per serving: Calories 346Kcal; Fat: 0g; Carbohydrates: 85.6g; Protein: 0g

15. Cabbage and Carrot Fermented Juice

Preparation time: 15 minutes + 4-6 days processing time

Cooking time: 0 minutes

Servings: 2 quarts

Ingredients:

- ½ head cabbage, sliced
- 3 carrots, grated
- 1 tablespoon ginger, grated
- 2 teaspoons sea salt
- Bottled spring water for soaking vegetables
- Gears/Materials:
- 2-quart jar
- Cheesecloth or kitchen towel
- Rubber band
- Long handle spoon for stirring

Directions:

1. Place the cabbage, carrots, ginger, and sea salt in a 2-quart jar.

2. Fill the jar with spring or well water.
3. Place cheesecloth or a kitchen towel over the jar and secure it with a rubber band to keep the bugs out.
4. Leave the jar in a warm, dark place for four to six days, stirring well twice a day. Bubbles and grayish foam will form on the surface of the liquid, which is completely normal and should not be interpreted as spoilage. When the juice is finished, it will smell sour, yeasty, and vinegary (not rotten).
5. Strain the juice off the vegetables and either drink immediately or pour into a sealable jar or bottle and keep in the refrigerator for up to one week.

Per serving: Calories 31Kcal; Fat: 0.1g; Carbohydrates: 7.1g; Protein: 1.2g

Pickling Recipes

9. VEGETABLES

16. Pickled Cherry Tomatoes

Preparation time: 10 minutes

Cooking time: 10 minutes

Servings: 4

Ingredients:

- 4 cups cherry tomatoes
- 2 cups water
- 1 cup vinegar
- 2 sprigs fresh rosemary
- 2 garlic cloves
- 1/2 tsp salt

Directions:

1. Add vinegar, water, and salt in a saucepan and bring to a boil over medium heat. Turn heat to low then simmer for 10 minutes.
2. Pack cherry tomatoes in clean jars.
3. Add garlic cloves and rosemary on top of the tomatoes.

4. Pour hot brine over tomatoes. Leave 1/4-inch headspace.

5. Seal jar with lids. Process in your water bath canner for 10 minutes.

6. Remove jars from the water bath and let them cool completely.

7. Check seals of jars. Label and store.

Per serving: Calories 45Kcal; Fat: 0.5g; Carbohydrates: 8g; Protein: 2g

17. Garlic Pickles

Preparation time: 10 minutes
Cooking time: 20 minutes
Servings: 10
Ingredients:

- 12 garlic heads (separated into cloves, peeled)
- 1 tablespoon of pickling salt
- 2 ½ cups of white vinegar
- 1 tablespoon of dried oregano
- 1 cup of white wine
- 5 dried red chili peppers
- 1 tablespoon of sugar

Directions:

1. Clean the jars and put a chile pepper in each one.

2. In a saucepan, combine the wine, vinegar, oregano, salt, and sugar and bring to a gentle boil for a minute.

3. Remove your pan from the heat and add the garlic.

4. Fill the sterilized jars halfway with the mixture, allowing a half-inch headspace.

5. Clean the rims and remove any air bubbles.

6. Place the lids on the jars then attach the bands, ensuring sure they are tight.

7. Process the jars for 10 minutes in a hot water canner that has been prepared.

8. Remove the jars from the oven, set them aside to cool, and then label them.

Per serving: Calories: 92.3Kcal; Fat: 0.2g; Carbohydrates: 14.7g; Protein: 2.4g

18. Pickled Carrots

Preparation time: 10 minutes
Cooking time: 10 minutes
Servings: 8
Ingredients:

- 1 lb. carrots, peeled and sliced into sticks
- 1 tbsp sugar
- 1/3 cup water
- 2/3 cup apple cider vinegar
- ½ tsp sea salt

Directions:

1. Pack sliced carrot sticks into the clean jar.

2. Add water, vinegar, sugar, and salt into the small saucepan and cook over medium heat until sugar is dissolved.

3. Pour hot brine over carrots in a jar.

4. Seal jar with lid and store in the refrigerator.

Per serving: Calories: 33Kcal; Fat: 0g; Carbohydrates: 7.3g; Protein: 0.5g

19. Pickled Cucumbers

Preparation time: 10 minutes
Cooking time: 60 minutes
Servings: 6
Ingredients:

- 1 cucumber, thinly sliced
- ½ cup water
- ½ cup apple cider vinegar
- 1 tbsp sugar
- 1 ½ tsp kosher salt

Directions:

1. In your medium bowl, mix together water, vinegar, sugar, and salt. Stir until sugar is dissolved.

2. Add sliced cucumbers into the bowl and let soak for 1 hour.

3. Pour pickled cucumbers into the clean jar and seal the jar with a lid.

4. Once a jar is open then store it in the refrigerator.

Per serving: Calories: 19Kcal; Fat: 0.1g; Carbohydrates: 4g; Protein: 0.3g

20. Pickled Jalapeno

Preparation time: 10 minutes
Cooking time: 15 minutes
Servings: 2
Ingredients:

- 10 jalapeno peppers, sliced into rings
- ½ tsp oregano
- 1 garlic clove, crushed
- 3 tbsp white sugar
- ¾ cup vinegar
- ¾ cup water
- 1 tbsp kosher salt

Directions:

1. Add water, oregano, garlic, sugar, vinegar, and salt into the saucepan and bring to a boil over high heat.
2. Stir in jalapeno peppers. Remove pan from heat then let it cool for 10 minutes.
3. Pour pickled jalapeno with brine in a clean jar. Seal the jar with a lid then store it in the refrigerator.

Per serving: Calories: 120Kcal; Fat: 1.1g; Carbohydrates: 24.8g; Protein: 1.2g

21. Pickled Radishes

Preparation time: 10 minutes
Cooking time: 10 minutes
Servings: 6
Ingredients:

- ½ lb. radishes, remove stem & root & cut into 1/8-inch slices
- 1 bay leaf
- ½ tsp ground black pepper
- 1 tsp mustard seeds
- ¼ cup water
- ½ cup sugar
- ½ cup apple cider vinegar
- 1 tsp salt

Directions:

1. Add sliced radishes into the clean jar.
2. Add vinegar, sugar, water, mustard seeds, black pepper, bay leaf, and salt into the saucepan and bring to boil.
3. Pour hot brine over sliced radishes.
4. Seal jar with lid and store in the refrigerator.

Per serving: Calories: 76Kcal; Fat: 0.2g; Carbohydrates: 18.5g; Protein: 0.4g

22. Pickled Sweet Peppers

Preparation time: 10 minutes
Cooking time: 5 minutes
Servings: 4
Ingredients:

- 2 cups sweet peppers, sliced
- 4 garlic cloves, minced
- 2 tbsp sugar
- ¾ cup water
- ¼ cup rice vinegar
- 2 tsp salt

Directions:

1. Place sliced sweet peppers into a clean jar.
2. Add vinegar, water, sugar, garlic, and salt into the small saucepan and cook until sugar is dissolved.
3. Pour hot brine over sliced sweet peppers.
4. Seal jar with lid and store in the refrigerator.

Per serving: Calories: 56Kcal; Fat: 0.2g; Carbohydrates: 11.5g; Protein: 0.8g

23. Pickled Asparagus

Preparation time: 10 minutes
Cooking time: 10 minutes
Servings: 4
Ingredients:

- 1 lb. fresh asparagus spears, trim ends
- 3 fresh dill sprigs
- 2 garlic cloves, peeled
- 1/2 tsp black peppercorns
- 1 1/2 tsp sugar
- 1 cup water

- 1 1/2 cups vinegar
- 2 tbsp salt

Directions:

1. Pack asparagus spears into the jars.
2. Add water, sugar, vinegar, and salt into a saucepan and bring to boil over medium heat.
3. Stir until sugar is dissolved.
4. Pour the hot water mixture over the asparagus. Leave 1/2-inch headspace.
5. Seal the jar with lids.
6. Let it cool completely then store in the refrigerator.

Per serving: Calories: 40Kcal; Fat: 0.1g; Carbohydrates: 6g; Protein: 2g

10.   FRUITS

24.   Yummy Blueberry Pickle

Preparation time: 12 hours 30 minutes
Cooking time: 15 minutes
Servings: 3 jars
Ingredients:

- 3 long cinnamon sticks
- 6 cups fresh blueberries
- 1 cup brown sugar
- 1 cup white sugar
- 1 ½ cups red wine vinegar
- 1 teaspoon whole allspice berries
- 1 teaspoon whole cloves

Directions:

1. Place the spices – allspices, cloves and cinnamon sticks at the center of the cheesecloth and tie it tightly. Pour the vinegar into a large pan and place the tied cheesecloth in the pan as well. Bring a boil and let simmer for 5 minutes for the flavors of the spices to infuse.
2. Stir in the blueberries and cook for 5 minutes without stirring to ensure they remain intact. Remove from heat then let stand for 12 hours.
3. Drain the berries over a bowl and transfer the vinegar liquid into a saucepan without the cheesecloth.

Stir in the two cups of sugar until dissolved and simmer until it thickens into a syrup, for about 5 minutes.

4. Pack the berries into prepared jars and top with the sugar-vinegar syrup. Cover and process for canning.

Per serving: Calories: 26.5Kcal; Fat: 0.1g; Carbohydrates: 6.8g; Protein: 0.2g

25.   Watermelon Pickles

Preparation time: 30 minutes
Cooking time: 10 minutes
Servings: 4 pints
Ingredients:

- 2 pounds of watermelon rind
- 4 cups of sugar
- 2 cups of white vinegar
- 2 cups of water
- 1 sliced lemon
- 1 cinnamon stick
- 1 tablespoon of whole cloves

Directions:

1. Trim dark green and pink flesh from rind; cut into 1-inch cubes.
2. Combine ¼ pickling salt and 1 quart of water.
3. Heat and stir until salt is dissolved.
4. Pour saltwater over rind cubes. Leave overnight.
5. Drain and rinse cubes.
6. Place in a heavy pot or kettle.
7. Cover with cold water and cook until tender; drain.
8. Combine sugar, vinegar, water, and lemon slices in a heavy pot.
9. Put the cinnamon and cloves in a cheesecloth bag and put the bag in the vinegar mixture.
10. Simmer the mixture for 10 minutes and remove the spice bag.
11. Add rind cubes to the vinegar mixture and continue cooking until cubes are translucent.

12. Pour into hot, sterile, pint jars, dividing syrup evenly and leaving ½-inch headspace.

13. Can jars in a boiling water bath for 15 minutes.

Per serving: Calories: 70Kcal; Fat: 0g; Carbohydrates: 17g; Protein: 0g

26. Tart Cherry Pickle

Preparation time: 2 hours 10 minutes
Cooking time: 0 minutes
Servings: 1 jar
Ingredients:

- 2 cups sour cherries with seeds
- 2 cups white wine vinegar
- 1 teaspoon kosher salt

Directions:

1. Thoroughly wash the cherries and drain them completely. Spread them on a baking tray or other wide tray and let dry in the sun for about 2 hours.

2. Pack the cherries in a storage jar, sprinkle with salt and cover with vinegar. Tightly seal the jar and set it in a cool and dry jar.

Per serving: Calories: 28.9Kcal; Fat: 0.2g; Carbohydrates: 6.9g; Protein: 0.6g

27. Spicy Avocado Dill Pickle

Preparation time: 15 minutes
Cooking time: 10 minutes
Servings: 2 jars
Ingredients:

- 3 avocados (not very ripe), peeled and cut into eights, lengthwise
- 2 habanero peppers
- ½ teaspoon habanero pepper flakes
- 2 cloves garlic, squashed and cut in two
- ½ teaspoon black peppercorns
- 1 teaspoon mustard seeds
- 2 teaspoons fresh dill, chopped
- ¾ cup sugar
- 2 teaspoons rock salt

- 1 ½ cups water
- 1 ½ cups white wine vinegar
- 1 ¼ cup distilled white vinegar

Directions:

1. Add the water and vinegar to a medium-sized saucepan over medium to high heat. Stir in the pepper flakes, mustard seeds, black peppercorns, dill, salt and sugar and bring to a gentle boil. Once the salt and sugar have dissolved completely, turn off the heat and let cool.

2. Meanwhile, divide the avocado, garlic and habanero peppers between two jars and pour in the cooled vinegar mixture, leaving ¼ inch of head space.

3. Tightly seal the jars and refrigerate.

Per serving: Calories: 106.5Kcal; Fat: 0.3g; Carbohydrates: 26.2g; Protein: 0.4g

28. Apricot Pickle

Preparation time: 25 minutes
Cooking time: 5 minutes
Servings: 12
Ingredients:

- ¾ C. white wine vinegar
- ¾ C. water
- 3 tbsp. turbinado sugar
- 1 tsp. yellow mustard seeds
- 2 C. dried apricots
- ¼ C. dark raisins
- 1 bay leaf

Directions:

1. In a small-sized non-reactive saucepan, add the vinegar, water, sugar, and mustard seeds and bring to a boil, stirring occasionally.

2. Meanwhile, in the bottom of 3 (½-pint) hot sterilized jars, place the apricots, raisins, and bay leaf.

3. Pour the hot vinegar mixture over the pear pieces, leaving about ¼-½-inch space from the top.

4. Slide a small knife around the insides of each jar to remove air bubbles.

5. Wipe any trace of food off the rims of jars with a clean, moist kitchen towel.

6. Close each jar with a lid and screw on the ring.

7. Arrange the jars in a boiling water canner and process for about 10 minutes.

8. Remove the jars from the water canner and place them onto a wood surface several inches apart to cool completely.

9. After cooling with your finger, press the top of each jar's lid to ensure that the seal is tight.

10. Place the jars of pickles in the refrigerator for up to 1 month.

Per serving: Calories: 34Kcal; Fat: 0.3g; Carbohydrates: 7.7g; Protein: 0.5g

29. Grapes Pickle

Preparation time: 25 minutes
Cooking time: 5 minutes
Servings: 16
Ingredients:

- 1 C. white sugar
- 1 C. apple cider vinegar
- ¼ C. water
- 1 cinnamon stick
- ½ vanilla bean
- ¼ tsp. cloves
- ¼ tsp. black peppercorns
- 1/8 tsp. yellow mustard seeds
- 1 lb. red grapes, trimmed

Directions:

1. In a small-sized non-reactive saucepan, add sugar, vinegar, and water over high heat and bring to a boil, stirring occasionally.

2. Meanwhile, in the bottom of 2 (1-pint) hot sterilized jars, place the spices and top with grapes.

3. Place the vinegar mixture over the green beans, leaving about ¼-½-inch space from the top.

4. Slide a small knife around the insides of each jar to remove air bubbles.

5. Wipe any trace of food off the rims of jars with a clean, moist kitchen towel.

6. Close each jar with a lid and screw on the ring.

7. Arrange the jars in a boiling water canner and process for about 10 minutes.

8. Remove the jars from the water canner and place them onto a wood surface several inches apart to cool completely.

9. After cooling with your finger, press the top of each jar's lid to ensure that the seal is tight.

10. Place the jars of pickles in the refrigerator for up to 1 month.

Per serving: Calories: 69Kcal; Fat: 0.1g; Carbohydrates: 17.6g; Protein: 0.2g

30. Currant Pickle

Preparation time: 20 minutes
Cooking time: 35 minutes
Servings: 8
Ingredients:

- 2 C. dried currants
- 1 C. sherry vinegar
- 2 tsp. mustard seeds
- 1 tbsp. fresh thyme
- ¼ C. granulated white sugar
- ¼ C. brown sugar

Directions:

1. In a large-sized non-reactive saucepan, combine all ingredients over medium-high heat and bring to a boil.

2. Then adjust the heat to low and simmer for about 30 minutes, stirring occasionally.

3. Remove the saucepan of currant mixture from heat and transfer into 1 (1-pint) hot sterilized jar.

4. Slide a small knife around the insides of each jar to remove air bubbles.

5. Wipe any trace of food off the rims of the jar with a clean, moist kitchen towel.

6. Close the jar with a lid then screw on the ring.

7. Arrange the jar in a boiling water canner and process for about 10 minutes.

8. Remove the jar from the water canner and place it onto a wood surface several inches apart to cool completely.

9. After cooling with your finger, press the top of the jar's lid to ensure that the seal is tight.

10. Place the jar of pickles in the refrigerator for up to 1 month.

Per serving: Calories: 61Kcal; Fat: 0.3g; Carbohydrates: 15.1g; Protein: 0.6g

Conclusion

If you have always liked the idea of fermented and pickled food, then you are not alone. Most people across the globe have begun to eat more fermented and pickled food since they know the benefits of these foods. If you are new to fermenting and pickling, you can use this book as your guide. This book has all the information you need about these methods. It introduces the concept of fermenting and pickling and their benefits.

The book also has different recipes you can use at home. These recipes are simple and give you the right quantities of ingredients you need to use. Ensure to follow the recipes to the tee since incorrect measurements and temperatures spoil the food. These foods harm your body. I hope you find the recipes easy and enjoy the process of fermenting and pickling.

Book 4
PRESSURE CANNING AND PRESERVING FOR PREPPERS

The Essential Guide for Pressure Canning and Preserving Foods To Be Self-Sufficient in Any Emergency

Jonathan Henry

Introduction

Canning is a method of preserving various foods by putting them in jars or cans and heating them to a certain temperature. High heat kills bacteria and inactivates enzymes to protect the food's safety and quality.

If done correctly, canning is an essential and safe technique for food preservation. The canning procedure includes putting items in jars and heating them to a temperature that kills bacteria that might cause illness or spoilage. Enzymes that might ruin the food are likewise inactivated by canning. During heating, the air is forced out of the jar, and a vacuum seal is established when it cools. The vacuum seal prevents air from entering the product and decontaminating the food with bacteria.

11. Water Bath Canning

Water-bath canning, often known as "boiling water bath," is a simpler technique of preserving homemade pickles, jams, jellies, syrups, and sauce in jars. You may keep the fresh taste for a year by heating the jars in hot water at the end of the procedure. The delectable high-acid menu has sweet and savory options. Items that may be properly preserved with the water bath canning technique include fruits, jams, relishes, fruit spreads, salsas, fruit juices, most tomatoes, vinegar, pickles, chutneys, sauces, and condiments. Water bath canning is suggested for such foods because these popular foods contain significant acid levels, or the recipe includes the proper acid balance. Making shelf-stable jams and pickles in the home is as simple as boiling water bath canning. It's essential to remember that water bath canning is only suitable for high-acid foods. Meats, fish, chicken, chili and beans, maize, and other low-acid vegetables need a higher heat (240°F) within the jars than the boiling water canning (212°F) and hot enough to kill dangerous germs are not suitable for water-bath canning. Pressure canning is required for low-acid foods.

12. Pressure Canning

Pressure canning is an in-house food preservation method that involves using specific equipment to prepare food at a greater temperature than traditional water bath canning. It's mainly used to can vegetables and meats without adding high-acid ingredients such as pickles. Low-acid items like vegetables and meats are ideal for pressure canning. You'll need to learn how to use a pressure canner if you want to can green beans, soups or meats. The pressure canning technique is similar to boiling-water canning, but the equipment is different. You must use a pressure canner to jar the food when a recipe calls for it. You can store peas, stews soup, asparagus and more using a pressure canner (similar to but not the same as a pressure cooker). Because the procedure renders these items shelf-stable, they may be used to create homemade equivalents of canned stocks & vegetables seen in the supermarket's produce section. Because you may select the ingredients, the handmade version might be a better product (because of low or no salt or not adding preservatives).

Modern pressure canners have removable racks, an automated vent lock, a vent pipe and a safety fuse. To guarantee safety, always use canners approved by the UL (Underwriters Laboratory). Fortunately, companies have greatly improved safety features and the materials used to build pressure canners so that one can pressure green beans, fish, maize, pork, and other low-acid items without fear of a kitchen explosion (always with a pH of more than 4.6).

13. History

To preserve food from spoiling, canning is used to store it in vessels that are hermetically sealed and sterilized by heat. In response to a government request for a way to preserve food for an army and naval use, Nicolas Appert of France devised the technique in 1809 after extensive study. It was found that Appert's procedure was to firmly seal a container of food, heat it to a specified temperature, and keep the container sealed until it was ready to be used. Before Louis Pasteur could explain why the food so handled did not rot, the heat killed the bacteria already in the meal, and the sealing prevented other microbes from entering the jar. England's Peter Durand invented tin-coated iron cans in 1810 and supplied the Royal Navy with huge numbers by 1820. The European canning technologies quickly spread to the United States, and that nation soon became the world's leading producer of automated canning operations and the total can output. In the late 1800s, Samuel C. Prescott and William Underwood of the United States described exact time-temperature heating criteria for sterilizing canned goods, which laid the scientific foundations for modern canning.

In the beginning, cans were made from a sheet of tin-plated iron that was manually soldered at the top and bottom before being rolled into a cylinder. The contemporary sanitary or open-top can, whose component components are linked by interlocking folds that are crimped or pushed together, supplanted this design in the early twentieth century. Soldering can also be used to seal the body seams. Polymer sealing compounds are applied to the end, or lid, seams. The contemporary tin can is 98.5 percent steel with a thin layer of tin on top (i.e., tinplate). Hundreds of cans per minute are produced on fully automated lines of machines.

While tin cans have long been used to store numerous types of food and beverages, aluminum cans are becoming more popular since they are lighter and don't corrode like tin cans. Impact extrusion is used to make aluminum cans; a stamping die punches out the can's body from a single metal sheet. A second piece serves as the lid for this seamless component, which has a rounded bottom. Aluminum is also utilized to make the tabs on pop-top cans. Aluminum cans with steel covers are known as bimetal cans.

In order to preserve food as soon after it has been harvested as feasible, canneries are typically built near the locations where it is being grown. Cleaning and preparing the raw food material; blanching it; filling containers; sealing and sanitizing the cans; labelling and storing the final items are all steps in canning. Water or high-pressure water sprays are commonly used to clean raw food, which is then processed into various forms, such as peeling, slicing or pureeing. All but a few fruits and vegetables must be blanched before canning in order to soften the tissues and make them malleable enough for packing. This technique also serves to inactivate enzymes that might induce unwanted changes in the food before canning. Blanching can also be used as a final or supplementary cleaning step.

In order to remove as much air as possible from cans, they are mechanically filled by machines with solid contents and, in many circumstances, an accompanying liquid (typically brine or syrup). Food is heated in an exhaust box to expand it and force out the residual air; therefore, following sealing, heat sterilization and cooling of the cans, the condensing contents form a partial vacuum inside the container. The cans are mechanically emptied by vacuum-can sealing devices when certain items are vacuum-packed.

As soon as the cans are empty, a machine seals and close them; the can cover is rolled into place and then flattened, and the flange on the can body and the curl on the can cover are wrapped together. To guarantee a hermetic seal, a tiny coating of sealing material is spread between the two metal layers. If there are any microbes still present in the sealed cans, the cans are sterilized, which means they are heated at high temperatures and for a lengthy period of time to kill them. High-pressure steam kettles, or cookers, are used to heat the food to roughly 240° F (116° C) for the majority of the time. To cool the cans down, they are placed in cold water or air, and the labels are then applied.

Putting food in a can protects most of its nutritional value. Vitamins A, C, D, and B2 are unaffected, as are proteins, carbs, and lipids. The quantity of heat used in canning affects the amount of vitamin B1 that is retained. During the canning process, some vitamins and minerals may disintegrate into the brine or syrup, but if taken, they preserve their nutritional value.

Pressure Canning Benefits

Pressure canning offers a lot of benefits:
- You can preserve a wide range of locally grown or raised vegetables, poultry, meats, and shellfish.
- Bulk fruits, meats, and poultry can be purchased at a discount.
- It's easy to stock your pantry with home-canned convenience foods, such as soup base and pie filling ingredients like squash or chickpeas, lentils, and chickpeas.
- In the event of a power outage or freezer malfunction, your canned goods will not go bad.
- To reduce the amount of waste you produce, save your jars and reuse them. Modern glass canning containers can last many years if properly cared for.
- The ability to brag. There's nothing quite like showing off your pantry's shelves full with jars of home-canned treats.

Tools For Pressure Canning

14. Equipment And Instructions For Operating Pressure Canning

Before diving into the instructions, let us quickly take a look at some equipment you need to begin pressure canning. The following are the basic equipment required to begin pressure canning.

a. Pressure Canner

A pressure canner is a large pot but the difference between this canner and the water canner is that the pressure canner is a stainless-steel, heavy-duty pot that is made strong enough to endure extreme steam and pressure. The lid of this canner comes with a vent and also a rubber seal to stop any air from seeping into the can and disrupting the process. A rack is also included with the pressure canner and serves the same purpose as the rack in the water canner.

One more thing to make a note of is that there are two types of pressure canners. One comes with a dial and the other comes with a weighted gauge. In my opinion one is not better than the other and they both provide the same end result.

b. Canning Jars

There are three parts of a jar: the metal screw band, the metal lid, and the jar. The jar is where you put the food that you want to process. Some of the types of jars that can be used for canned food items include Mason jars and Ball jars. You could also use any type of jar that is threaded and comes with a self-sealing lid. These jars also have a wide opening, approximately about three inches, so that you are able easily empty and fill them.

Jars can come in many sizes ranging from ½ a pint all the way up to ½ gallon. They can be reused numerous times until they wear out. You will know that a jar is worn out if it has any type of chip or fraction within the glass. If the jar is even slightly chipped then it will disrupt the seal and possibly break in the canner while you are in the process of canning your food.

c. Canning Rack

The rack is used to keep jars off the bottom of the canner during the whole process. This allows steam to circulate in each jar and ensures even heating.

d. Lids

The lid is one of the most important parts when it comes to sealing the jar and keeping out the air. The jars that are sold in today's market come with a two-piece lid that has a self-sealing compound that is basically a metal disc and a ring.

Since the lid is small and thin and is easily softened when it is heated, it is a must that you dispose of the lid once you are done using it. But your metal screw bands/rings can be reused numerous times because their job is just to hold the lid in place while it's being processed.

e. Headspace Measuring and Air Bubble Remover Tool

This is your best friend when you're canning. It's an inexpensive tool with measurements on one end and a flat tip to remove air bubbles on the other. It ensures the proper amount of free space in each jar for food expansion and contraction during processing and vacuum sealing.

f. Widemouthed Jar Funnel

Save additional work cleaning residue off each jar rim by getting all the food in the jar the first time. Using a funnel means you waste less food and time and helps maximize jar space.

g. Magnetic Lid Grabber

Get lids out of boiling water safely by using this tool to magnetically grab one jar lid at a time. This is another handy tool Grandma would have loved to have back in the day!

h. Waterproof, Heat-Resistant Canning Mitts or Jar Grabber

Dish towels and pot holders conduct heat when wet, but a waterproof mitt or a jar grabber keeps your hands safe from burns. These tools help you maintain dexterity when handling wet, boiling-hot jars.

i. Large Slotted Spoon and Ladle

While many jars can be filled using a ladle, a slotted spoon helps balance the ratio of liquids to solids in each jar, which is essential to maximizing jar space.

j. Dish Towels And Cutting Boards

Granite and stoneware countertops are naturally cool. If you put scalding hot glass jars directly on granite or stoneware, they may fracture, crack, or shatter. Keep processed hot jars away from direct contact with cool granite or stoneware countertops by placing them on a cutting board covered with dish towels. Doing so prior to filling jars prevents the countertop surface from decreasing the temperature of warm glass jars. The cutting boards elevate jars off cold countertops and dish towels soak up water.

k. Clean Terrycloth Washcloth

Reserve a separate washcloth for each recipe to wipe jar rims and screw threads when canning. While any material will work, terrycloth is the best for absorbing moisture and capturing residue during cleaning.

l. Distilled White Vinegar

Vinegar is a canning and kitchen staple that naturally kills bacteria. Wet a washcloth in warm water, wring it out so it's just damp, and then dip it in vinegar prior to wiping jar rims and screw threads. Add 1 ounce (2 tablespoons) vinegar to the water in your pressure canner prior to processing. The vinegar prevents mineral deposits from forming on your glass jars.

m. Timer

Have a reliable timer in the kitchen to properly track cooking and processing times.

n. Permanent Marker

After lids have been sealed and jars have been cleaned, label each lid with the recipe or food and the month and year it was preserved.

o. Pressure Gauge

This lets you know how much pressure is placed on the food (this is vital to ensure that your food is preserved correctly). Different pressure gauges are designed for different pressure ranges.

p. Weight Or Regulator

This is used to monitor and maintain the same pressure.

q. Safety Goggles And Face Masks

These help avoid accidents when opening the canner so that you don't accidentally inhale hot steam. Also, they will help avoid food splatters against your face.

Having all equipment is not a must. The most important thing is to have at least some experience when you are learning how to pressure can food for the first time. Also, be sure that you follow the rules and regulations for temperature and pressure. If you don't, you can risk getting burned, injured or sick.

15. Brands And Types Of Pressure Canners

When it comes to pressure canners, there are two brands that dominate the market, All-American and Presto. Both All-American and Presto pressure canners have their pros and cons. Ultimately, it is the customer's decision on what model makes them feel most comfortable.

All-American pressure canners come in a variety of sizes, which is perfect for people who plan on making large batches at a time. Their largest size will can 19-quart jars at a time, while their smallest holds only four. With this variety of sizes comes a variety of prices. Be prepared to spend more money on larger canners. All-American canners should only be used on a gas range instead of an electric one, so there is no stove damage. A feature of the All-American that makes them more user-friendly is their weighted gauge. Instead of having to manually adjust the heat, the weight on the valve regulates the pressure.

Presto pressure canners only come in two sizes which are the 16-quart liquid capacity model and the 23-quart liquid capacity model. The Presto brand canners work with both gas and electric ranges. This fact, along with their small size, makes Presto more versatile than the All-American canners. The gauge is a dial gauge instead of a weighted one, and the pressure must be manually handled. This is better for people who wish to can in higher altitudes. Newer models have a button feature that drops down to inform you when the canner is safe to open.

As far as price goes, the Presto brand runs cheaper, and is more commonly available in stores such as Walmart. Presto canners do require the additional expense of replacing the rubber gasket around the inside of the lid. Gasket replacements are not very expensive however, and are only needed every few years. Keep in mind location when choosing between the two brands as well. High altitude places will prefer the presto while lower altitudes can enjoy the weighted gauge feature of the All-American.

The decision between the two is also dependent on batch sizes. Investing in a larger All-American pressure canner will be the smarter option for those who have a good amount of canning orders to do in a short time. Presto canners are better for casual canning. Both brands are well built and last a long time.

Just because All-American and Presto are the most well known brands on the market, does not mean they are the only brands. Mirro, while not as popular, is the only brand other than the two aforementioned brands that are most recognized by professionals in the field of canning. Mirro, like Presto, only comes in two sizes: Both of these sizes have weighted gauge features like All-American canners.

A pressure gauge is supposed to monitor and help regulate pressure inside of the canner. There are three different models of gauges that you can find on a pressure canner. The first and oldest is a dial gauge that is used to measure the pressure within the pot. The downside to this is that it can't control the pressure. A weighted gauge is the opposite: It controls the pressure but can't measure it. Lastly is a dual-gauge, which is a hybrid of the two. It has a dial for reading the pressure levels, but also utilizes weight to regulate that pressure.

A dial gauge pressure canner uses a dial to display the pressure that is present within the canner. As the temperature, as well as the pressure, builds up within the canner, the dial rises. Some gauges can show a half or a 1-pound increase in pressure while others are only marked for 5-pound increments. These pressure canners come in handy if you want to determine the pressure increments at higher altitudes. For instance, the pressure required for meats and vegetables is around 11 pounds if the altitude is less than 2000 feet. Unless you carefully monitor the gauge and adjust the heat, you cannot maintain the desired pressure within the pot. The gauges of these canners should be checked at least once a year to ensure their accuracy.

Similarly, a weighted gauge pressure canner uses a weight that regulates the pressure building up or present within the canner. These pressure canners have a single flat disc that has different markings for pressure such as 5 and 10. Some models of weighted gauge pressure canners have metal rings that can be stacked to regulate the pressure within the canner. For instance, if only 10 pounds of pressure is needed, two rings of 5 pounds each can be added. As the pressure starts building within the pot, the pressure causes the weight to jiggle. This is also an indicator the desired temperature is achieved within the pot. Some weights will jiggle a few times while others do it continuously. At altitudes of over 1,000 feet, don't forget to increase the pressure by 5 pounds.

The dual-gauge is just using both methods. Since weighted gauges are less hands-on, the dial gauge is mostly there to keep track of where the pound per square inch or PSI is at. It can be a backup if something goes wrong, but to be honest, it is kind of useless. Modern Presto canners are mostly dial gauge, but they've made their pot compatible with dual-gauges. The weights are sold separately. This is helpful for people who prefer the dial gauge way, but aren't close enough to a local extension service to get their dial checked every year.

16. Parts Of A Pressure Canner

A pressure canner consists of several parts that are specially designed to help regulate the temperature as well as the steam pressure present within the canner. Understanding the different parts and the specific functions they perform will leave you better equipped to use your pressure canner. In this section, let's look at all the different parts of a pressure canner.

r. Pressure Regulator

This part helps maintain and regulate the pressure within the canner. A peg usually holds the regulator in place. This feature ensures the pressure does not exceed 15 pounds within the canner.

s. Adjustable Pressure Regulator

Some pressure canners have adjustable regulators to adjust the pressure within the pot. Such regulators give you the option to decide whether the pressure within the pot should be 5, 10, or 15 pounds. If the pressure regulator starts a gentle rhythmic rocking motion, it signals that the ideal pressure is maintained within the pot.

t. Vent Pipe

The vent pipe is an important part of a pressure canner because it helps release excess pressure in the pot. It is a small opening where steam and pressure are vented out from the pot during the canning process. In some models, the vent pipe might be present on the lid itself. Ensure that you always check the vent pipe after every use because, at times, food or foam can clog it which prevents it from functioning effectively.

u. Air Vent

The air vent is essentially a visual indicator of the pressure that's building up in the canner. Once sufficient pressure is present within the pot, the cover locks itself. This means opening it becomes impossible in any type of pressure canner. This is also a safety feature put in place to ensure the device is always closed under extreme pressure. The cover lock and air vent drop when the pressure inside the canner reduces.

v. Locking Bracket

The locking bracket is present within the body of the pressure canner. This engages with the air vent to ensure the cover cannot be opened when pressure is present within the pot. All the pressure canners that were manufactured before 1978 do not have this feature.

w. Sealing Ring

The sealing ring helps seal pressure within the body of the canner to ensure the pressure doesn't escape. It fits right around the pressure canner's cover and offers a tight pressure seal. It's present between the lid and the body of the pot. Sufficient pressure will not build within the canner if this ring is broken or not in place. It can handle the heat only from the pressure canner for as long as there are no tears or cracks in it.

x. Pressure Dial Gauge

The dial gauge is a readable dial with a pointer that indicates the pressure present within the canner. You cannot use this to regulate the pressure. Instead, it is simply used to check the pressure within.

y. Cooking Rack

The cooking rack is used for elevating food away from the liquid present in the pot. It also helps separate foods that you don't want to mix. You can use it for sterilizing as well. The cooking rack makes sure the jars or containers do not touch the bottom or the walls of the canner.

z. Overpressure Plug

Another safety feature added is an overpressure plug. Any food clogging the vent pipes makes it difficult for the excess pressure to be let out of the body. In such instances, the steam will be automatically redirected from the overpressure plug. This plug usually pops out in case this happens. Heed it as a warning that you need to release the pressure from the part.

Pressure Canning Methods

17. Methods

One of the most vital guidelines for pressure canning is ensuring that it is done appropriately to achieve desired results. The following steps will teach you pressure can go without any hitch:

aa.   Canning

- To begin the canning process, center your canner on your heat source and add water. If you are using cold or raw pack foods, then you would want to begin with cool water. Contrastingly, if you are using hot pack foods, where the jars are hot and the food inside of them is hot, then you should begin with hot water. This is done to avoid heat stress on your jars.
- Next, you should ensure 3 inches of water in the bottom of your canner. Since it might be difficult to see the inside of your canner just by looking inside, you should use your measurement ruler, which helps you judge how much water is in the bottom of your canner.
- Take your rack and place it inside the pressure canner. This will help you avoid the jars touching the bottom of the canner, which gets very hot during the canning process.

- In addition, you should employ the use of a jar lifter to place the jars in the canner. The jar lifter is easier to use to avoid any mishaps. However, if the product is cold you can still use your fingers – although the jar filter is recommended in any case. When you are doing a hot pack, the jar lifter protects your hands from burns during the canning process.
- Now to the actual canning procedure, if you are using a 16-pint canner, this means you can put about 8 pints on the bottom of your regular pressure canner (again depending on the size of the canner too). You should check your manufacturer's instructions to see how many jars your canner can hold. Next, add a rack and then layer it with another 8 pints of jars (if available) on the second layer.
- For those who do not own racks, you can stagger your jars inside the canner or offset them in a position that keeps them apart from each other. This means that they should not be placed on top of each other. If you are using a second layer, as soon as you get your jars inside, add the next rack, followed by the next layer on top of that.
- When you get the jars into the pressure canner and get it filled, put the lid of the canner on. To do this, match the arrows on the lid to the canner. There is an arrow on the lid as well as on the pressure canner. Once the arrows are matched, turn the lid so that it locks in place. If you are using the canner that uses the clamps, bring the clamps up on opposite sides and barely get hold of them to ensure that they are fitted in on top. To this for all of the clamps and ensure that they are tightened to prevent steam from escaping. If you are using a canner that has a turn-on lid, you should match your arrows – which are usually by the handles – and turn it on so that it locks securely.
- Once you have the jars filled in the canner and the canner lid is on, you should make certain that your vent port is open. Next, turn the heat of your stove to high. Leave the stove on high heat 'til the canner comes up to pressure and begins emitting steam through the vent port.
- When the steam becomes a steady stream, let it go for 10 minutes. At the end of 10 minutes, put the dead weight on if you are using a dial gauge canner. If using a weighted gauge canner, put it on the weight that you need. If using a weighted gauge canner, you would want to listen for jiggles when it is up to about 10 pounds of pressure.
- Note that you need to time the process of canning when the pressure reading on your dial gauge shows that the recommended pressure has been obtained or when the weighted gauge starts to jiggle.
- Regulate the heat source to maintain a steady pressure at or slightly above the correct gauge pressure. If the pressure drops below the recommendation, then the canner must be brought back up to the recommended level and the timing starts over again.
- Also, you should note that quick and large pressure variations during processing may cause unnecessary liquid loss from jars. Review the manufacturer's instructions for weighted gauge canners to ensure that your weighted gauge is properly adjusted. It is wise to perform a dry run before you proceed to the actual process. This helps to ensure that your pressure canner is in a good working condition, and you are comfortable with the process of how it works as well as knowing how your heat source works with the canner.

bb. Cooling

- When the time process is completed, turn off your heat and remove the canner from the heat source to cool down. Allow the canner to cool all the way to ensure that it completely depressurizes inside. In addition, it is important to allow the pressure to drop naturally. Avoid putting it in cold water, applying cold clothes, or taking it out into cold air.

- For the cooling period, heavy-walled canners require about 30 minutes if they are filled with pint jars and 45 minutes if they are filled with quart jars to cool down. In contrast, thin-walled canners will cool a little bit more rapidly.
- When the pressure on the dial-gauge drops all the way to zero, then you can remove the weight from your vent port. You can also check it to make sure that it is down. If there is no hissing noise when you tip it, then there is a chance that the pressure is completely out. If you are using a weighted gauge canner, tip the weighted gauge and ensure that there is no hissing sound in the canner.
- When the pressure canner is completely down and cooled, you should wait for about 10 minutes before you unfasten the lid. This is to ensure that there is nothing stuck inside the vent port that might cause any problems.
- After 10 minutes, unfasten the lid and tip it away from your face to avoid getting burnt by the steam. Remove the jars with the lifter; place them on a towel or a cooling rack to allow them to cool. Note that you need something to put the jars on, because they are very hot and you should protect your counter surface.

- Next, allow the jars to cool for 12 hours before moving them again so that you do not compromise your seal. Jars should be cooled in an area away from drafts because the air blowing on the hot jars can cause thermal breakage. In addition, ensure you do not rush your cooling process or your jars may break.

cc. Storing

- When you complete the actual canning process and your jar has cooled for 12 hours, you can then check your seals. One way to do that is to inspect the jar and check if the jar lid is pulled down and is concave. Another way is to press on it and see if there is any give in the lid of the jar. You can also take the back of your spoon and tap on the lid to see if something sounds different.
- If you have a jar that does not seal properly afterwards, there are a handful of things you can do. First, within 24 hours from the time that you finished processing it, you can reprocess the jar. What you need to do is to put a new lid on it before you process it. Also, check the edge of your jar to make sure that there are no nicks, which would prevent the seal from forming at all. If you do not want to reprocess the ill-sealed jar, you can adjust the headspace in a way that it is an inch and a half and put it in the freezer or store it in a refrigerator for 3 to 4 days.

- Rings may also be removed from the jars before storing. In fact, it is recommended that you remove the ring so that you do not get rust accumulation on the inside of the ring, which can compromise the seal.

Additionally, you should ensure that your jars are stored in a cool, dry place. You need to make certain that they are labeled. On the label, you should include what the content of the jar is, because it may be difficult to remember when you canned all your foods. You should also add any special things you did for the recipe – if you put salt or other ingredients. You also need to put the date that the food was processed and how you processed it.

18. Important Considerations While Canning

If you have a canner and other equipment, canning at home is easy. That said, certain external factors are also responsible for the longevity of the food you canned. Three important factors that home canning enthusiasts must pay attention to are altitude, temperature, and acidity. These three factors make all the difference between a successful attempt and a poorly canned jar of food.

dd. Acidity

To determine how acidic or alkaline things are, a scientific measure known as the pH scale is used. The markings on this scale extend from 0 to 14. If the pH is between 0-6, it is known to be acidic, with 7 being neutral and above that is what is known as basic or alkaline pH. The stronger the acidic pH, the closer to 0. Are you wondering what this has to do with canning? An important benefit of pressure canning is it helps eliminate botulism-causing spores and bacteria. Acidity plays a vital role here. Common foods that are low in acidity score are milk, fresh vegetables, red meats, seafood, and poultry. Their pH is above 4.6. Any other ingredient with such a weakly acidic pH must be sterilized at temperatures between 240-250°F to ensure the harmful spores are killed. This is perfectly attainable while using pressure canners. The only exception to this is tomatoes because of their high acidity. Other high-acid foods such as jams, pickles, fruits, jellies, and such usually have a pH lower than 4.6. These can be canned using a regular water bath canner.

ee. Temperature

The boiling point of water is 212°F. Regardless of the time spent boiling the water, it will not exceed this temperature. After the water reaches its boiling point, evaporation starts. This is a primary reason why water-bath canning is not the best method for preserving and canning low-acid foods. When water is heated up in a closed container, the temperature increases. This is due to the added pressure in the form of evaporating water. Due to this simple mechanism at play, pressure canning is ideal for any type of food. While using a pressure canner, there is an additional 10-11 pounds of pressure that increases the water beyond its boiling point and brings it up to 240°F. This is the temperature desired for destroying botulism-causing bacteria and their spores. It effectively halts their germination cycle by destroying all their traces from the food within the jars.

Certain factors reduce the temperature present within the pressure canner. One such thing is an inaccurate dial reading or low temperature of the air present within the canner. This is one of the reasons why the canner must be allowed to vent for at least 10 minutes. This helps expel the cold air present within. Before you place the weight or the pressure regulator, ensure that you let the pressure canner vent for a while. If the pressure canner has dial gauges, then make sure you check the gauges annually to maintain their accuracy.

ff. Altitude

The next important external factor that you must pay attention to while home canning is the altitude. It's repeatedly mentioned that the boiling point of water is 212°F. However, did you know that this is the boiling point of water at sea level? When the altitude increases water can boil at a lower temperature. This is why you need to pay attention to altitude while canning. The time or temperature has to be changed accordingly depending on the altitude to ensure harmful pathogens are not present in the jars you are canning.

As the altitude increases the time taken for canning along with the temperature to be maintained during this process will increase. While using a pressure canner, the time taken for canning prescribed by most recipes will stay the same. That said, the pounds of pressure that need to be applied have to be increased. If you are using a weighted gauge pressure canner and are at an altitude of over 1000 feet, then food is normally sterilized at 15 pounds pressure. If the altitude is between 1,000-2,000 feet, 11 pounds of pressure is sufficient to attain the same results. However, the pressure must be increased to 12 pounds if the altitude is between 2,000-4,000 feet. Similarly, for an altitude of 4,000-6,000 feet, the pressure needed is 13 pounds whereas it is 14 pounds when the altitude is between 6,000-8,000 feet.

Learning about this is needed because the cooking time is crucial to ensure the ingredients are properly sterilized and processed.

gg. *Risk Of Botulism*

Botulism is a type of food poisoning that's caused by a specific strain of bacteria known as *Clostridium botulinum*. Spores of this specific bacteria are commonly present on all food surfaces. Chances are you have heard of the risk of botulism in canned foods. It usually occurs upon the consumption of improperly canned food. It probably makes canned food seem risky but with a few safe practices, you can eliminate this health hazard.

If the spores of this bacteria are present on all surfaces, then shouldn't eating any food be harmful? Well, the thing is, these spores are harmless when present on the surface of fresh foods. Understand that there is a difference between harmless spores and a full-blown infestation of the bacteria. Under the right conditions, these spores germinate, multiply, and diet. This cycle keeps repeating until they have fully contaminated the food. As these bacteria multiply and die, they release a toxic compound causing botulism. This renders the food unfit for consumption.

The absence of oxygen and low temperature are the two external factors the spores of botulism-causing bacteria need to develop. The ideal temperature for their germination is between 70-120°F. Canned foods meet both these basic needs. Therefore, you need to be extra careful while canning foods, especially ones with low acidity. When food is canned using a pressure canner, the pressure within the canner helps increase the temperature of water beyond its boiling point. The temperature within it can be up to 240° F, which is sufficient to destroy the spores of this harmful bacteria.

Safety Criteria for Pressure Canning

Pressure canning is a difficult process. If you have tried water bath canning and understand the process completely, you can go try pressure canning. Make sure to keep the following safety measures in mind.

1. Make sure that your pressure canner, the canning jars, the removable rack, the seal, and everything else involved in this process are thoroughly clean.

2. The canner you select must be suitable to carry the size of the canning jars.

3. All your canning jars should be sterilized.

4. Avoid heating the canning jars in the pressure canner if the food inside the jar is cold, or else, the canning jar might break.

5. Do not cover the vent of the pressure canner right after turning the heat on and sealing the lid. Wait for the pressure canner to start producing the steam, and then cover its vent.

6. Before opening the pressure canner, after it's done, make sure to release all this steam from inside, and then remove the lid.

7. Wear gloves while dealing with the pressure canner and the canning jars.

8. Always keep the jars in an upright position on a leveled rack.

9. Avoid adding foaming-producing food to the canning jars; otherwise, the jars might spill.

While pressure canning, always leaves one-inch space above the food inside the jar to allow expansion without a spill.

19. Spoiled Canned Food

Do not taste food from a jar that is unsealed or shows signs of spoilage. Examine a jar of food carefully before using it to ensure a vacuum seal is present. If the lid is concave, that indicates the jar is sealed. Do not use any jar of food that has a bulged lid or does not require a can opener for the lid to be removed.

Food spoilage produces gases that cause the lids to swell and break their seals, so examine canning jars of food for other signs of spoilage. Jars with spoiled food should be treated well before disposal because they may contain botulinum toxin, which is very hazardous to the health of any living being. Keep the spoiled food in its jar and place it in a shopping bag. Secure the bag and place it in the regular trash container and dispose of it at a landfill. Open and leaking jars of spoiled home-canned food should be detoxified before disposal. Home-canned food that shows the signs of spoilage must be discarded in a manner that no human or animal will come in contact with the botulinum toxin, whether it is ingested or enters the body to the skin.

20. How to Clean and Sanitize Canning Jars

If you intend to can your foods, there are various safety precautions to take. It is critical to properly wash and sterilize your canning jars. Improperly carrying out these tasks, or using non-safe cleaning chemicals, might result in major health problems. Cleaning products that do not include harsh chemicals are regarded as safe. Safe detergents will not contaminate your food or canning jars.

hh.   Cleaning and sanitizing materials for canning jars

- Basin or bucket
- Dishwashing liquid
- tongs
- vinegar (white)
- Fresh dish towels

- cloths for cleaning
- Pressure canner

ii. Cleaning

Before sterilizing your canning jars, thoroughly wash and clean them.

If your jars develop scaling or hard-water film, soak them in a bucket or basin of hot water and white vinegar.

You may hand-wash your canning jars or put them in the dishwasher. In any case, be certain that all soap residue is gone.

jj. Sterilizing

The jars and lids, like meat, may harbor germs that grow and damage your meat. As a result, all canning equipment must be thoroughly disinfected.

The canning procedure itself is the best way to sterilize jars and lids for pressure canning. To begin, jars and lids must be cleaned; however, the additional sterilizing step can be omitted.

kk.   Cleaning the Lids and Screw Bands of Canning Jars

Contrary to common belief, metal and rubber lids are not reusable. They should be replaced every time you can food.

Screw bands do not need to be replaced because they are never in touch with food. Instead, hand-wash them in hot water with a few drops of liquid dish soap.

The first step after washing screw bands is to make sure they are completely dry. Use a dry napkin for this, then place it upside down on a clean kitchen napkin for a few hours before using. This will help to keep the bands from rusting.

ll. Jars Should Be Examined To Ensure A Good Seal.

After 12 to 24 hours of chilling, the jars must be examined for good sealing before being stored. Remove the screw bands and examine the seal using one of the methods listed below.

Apply pressure to the center of the lid with your finger or thumb. If the lid does not move down or up, it is properly sealed.

Lift the jar using the lid as a handle. If the lid does not come off, the container is properly closed. When checking the seal, lay a hand below the jar to hold it if it comes away from the lid, or place it on a napkin-lined table for cushioning.

Picking up the jar and inspecting the lid at eye level is another way to ensure proper sealing. If the lid is slightly bent downwards in the middle, the jar has properly sealed.

mm.   Pressure Canner Maintenance And Storage

Inside and out, clean the rack and canner. To keep moisture during storage, place ripped newspaper or paper sheets in the pot's base. Place the rack in the canner.

Take extra care not to damage or distort the canner lid while washing it. Remove the gasket to clean it. Dry the lid and gasket thoroughly. Examine the gasket for any signs of deterioration. If the gasket is fractured or damaged, replace it.

nn.   What Are The Factors Influencing Processing Time?

- Acid level

- Size of the food cuts
- Jars' original temperature
- Is the meat boneless or has bones?
- Size and structure of the jar
- Viscosity
- How tight is the food arranged in the jar?
- The temperature of the food is being processed.

oo.   *Inspect for Spoilage*

Before using canned products, check sure they have been properly examined for symptoms of rotting. It's a good practice to check your canned goods for signs of spoilage on a regular basis, but double-check them before use. If there are signs of deterioration, the food should be thrown properly. If you are unsure whether a food is spoiled, do not try to judge spoilage by tasting it; instead, throw it away to be safe.

pp.   *Canning Storage*

Wipe off any residue on the jars and lids after verifying for a proper seal.

Label the jars with the contents and the processing date. Apply a label to the jars or write on a piece of masking tape to write the data. A black marker can be used to write the item and date on the surface of the lid.

Keep the jar somewhere dry, cold, and dark. If the area is damp, the lids may rust, weakening the seal. If food is exposed to a lot of light or heated temperatures, it will lose its look and taste.

Common Problems And How To Solve Them

There are a couple of conditions that can lead to catastrophic failures, such as:

21. The Altitude

The pressure of operation at sea level differs from any distance above that, so you want to make proper adjustments. At higher altitudes, the pressure inside the canner is lower, and therefore temperature. The higher you are, the higher the pressure you need. Thankfully, you do not have to do the math here. There are plenty of reliable instructions to be found online about altitude adjustments.

22. When The Pressure Canner Is In Operation, There Is Air Inside The Device

The trapped air in your pressure canner lowers the temperature obtained depending on the pressure, resulting in underprocessing and potential food poisoning or botulism. Therefore, the USDA recommends that you must vent your pressure canner for about 10 minutes before pressurizing again.

- Do not cover the steam vent or vent pipe to vent your canner. If your model has a petcock, open it after filling up the canner and lock it in place.

- Then, heat the canner at a high temperature until the water starts boiling, and steam comes out through the vent pipe or petcock. When you see the funnel shape of steam coming from the canner, set the timer to 10 minutes.
- After the time is up, you can allow your canner to pressurize again. Close the petcock, or put the weighted gauge or counterweight over the vent pipe.

23.   Sometimes, An Incorrect Dial Gauge Is Also Used

So, check the dial gauges for accuracy every year before use. If the gauge is off by over two pounds at 5, 10, or 15 pounds pressure, it is time to get a new one. If there is a deviation below two pounds, you can make adjustments to ensure that you achieve the right pressure in your canner.

24.   Exhausting Steam From The Pressure Canner

It is necessary to vent steam for 10 minutes in the beginning. After venting, you can close the valve or put the weight on the vent. If the steam isn't vented, it can create a discrepancy between the temperature in the canner and what is displayed on the pressure gauge.

25.   Using Cold Water On The Outside Of The Pressure Canner

You may be wondering whether you can use cold water outside your pressure canner to cool the jars down more quickly, in turn, making it so you can preserve a new batch faster. Well, this is not a good idea. Part of the preserving process involves it cooling naturally at room temperature. If the cooling is rushed, your foods can spoil and could be unprocessed. Rapid cooling also increases your risk of breaking the glass jars.

26.   Weighted Gauge Pressure Canners Vs. Dial Gauge Pressure Canners

While the weighted and dial gauge are accurate when cared for according to the manufacturer's instructions, the weighted gauges tend to be even more accurate. Some people like the visual representation of the pressure dial to tell them what pressure they are at. The weighted gauge lifts and makes a sound, which some people like more.

A dial gauge will need to be tested periodically. While the weighted gauge doesn't need to be tested, it requires cleaning to ensure proper functionality. The dial gauge can be more efficient at different altitudes as the dial can be adjusted more easily to accommodate altitude differences.

27.   If Canner Drops Below The Recommended Pressure During Processing

For proper processing, the canner must remain at the designated pressure for the duration of the food being processed. So, you won't want to start your processing timer until your canner has reached the proper pressure. If your canner dips below the designated pressure, you'll have to start the timer all over again.

28.   In Case You Do Not Get The Headspace Right, What Should You Do?

Getting headspace right isn't a food safety issue right off the bat. But it can prevent you from getting a seal. And, it can prevent you from getting a seal that fails on the shelf, which might cause a food safety issue. And, it can prevent discoloration of food at the time of the jar — which though still safe, is unsightly.

29.   What Happens If I Put Too Much Water In My Pressure Canner?

You may want to ask me, does adding extra water in the jars reduce the canning quality?

Well, extra water in the pressure canner may not appear to be seemingly harmful; nevertheless, you must make the error of adding too much water inside the jars that you want to use for canning. This is because when you put too much water inside the jar, you eventually reduce the quality of canning.

30.   Why Do I Lose Liquid When Pressure Canning?

You must understand whenever a pressure canner reaches the recommended pressure; you have to lower the temperature to maintain that pressure without making sharp alterations. Removing jars from the canner too quickly after processing causes stress that sends liquid out of the jar.

Conclusion

Pressure canning is a specific preservation process that can be done with the help of special equipment that can preserve foods at higher temperatures. Food processing at a higher temperature saves the food from future spoilage. Pressure canning can be used to preserve low-acid fruits and vegetables. It is a controlled manner of applying high temperature and pressure to the fruits and vegetables to preserve and protect them from contaminants. Fruits are kept inside individual containers and put into the pressure cooker in water. The water heats up and increases both contents' temperature and pressure. The heat and pressure cook the fruits or vegetables and sterilize them for microbe-free formula. The pressure also seals off the containers and keeps the jars airtight. The pressure and temperature from the steam tenderize the food and keep it safe from spoiling agents like moisture and yeast. Fruits, vegetables, and meat can be well preserved this way.

Book 5

WATER BATH CANNING AND PRESERVING FOR PREPPERS

The Essential Guide for Water Bath Canning and Preserving Foods To Be Self-Sufficient in Any Emergency

Jonathan Henry

Introduction

Water bath canning is easy to safely preserve food with high acidic levels. Water bath canning is called "boiling water canning" or "hot water canning." It is the simple process of boiling jars in a large pot of water for a specified time. Within the pot, the jars are boiled evenly on all sides to ensure the food is thoroughly cooked. After the jars have been boiled and properly sealed, they no longer have to be refrigerated. They will be safely preserved until the jar is opened again as long as they are stored in a cool and dry place.

Products that is canned in a water bath canner will theoretically last forever. If the seal is intact, the food is still edible. This doesn't mean that the food will be delicious forever, though. After a year, the flavor will start to go downhill and the overall quality will diminish. That's why it's recommended to eat home canned goods within the following 12 months after its processing. I always recommend labeling the jar with the date and having an organized storage system where the oldest products are the easiest to get to and use.

Water Bath Canning Benefits

The canning process has many advantages over the water bath process. The water bath process preserves the foods well with minimal investment and effort. Here are the benefits of water bath canning for someone who wants to try it.

31. Kills Of Microbes

Food is a common growth ground for microbes and pathogens. The rule to eat safe and non-contaminated food is to keep the food safe from microbes. The water bath canning process makes your food sterile and safe, along with making the food delicious. Many microbes like Escherichia coli and Salmonella enterica are killed by the boiling and heated action of water bathing during canning. Moreover, the high acidity of the foods and the water activity of the canner also kills off the pathogens so that the canned food is not spoilt easily and is safe to consume.

32. Drives Out Air And Creates A Vacuum

The main reason for the food spoilage is its prolonged contact with the air. The air is a vector of air-borne microbes and pathogens. The water bath technique during canning keeps the food safe from the air as it creates a vacuum and seals the food chemically inside the jar. The vacuum caused inside the jar due to the water bath boiling action ensures that the food is not exposed to oxygen. When the food is not exposed to oxygen, it does not degrade in color or appearance of flavor. Canned food with a water bathing technique maintains its nutritional and physical quality. The vacuum ensures that there is no re-entry of air into the food inside the jar.

33. Increases Shelf Life

Water bath canning is known to increase the length of the shelf life of a fruit or vegetable as a preserve. The process not only kills the microbes that may be responsible for the spoilage of food, but it also inactivates the enzymes of the food and as secreted by the microbes so that the food remains preserved for a long time. The fruits and veggies you would see spoilt after 3 or 4 days are preserved for around a year so that you can eat them whenever you wish. The longer shelf life of the preserves saves a lot of food for you and opens up avenues of taste for you.

34. Safe Procedure

Many procedures protect and preserve food for a long time. However, the water bath canning process is safer than other processes. The pressure canning method depends on the build-up of pressure inside the pot, and this can be dangerous if the build-up is not tracked properly. On the other hand, the water bath canning process is also very cheap and easy as it only needs a large pot like the Dutch oven and a wire rack. The set-up is very simple, and you can easily use this method at home. The procedure is safe as it does not lead to mishaps and accidents when you use the right equipment and stick to the right precautions for the process.

35. Eat Healthily

The goal of any food preservation process is to maintain the nutritional quality of the food and its appearance when eating them later. You will get many artificially preserved foods near you. However, artificially preserved foods are unhealthy alternatives to home-canned foods. The water bath technique helps you preserve the food items in their natural forms and with only natural preservatives like oils and syrups. You can control the number of preservatives and other ingredients added to the fruits or vegetable preserve. This helps you monitor what you eat and ultimately eat healthily.

There are multiple advantages of water bath canning that you can experience if you keep canning foods. Canning foods at home with the help of a water bath helps you preserve foods on a budget and reduces your dependency on supermarkets and brands.

Tools For Water Bath Canning

36. Essential Tools

As with any trip, embarking on the journey of home canning requires some specific gear. You won't need a new sleeping bag or a tent, but just like those tools, the canning equipment you purchase will be used over and over—for years, if not decades. So, although a little up-front investment is required, it will provide returns for years. In truth, you probably already have almost everything you need right home and can purchase the remainder for under $100.

a. Water Bath Canner

Water bath canners are large pots wide enough to hold multiple jars at a time and are tall enough to cover the jars with 2 inches of water. They are inexpensive; usually you can find a basic setup, which includes a rack for the jars to sit on, for about $50. Larger 21-quart canners hold 7-quart jars or 9 pint jars. This is the right size for you if you make large batches of pickles or canned tomatoes. Smaller 12-quart canners hold 4-quart jars or 7-pint jars, which is the perfect size for processing small-batch jams or sauces. Be aware that some water bath canners are not appropriate for certain types of stoves—for instance, induction or glass-top stoves. Check your range owner's manual before choosing a specific canner.

Any large stockpot can be used for canning, but it might be difficult to find a suitable size, as most are tall and narrow or short and wide, neither of which will do the trick.

b. Canning Rack

You need a rack to keep the jars off the bottom of the pot. Most canners come with an aluminum rack. These work great but will rust over time. If you plan to do a lot of water bath canning, splurge on a stainless-steel rack.

You must purchase a separate canning rack if you use a stockpot as a water bath canner. Canning racks of all sizes can be found online, usually for less than $25.

c. Large Pot

Because most foods need to be cooked before canning, you need a large pot. A 5-quart pot is large enough to prepare small batches of jams, pickles, sauces, etc. However, I recommend investing in an 8-quart or larger pot or Dutch oven. The larger pot reduces the chances of jam or pickles boiling over—and of you getting hit with hot, splattering jam. Plus, a larger pot ensures that all the ingredients are heated, thus helping make your home-canned product safe. Avoid aluminum or cast iron; choose enamel, ceramic, or stainless steel. Aluminum and cast iron react with acid ingredients, giving your products an unwelcome metallic taste.

d. Canning Jars

It is imperative to have approved canning jars with two-piece lids. Although Mom may have used empty mayonnaise or pickle jars, please refrain from following this tradition. These days, jars used in commercial canning are designed for a single use only and not the home canning process. The glass is not as heavy nor as sturdy as that of approved canning jars. It's not worth the risk of shattered jars and injuries from glass shards.

e. Lids And Rings

New boxes of approved canning jars come with two-piece metal lids, including a sealable lid and the ring that keeps it in place on the jar. You can also purchase additional rings and lids separately. Most sealable lids are designed for one use only, so do not try to reuse them. Rings can be used repeatedly, but because they are metal, they may become rusted or bent, which must be discarded. Reusable plastic lids are fairly new to the market; they require a slightly different sealing technique, so follow the individual brand directions.

f. Towels

I recommend placing tea towels or terrycloth dish towels on the counter to cushion the jars when setting them down. Towels help keep jars from slipping while they are being filled and insulate hot jars after processing. Dipped in water or white vinegar, a clean towel should be used to wipe down jar lips after filling but before adding the two-piece lids. Vinegar is especially helpful when you are canning items that may be greasy; otherwise a towel moistened with water works fine.

g. Jar Lifter

A jar lifter grabs the hot jars and helps you lift them from the water bath canner. It is a handy implement and the most effective way to remove hot jars without burning your fingers.

37. Nice To Have Equipment

Although not necessary, some tools make your canning experience easier, more enjoyable, and less messy.

h. Food Scale

Some people consider a food scale a necessity. However, most recipes include ingredient amounts in cups or by number of items and weight. A food scale might come in handy when you aren't quite sure about how large to chop the fruit or whether you have enough product on hand to make the recipe. Check ingredient weights with a food scale in these situations.

i. Funnel

A wide-mouth jar funnel is my favorite canning implement. While you can fill jars without a funnel, using one makes the job easier and less messy. Look for a specially designed funnel to fit both regular and wide-mouth canning jars.

j. Bubble Remover

This implement is designed to remove bubbles from filled jars and is most often used when canning fruits or pickles. Any long, nonmetallic device, like a chopstick, can be used instead, but the bubble remover is thin and thus easier to use and more effective.

k. Magnetic Lid Grabber

Although it is no longer necessary to sterilize jar lids before use, the lids do need to be clean, so many of us still preheat them in simmering water. This tool lets you grab the lid and lift it out of the water, saving you from scalded fingers. You can use tongs to pick up the lids, but this tool works like magic.

l. Headspace Measuring Tool

Every canning recipe requires a specific bit of headspace, an empty area between the top of the container and the lid. This angled tool measures just how much headspace you have so you can adjust the product amount if necessary. The screw rings on the jars usually do this as well, with the bottom ring indicating ½-inch headspace and the top ring indicating ¼-inch headspace. Or you can always use a ruler.

m. Digital Thermometer

If you make lots of jam and fruit preserves, a candy or deep-fry thermometer helps make sure you have reached the gelling point. The gelling point is 8 degrees above the boiling point. Other ways to check for jam gelling, like the plate method or the spoon method, are less precise but can be used in a pinch. A thermometer assures that your jams are perfectly set, neither too syrupy nor too thick.

n. Camp Stove

A camp stove falls into the must-have category if you have an older glass-top stove that isn't safe for canning. But even if that isn't a concern, a camp stove can make canning on a hot summer day a much more enjoyable experience. Using a camp stove moves the processing heat out of your kitchen and gives you an excuse to spend time outdoors, enjoying the day.

o. Cheesecloth Or Jelly Bag

Using fine-weave cheesecloth or a jelly bag is the easiest way to strain fruit for jelly. Cheesecloth also comes in handy when using whole spices in pickling or when infusing syrups and vinegars.

Water Bath Canning Method

38. Step 1: Preparation

The first thing you should always do before starting to can is clean. Clean absolutely everything from the jars to the canner itself. This may seem like overkill and it absolutely is. A good philosophy to have when it comes to canning is that it's better to be safe than sorry. If your utensils have been sitting in storage for half a year, it's likely to have accumulated some dust. You won't want to pour food into dusty jars. Not only could it be dangerous for bacterial reasons but it's not very appetizing either. When you are done washing all of your equipment make sure to thoroughly dry it off.

While a canner's worst fear is botulism, a canner's worst enemy is rust. Cleaning your equipment before use is a great time to check it over for any possible rust. Rust can ruin the integrity of the canner and cause holes where you don't want them. Canners are supposed to last decades if they are properly maintained. The last thing you'll want to do is have to replace your expensive equipment because it's faulty. This is why canners need to be stored in a similar location to the canned goods. The right conditions will keep it safe from any possible rust or even mold.

If the processing time for your goods is less than 10 minutes you'll need to sterilize the jars. To do this, place the empty jars in the water bath canner right side up and fill the canner with water. This should come to about 1 inch above the jars. Boil the water for 10 minutes. (Add one minute every 1,000 feet above sea level where you are located.) When this is done, remove the jars from the canner using a jar lifter. Drain the hot water from the jars and dry them off before adding food. You can leave the water in the canner and use it to process the food.

If you don't need to sterilize the jars, you still need to make sure they are warm before the food goes in them. In this case you can fill the water bath canner 1/3 of the way. Place the jars upside down and let the steam keep them warm. (You can also just wash them in a dishwasher and keep them in there until you're ready to use them.) The lids and screw bands should also be warm. An easy way to do this is to put them in a warm bowl of water.

39. Step 2: Heating

After you have filled the jars and checked them for air bubbles, it's time to put them in the canner. Using a jar lifter, slowly place the jars of food into the water bath canner. Evenly space them out on the rack so they aren't touching. The rack should assist with this. If you have a water bath canner, your rack should be able to rest on the sides of your canner. Once your rack is loaded, you can lower it down so the water is now covering the jar lids. Add water until there are 2 inches of water above the jars. It's important for the process that the water can freely move around the jars.

The time doesn't start until the canner is at a boil. When this starts to happen place the lid over the canner and have it come to a full rolling boil. It's best to measure the cooking time exactly so use an app on your phone or an actual kitchen timer. You'll definitely want an alarm if the process is going to take more than half an hour. If you choose to just pay attention to the clock you may accidentally over-process the food. The canner is going to reach temperatures of 212 °F, so make sure you don't accidentally burn yourself on the canister.

Processing times can change depending on your altitude. Most recipes only provide the processing times for locations under 1,000 feet above sea level. If you live in high-altitude places like Colorado, this could be a problem. The reason why altitude can affect processing times is because of the change in atmospheric pressure. By every 1,000 feet, the atmospheric pressure is reduced. This will make water boil at a lower temperature than 212 °F. Since water is boiling at a lower temperature, it's going to take longer to cook. It's important to research your altitude before you begin canning and change the processing times accordingly.

If you have a long processing time, it is vital for the canner to keep up the boiling. Every once in a while, lift up the lid and look inside to make sure the canner is doing its job. The pot is supposed to be full of boiling water though, so be very careful. If you've noticed that the water is no longer at a full rolling boil, add some more boiling water to the canner to help it maintain its process. Be careful when adding in the boiling water, as you don't want to spill any and end up with any serious burns.

40.   Step 3: Cooling

Once your timer goes off you can turn the heat off. The water bath canner will still be hot so be careful as you lift up the rack. Always wear protective gear around a heated water bath canner. You don't need goggles or anything dramatic like that, but oven mitts are a must have. Make sure not to shake the jars too much when you are lifting up the rack. The sealing process is still relatively fragile at this stage and you could mess it up. Before you take the jars out, give them a minute or two to cool down.

Grab your trusty jar lifters and slowly take the jars out one by one. The jars are still going to be very hot so make sure to put them on a wooden board or thick towel. You don't want to end up with any scorch marks on your counter. The jars should be in an upright position, as putting them in any other position will mess with the sealing process. There also needs to be a couple of inches between the jars so that air can freely circulate around them. Make sure they aren't located in a spot with a draft; cold air could break the hot glass of the jars and ruin all of your hard work.

In the next couple of minutes, the jars will start to cool. As they do this the sealing process begins. You'll most likely hear a pop. This comes from the seal of the inner lid pulled down and resulting in a satisfying "ping" sound. Make sure not to touch the jars during this cooling process. The worst thing you can do at this point is to press down on the lid. It will mess up the seal and make all of your hard work for nothing. The jars should be left alone for about 24 hours.

After the 24 hours of waiting comes the moment of truth. Press down on the lid to see if the sealing process was a success. If you find that the lid is sucked down and does not pop back up when you press down, congratulations—you did it! If it does pop up, it's not that big of a deal. The seal may not have worked but the food is still good. Just put it in the refrigerator and eat it in the next few days. You could also try to re-process it, but that might result in an overcooked taste and texture.

41.Step 4: Storing

Before you start canning you should already know where you are going to put your canned goods. Canned food needs a cool and dry environment to stay preserved. This can be a cellar or a temperature-controlled garage. It can also be a regular pantry; just make sure there is no direct sunlight. Another huge issue is using a location with any sort of humidity. If you're storing your canned goods in a cellar, there can't be any hot pipes around. This can result in the steam that will pop the sealed lid straight off. Your location should also have enough room for your cans to stay organized. If you make more cans than your space allows, you could end up having to store them in a place that isn't ideal, and lose productivity.

Once you have a location, it's time to store your first batch. Make sure to take off the screw band. This won't affect the actual seal and the lid will stay put. The problem with keeping the screw band on is that it could rust over and ruin your jar. It can also make it impossible to open the container safely. If you're having trouble removing a screw band, it's not the end of the world. Just keep it on and check on it every once in a while to make sure no rust is forming. If you try to force it, it can ruin the seal.

After removing the screw bands you're not yet done. The jars need to be labeled. I suggest adding the date that they were canned, the type of food in them, and any ingredients that went into them.

The ingredient list might only seem necessary if you're planning on selling the goods, but it can come in handy even if you're not; when you're trying out different recipes, you want to know which ingredients worked best for you. When you are putting on the date, the year is just as important. You don't want to accidentally eat something that's seven years old. It won't kill you but it probably won't taste good.

The USDA recommends eating your canned goods within a year. After this point, the food quality will go down. You'll end up missing out on the nutritional value along with the taste. (However, in the case of an apocalypse, you may be happy you saved strawberries from 30 years ago.) So ultimately the decision whether to throw the food away after it has peaked is up to you. When you're done with a jar, make sure to discard the lid, wash the jar, and store it somewhere safe for the next harvest season.

42. Temperature Plus Time

Both temperature and time must be considered for a safe water bath product. Boiling water helps eliminate harmful bacteria, but there are two caveats:

The water must be continuously boiling throughout the processing period.

If the water temperature drops after the jars have been added to the canner, the processing has been compromised. This means that once the water comes back to a boil, the processing time must start over.

Products must be kept in the boiling water for the prescribed length of time.

The time period indicates how long it takes the heat from the boiling water to penetrate through the product and kill all harmful bacteria. You will find charts that show how long your particular products need to stay in the canner. In general, denser products like whole tomatoes require a longer time period (up to 90 minutes), whereas small, loosely packed products like salsa or relish need less time (about 15 minutes). Most jellies should be processed for 5 minutes in a boiling water bath. Jam and fruit butter need 10 to 15 minutes of processing time. Pickles in pint or quart jars are processed for 10 or 15 minutes, while quarts of sauerkraut need 20 minutes. Tomato sauce needs 35 minutes for pints and 40 minutes for quart jars.

Over a long processing time, there is a tendency to boil dry (that is, all the water evaporates), so it's recommended that you keep a kettle of boiling water on the stove while you are canning. This way, you can top off the water bath canner with boiling water and not reduce the water temperature, which would require you to start over.

Products processed at a high altitude need a longer time to be considered safe. This is because water boils at a lower temperature at a higher altitude, so the time is increased. To find out the altitude where you live and the altitude adjustments.

43. Eliminating Oxygen

The final piece of the water bath safety puzzle eliminates oxygen. When a jar with a two-piece cap is placed in a canner full of boiling water and processed for the proper length of time, all the air gets pushed out of the jar, forming a vacuum. Most bacteria cannot grow without oxygen, so this step helps keep the food product safe. The process of forcing the air out of the jar creates an airtight seal when the vacuum forms.

44. Avoiding Botulism

Botulism sounds scary, and it is. Botulism is an illness caused by the *Clostridium botulinum* bacteria. The bacteria's spores love to grow in a moist, low-acid, low-oxygen environment, where they produce a deadly toxin.

You can't smell or taste the botulism toxin, but ingesting it can be fatal or cause permanent nerve damage or paralysis. Luckily, there is a simple way to avoid the threat of botulism: Use high-acid foods, follow an appropriate recipe, and adhere to the necessary processing temperature and time. If you are ever in doubt about whether a product has been compromised, throw it out. It's not worth the risk.

Safety Criteria For Water Bath Canning

In regards to food preservation, most foodborne illnesses can be avoided if you:

- Wash your hands thoroughly before handling food; ensure all tools and surfaces used are also clean.
- Rinse produce under running water, rubbing the whole surface with your clean hands. Soaps or detergents are not necessary; the friction of the hands loosens bacteria holding dirt and grime, and running water washes it away.
- Don't allow the product to soak. Use sieves, or colanders, for small foodstuffs, and make sure to keep the layers shallowed; so, that all surfaces of each bean, berry or other food are rinsed as thoroughly as possible.

Whether by salting, sugaring, canning, or freezing, food preservation is the art of killing microbes or at least keeping them from reproducing to toxic levels.

Freezing or refrigerating food keeps bacteria from growing. Unluckily, there are at least two bacteria that can grow at refrigerator temperatures. High salt, sugar, and acid levels also keep bacteria from growing.

Only heat kills the microbes. If held for even a few seconds, a temperature above 160 °F [78 °C] is sufficient to kill viruses, parasites, and bacteria, except for one. The bacteria Clostridium produces heat-resistant spores that can only be killed above boiling temperature. Pressure canning produces the high temperature necessary to kill these spores.

Not all toxins produced by bacteria are affected by heat. Therefore, it is very important to always preserve good quality foods. Avoid:

- Split peels or skins
- Bruised fruit
- Evidence of insect attacks
- Nibbles by birds or animals

Ensure all foodstuffs are as fresh as possible and processed in a small, manageable batch as quickly as can be. In order to produce the highest quality preserved foods you need to process them on the same day as they are harvested and managed in a sanitary way. Again, food safety should be your first concern when preserving foodstuffs for future use.

45. Jar Sterilization

Do not afford to skip this step. While water bath canning may be the easier canning Direction, you need to remember the involved risks. If this process isn't carried out properly, you will take the risk of contaminating your food and putting your health at risk.

One of the measures needed to be carried out to protect the food you want to can is sterilizing your jars. A few people only recommend jar sterilization if you live in a high-altitude area. You should sterilize your jars, regardless of where you live—the extra effort won't hurt.

All foods that require processing, less than ten minutes, have to be filled into sterilized jars. The processing time differs with each recipe; please make sure you read through the recipe carefully.

This is how you should sterilize the jars:

- Place your empty jars, right side up, in the canning rack. The canning rack should be inside the water bath canner or stockpot.
- The water should be hot, not boiling.
- Bring the water to boil and let it boil for 10 to 15 minutes.
- Using the jar lifter or tongs, cautiously remove the sterilized jars one after another and drain them. Please keep in mind the jars are hot. Do not attempt to manage them with your bare hands.
- Replace all water in the canner with fresh water.

Once you have successfully sterilized your jars you can proceed with the following steps.

It is not necessary to sterilize the seals and lids in boiling water. You can always wash these with hot water and detergent. Be sure you wash them thoroughly to ensure that all the detergent has been removed. Remnants of detergent can cause unnatural flavors in the food; this is also why the washing Direction isn't the best way to sterilize your jars.

Also, you must sterilize your jars when you reuse them. Keep in mind that you can only reuse the glass jars—not the lids and seals.

46. Food

Remember, the water bath canning Direction is only for high acid foods. These foods have already been preserved by their naturally high acid levels, which makes the preservation process slightly easier for you, the beginner.

High-acidic foods are mostly fruits: (cranberries, cherries, raspberries, etc.) and fruit juices (especially from citrus fruits), jellies, jams, pickled vegetables (e.g., pickles or pickled sprouts), tomatoes that have been given additional acid, salsas, olives, etc.

Also, make sure the vegetables and fruits you plan to use are of the highest quality possible.

Before you cook your foods, you *must* wash them thoroughly to rinse any remnants of pesticides—or pests.

47. Equipment

When it comes to home canning, you must ensure all of your equipment is sterile before you start using them. You can boil your utensils for 5 to 10 minutes. You can wash them with detergent in hot water for the equipment not to be boiled (canning funnel, jar lifter, etc.). Once again, please make sure you wash the equipment carefully. Avoid using any old rusted utensils; throw those away and buy new utensils if you can.

48.   Yeast And Mold

Yeast and mold are common microorganisms found on the surfaces of fruits and vegetables. There are hundreds of species of yeasts and molds, and most of them can withstand different kinds of environmental conditions—this is why they are such a big problem. Their resilient versatility is the main reason these microorganisms can attack many kinds of foods—grains, meats, and fruits and vegetables.

Whether you are getting your produce from your homegrown garden, supermarkets, or the farmer's market, you need to make sure you check all fruits and vegetables for signs of yeast and mold. Preserving produce with these microorganisms could pose a serious risk to your health and the health of anyone else who will eat these canned foods. While canned food may have preservatives such as vinegar and lemon juice to prevent microorganisms from developing on the produce, they will not be able to treat already-infected fruits and vegetables. The best thing you can do is dispose of the infected fruits and vegetables and make use of fresh, clean ones instead.

Yeast often appears as a white or yellow, foam-like substance on the surface of fruits and vegetables. Molds are often dark green, grey, or even black. This usually occurs if the fruits or vegetables have been stored for a long time. You should also avoid storing your foods in warm, damp areas. Make sure, if you are growing your produce, to plan your canning efficiently. Try to preserve and can your food within a couple of days of harvest. If you find foods with yeast or mold on them, throw them out. Wash the remaining fruits and vegetables thoroughly before cooking them or trying to preserve them.

49.   Choose The Right Canner

The first step to safe home canning is choosing the right canner. First off, know when to use a pressure canner or a water bath canner.

Use a pressure canner specifically designed for canning and preserving foods. There are several types of canner out there, and some are just for cooking food, not for preserving food and processing jars. Be sure you have the right type of equipment.

Make sure your pressure canner is the right size. If your canner is too small, the jars may be undercooked. Always opt for a larger canner as the pressure on the bigger pots tends to be more accurate, and you will be able to take advantage of the larger size and can store more foods at once!

Before beginning to canning, check your pressure canner is in good condition. If your canner has a rubber gasket, it should be flexible and soft. If the rubber is dry or cracked, it should be replaced before you start canning. Be sure your canner is clean, and the small vents in the lid are free of debris. Adjust your canner for high-altitude processing if needed.

Once you are sure your canner is ready to go and meets all these guidelines, it is time to start canning!

50.   Check Your Jars, Lids, And Bands

As you wash your jars with soapy water, check for any imperfections. Even new jars may have a small chip or crack and need to be discarded. You can reuse jars again and again as long as they are in good condition.

The metal jar rings are also reusable; however, you should only reuse them if they are rust-free and undented. If your bands begin to show signs of wear, consider investing in some new ones.

Jar lids need to be new as the sealing compound on the lid can disintegrate over time. When you store your jars in damp places (like in a basement or canning cellar), the lids are even more likely to disintegrate. Always use new lids to ensure your canning is successful.

51. Check For Recent Canning Updates

Canning equipment has changed over the years, becoming more high-tech and therefore more efficient at processing foods. In addition to the equipment becoming more advanced, there have also been many scientific improvements, making canning safer when the proper steps are taken. For example, many people used to sterilize their jars before pressure canning. While this is still okay, it is unnecessary, as science has shown any bacteria in the jars will die when heated to such a high temperature in a pressure canner. Sterilization is an extra step you don't need!

52.   Pick The Best Ingredients

When choosing food to can, always get the best food possible. You want to use high-quality, perfectly ripe produce for canning. You will never end up with a jar of food better than the product itself, so picking good ingredients is important to the taste of your final product. Also, products that are past their prime can affect their ability to can them. If strawberries are overripe, your jam may come out too runny. If your tomatoes are past their prime, they may not have a high enough pH level to be processed in a water bath. Pick your ingredients well, and you will make successfully preserved foods.

53.   Clean Everything

While you may know your jars and lids need to be washed and sanitized, don't forget about the rest of your tools. Cleaning out your canner before using it is essential, even if you put it away clean. Make sure to wipe your countertop well, making sure there are no crumbs or residue. Wash your produce with clean, cold water, and don't forget to wash your hands! The cleaner everything is, the less likely you are to spread bacteria onto your jarred foods.

54.   Cool the Jars

Be sure to give your jars 12 hours to cool before testing the seal. Testing the seal too early may break as the jar is still warm, making the rubber pliable. Be sure to cool the jars away from a window or fan, as even a slight breeze may cause the hot jars to crack. Once cool, remove the metal band, clean it and save it for your next canning project.

55.   Canning Do's and Don'ts

Canning is relatively simple, but when not done properly, it can result in disastrous consequences. For you to truly be a master of this very important skill, let me provide you with some canning dos and don'ts you'll surely find helpful.

p. Be Organized

Did you notice studying the recipe is always the first step in the water bath and pressure canning methods above? This is because knowing what to do keeps you organized. When preserving food, you have to be organized since it could help your work go smoothly, and canning should be done as quickly as possible.

q. Spices And Seasoning Only As Specified

Do you know spices and seasoning are usually high in bacteria? Too many seasonings and spices on your food beyond what was required in the recipe could be unsafe.

r. Overripe Fruits and Vegetables Are A No-No

I have mentioned this before but let me just reiterate that canning can increase the life of the food, but it certainly couldn't increase its quality. Canning overripe fruits may become worse in storage.

s. No Butter And Fat Ever

You should not put these two in your home canned products as they do not store well. Adding them to your product will only decrease the food's life. In addition, butter and fat slow heat transfer during processing, resulting in an unsafe preserve.

Common Problems And How To Solve Them

Making errors not only wastes time, but may also be deadly. Fortunately, each of these mistakes is simple to avoid.

While canning is a terrific method to preserve the abundance of your summer garden, mistakes happen. But don't worry: these frequent blunders may be easily avoided.

56.   Overfilling Your Jars

Many recipes call for a quarter-inch to one-quarter-inch of headspace between the top of the jar and also the top of the liquid. You won't be able to create a good vacuum seal if you overfill your jar. As a result, your food may discolor or deteriorate sooner than expected.

57. Using The Wrong Jars

It's OK to repurpose store-bought glass jars...just not for canning. Canning jars are designed to withstand the high temperatures of the water bath and a certain level of pressure without shattering.

58. Reusing Lids

We believe in recycling, but then those canning lids are intended to be used just once. The rings will not form the same seal the 2nd time, making them dangerous.

59. Failure To Follow A Recipe

You'll want to adhere to authorized instructions since canning is about properly establishing a specific pH level within the jar. Otherwise, your shelf-stable foods may cause people to get ill.

60. Use Of The Water Bath Method Rather Than Using The Pressure Canning Method

This is an all-too-common blunder that may also be lethal. The water bath approach works well with high-acid foods like pickles and sugar-preserved goods like jam. To avoid botulism, low-acid items (such as soups or meats) must be processed in a pressure canner.

61. Not Disturbing The Air Bubbles

Did you know that before twisting the lid, you must first eliminate the air bubbles from the jar? It's particularly critical for thicker combinations like jam. The trapped air might increase your headspace, resulting in a poor seal. If you pop the bubbles, use a plastic tool (like metal tools can damage the jars).

62. Tightening The Lids Too Much

It's natural to want to tighten the bands to ensure that the contents are sealed but avoid the urge. Over tightened lids may cause buckled lids and poor seals by preventing air from escaping. Screw on the bands till they are fingertip tight, then leave the rest in the water bath.

Conclusion

Canning and preserving may be a procedure that benefits your food, nutrition, and finances in the long term. Still as a novice, you should be aware that this process will take time, money, and effort since it is time-consuming, needs work, and has a higher initial cost. And if you aren't aware of this, you may be dissatisfied in the end.

Canning is also one of the most important skills to produce nutritious meals for your family. It's a technique that will help many people save money on groceries while reducing their reliance on high-sugar, high-salt canned items from the supermarket. So, if you've been thinking about starting canning as a new and sustainable pastime for your family, now is the time to do it. You will undoubtedly profit from the various advantages that canning and preserving foods may provide over time.

Instead of jumping into canning and preserving foods immediately, as a novice, take it one step at a time. Begin by studying more about canning and preserving, planning your budget, and acquiring all necessary supplies and tools until you are ready to begin. In this manner, canning and preserving your goods at home would not be as stressful, difficult, or costly but would be a simple and gratifying procedure despite the initial outlay.

Some people believe that canning is only useful in an emergency. That is where they are mistaken. Canning is a fantastic way to preserve your food fresh for an extended period. Many people began canning as a pastime, but others have turned it into a way of life. You can create canned food without much effort, and the greatest thing is that it doesn't need much talent. These methods of preservation can keep your food fresh for a long time.

Book 6:

WATER BATH CANNING AND PRESERVING COOKBOOK FOR PREPPERS

The Complete Preppers Guide with 1200-Day of Quick, Easy, and Affordable Recipes to Keep Your Pantry Always Stocked.

Jonathan Henry

Introduction

What Is Canning?

Canning is a process of food preservation in which food is preserved in airtight jars at high temperatures for a long time, killing organisms and inactivating enzymes that would otherwise ruin the food. As the food cools, the heating process forces air out of the jar, establishing a vacuum seal.

Benefits of Canning

1. Food preservation is all about preventing food from going bad before it's eaten. Bacteria produce toxic compounds that infect our diet. Toxic and sometimes deadly cases of food poisoning are the end consequence.
2. When it comes to saving money, preserving fresh vegetables from the garden or farm is also a good idea. A variety of factors affect home-preserved food costs. All materials, equipment, fresh food, human energy, and fuel energy are included in the cost of producing and storing food.
3. The use of locally grown and seasonal food, the reuse of preserving jars, and improved packing and food miles are all ecologically beneficial components of this method.
4. Agricultural excess is one of the primary causes of food preservation.
5. It also prevents agricultural planning that isn't proper.

Types of Food Canning: Water-Bath and Pressure Canning

a. Water Bath Canning

It includes bringing food to a boil in water that has been canned, the process that is often referred to as "water-bath canning" is also known as "hot water canning." In the method of canning known as the water bath, the jar or can is "bathed" in hot water and allowed to reach a temperature of 212 degrees Fahrenheit for a certain amount of time.

For processing foods with a high acid content, use this procedure. Tomatoes (along with foods produced from tomatoes) and pickles are two examples of foods with a high acid content (as well as pickled food).

b. Pressure Canning

The method of canning under pressure is distinct from canning in a water bath, even though both use a kettle for heating the food. In contrast to the other method, which makes use of the kettle to heat the water, pressure canning uses the steam produced by the kettle. Simply said, all that is required of you is to put the jar inside the kettle and wait for it to achieve an internal temperature of 240 degrees Fahrenheit while maintaining a certain pressure. This pressure is displayed in pounds and measured using a dial gauge on the lid of the pressure canner.

How Does It Work?

Canning is a method of preserving food in jars for long periods at high temperatures, killing microorganisms and inactivating enzymes that can cause food to spoil. The heating process pushes the air out of the jar, creating a vacuum seal as the food cools.

When you heat a full, sealed jar, the food expands and releases steam, expelling air from the jar. As it cools, it forms a vacuum seal on the jar. Factors that can affect canning and shelf life are sugar content and acidity, and it's best to follow a canning recipe when you're just starting to help determine which method is correct for the food you will be preparing.

Tools Needed

- Water Bath Canner: a large pot with a lid and rack; it's usually used in canning high acid foods.
- Pressure Canners: usually mistaken as a pressure cooker. There are two kinds of pressure canners; the dial gauge and the weighted gauge. The dial gauge measures pressure through the dial gauge and the weighted gauge uses weights to measure and control pressure build-up. It also comes with wire racks. It´s used in canning low acid foods.
- For a bain-marie, a large pot that has a lid and grid for preserves.
- A good variety of glass jars.
- A jar lifter to remove these from the pot.
- Kitchen utensils: a wooden spoon, ladle, funnel, spatula, and long tongs.
- Clean handles and tea towels.
- The food you will put in the can.

Pros and Cons

a. Pros

- Chemically, canning modifies the food to protect it against germs, bacteria, mold, and yeast by altering the moisture or salinity levels. It also restricts the action of dietary enzymes. Together, these chemical reactions and the physical barrier of glass jars, seals, and lids efficiently prevent deterioration.
- Can store food in jars for up to two years on a shelf.
- Using locally grown or homegrown vegetables might be more cost-effective.

b. Cons

- It requires specialist equipment, which may be costly and difficult to store. The pressure canner serves as the water bath preservation pot, so it gets abundant usage.
- It may be baffling. The equipment is more sophisticated than other preservation equipment, and fewer individuals do it, making it harder to learn and understand. After a few attempts, you will discover it is no more difficult than regular canning. If you have never used a water bath before, this is a great start.
- Because the vegetables have been cooked, the texture of the surface changes.
- Canners need regular maintenance (a dial-gauge canner, for instance, should be examined for precision once a year).

How Is Food Preserved By Canning?

Canning is an excellent method to preserve fruits and vegetables from the garden or farmer's market while they are still in season. It can extend the bounty into the winter months when the local and seasonal items are not available.

Canning in both water baths and pressure cookers warms the food and generates a vacuum seal in the jar, killing any germs that could develop. The vacuum seal will prevent air from coming into touch with the preserved food, which might increase cell development and spoilage.

The term "canning" is a bit of a misnomer. Metal canning is no longer generally used in home canning as it is in industrial canning. Glass canning jars with properly constructed lids are the preferred preservation method.

Canning may be done in two ways: in a boiling water bath or a pressure canner. If you wish to ensure the preservation of food in sealed jars kept at room temperature, you must understand the differences between the two ways. The easier of the two procedures is boiling water bath canning. It only requires using a big, deep pot and canning jars and lids. The essential thing to remember about boiling water bath canning is that the technique is only safe for high-acid foods. What do you mean by high-acid foods? Fruits, vinegar-based pickles (including chutneys), fruit-based sweet preserves like jams and jellies, and tomatoes with extra acidity. To efficiently preserve the food in a boiling water bath, it must have a pH of 4.6 or below.

In a boiling water bath, you may process jars containing any of the high-acid food items. You must process all the other goods in a pressure canner, including non-pickled vegetables, soup stocks, and meats.

Heat processing in a boiling water bath helps preserve the food, but it does not ensure that the contents are safe to consume. The conclusion here is that the acidity of each jar's contents, rather than the heat of the processing, is what correctly preserves the food in a boiling water bath. When used with canning jars and lids, the boiling water bath generates a vacuum seal to keep molds out of the jars. Like store-bought canned items, you must store the opened jars in a refrigerator.

You could come across old-fashioned methods for sealing your canning jars, such as flipping them upside down while the food inside is still hot or putting them in the oven. It's not a good idea! Although the jars may have sealed, there is no guarantee that a real vacuum has been formed. Furthermore, the food within may not have reached the temperature of boiling water to the core using those ways. Canning periods (also known as processing times) are determined by the density of the food and the size of the jar, both of which influence how long it takes for all of the food to reach the temperature of the hot water in the surrounding area.

Which Food Can Be Canned and Which Cannot?

c. What Can You Can?

- Fruits
- Tomatoes
- Vegetables
- Meat, poultry, and fish are all options.
- Jellies and jams
- Fermented veggies and pickles

d. Food that shouldn't be canned

- Do not place frozen food in your pressure canner or water bath canning jars. This can cause a jar to explode.

- Do not use the sterilizing processes in your pressure canner or water bath on food items that contain raw meat, fish, poultry, eggs, or dairy products. They may contaminate raw meat and poultry with bacteria such as Salmonella and E.coli. Eggs may contain Salmonella and E. coli before they are cooked.

Tips and Tricks

e. Tips for Food Safety

1. Fresh food is best. Avoid any damaged or overripe product while it is at its optimal quality.
2. Pressure canner or boiling water bath? It is possible to preserve acidic foods such as pickles and tomatoes in a boiling water bath. It is necessary to use a pressure canner for non-acidic goods like soup stocks, unpickled vegetables, and meat.
3. Take advantage of the still-warm jars to fill them up. One at a time, fill the jars with hot food, leaving room at the top for the lids to seal. Once you've finished filling it, return it to the boiling water.
4. You will hear a popping sound if you do this. You should hear a popping sound and the lid should no longer pop up when the jar is thoroughly shut.
5. Overfilling containers: A decent recipe will tell you to leave an inconsiderable amount of headspace between the food and the jar's rim. Overfilled jars won't allow the canning lids to seal correctly. A few days in the fridge or enough headroom to seal it aren't deal-breakers if your jars are unsealed.

f. How to Avoid Canned Food Poisoning?

You should take great care when canning any food. Following instructions and processing methods are essential to prevent the deterioration and growth of botulism, a deadly form of food poisoning.

Harmful bacteria can multiply rapidly in the proper growing environment, including moist, low-acid food, temperatures in hazardous areas (40–120°F), and less than 2 percent oxygen.

Before serving canned food at home, inspecting the jar for any damage is crucial. The lid should be tight and still pressed in the center, indicating a good seal.

Some signs, such as the following, may show contaminated food:

- The lid has swelled.
- There are streaks of dry food on top of the jar.
- You see mold somewhere.
- Bubbles are rising in the jar.
- The color of the food is unnatural.
- The liquid has become cloudy.

Beware of eating such food items if any of the above signs manifest. When a jar has sealed well, it has to burst and buzz, similar to when you open a soda.

WATER BATH CANNING

Low Sodium and Low Sugar Recipes

1. Apple Butter

Preparation time: 10 minutes
Cooking time: 24 minutes
Servings: 24
Ingredients:

- 3 lbs. Fuji apples, cored and chopped
- ¼ cup water
- 1 tsp. ground cinnamon
- ½ tsp. ground ginger
- ¼ tsp. ground cloves

Directions:

1. Place apples, water, and spices in a slow cooker. Stir to combine.
2. Set your slow cooker on low and cook, covered, for about 6 hours.
3. Uncover the slow cooker and, with an immersion blender, mash the apples until pureed.
4. Loosely cover the pot with the lid.
5. Cook on low in the slow cooker, covered, for about 6–8 hours.
6. Divide the apple butter into 3 (½-pint) hot, sterilized jars, leaving about ½-inch space from the top.
7. Slide a small knife around the insides of each jar to remove air bubbles.
8. Remove any traces of food from the jar rims using a clean, moist kitchen towel.
9. Close each jar with a lid and screw on the ring.
10. Arrange the jars in a boiling water canner and process for about 10 minutes.
11. Take the jars out of the water canner and place them onto a wood surface several inches apart to cool completely.
12. After cooling, press the top of each jar's lid with your finger to ensure that the seal is tight.
13. Apple butter in a jar can be kept in the refrigerator for up to 2–3 weeks.

Per serving: Calories: 15kcal; Fat: 0.1g; Carbs: 4g; Protein: 0.1g

2. Pear Sauce

Preparation time: 10 minutes
Cooking time: 45 minutes
Servings: 40
Ingredients:

- 12 ripe pears, cored and quartered
- 6 cups water
- 1 tsp. ground cinnamon

Directions:

1. Add pears, water, and cinnamon into a large stainless-steel pan over medium heat. Cook for about 25–30 minutes, stirring occasionally.
2. Add cooked pear mixture into a high-speed blender and pulse until pureed.
3. Divide the pear sauce into 5 (1-pint) hot, sterilized jars, leaving about ½-inch space from the top.
4. Slide a small knife around the insides of each jar to remove air bubbles.
5. Remove any traces of food from the jar rims with a clean, moist kitchen towel.
6. Close each jar with a lid and screw on the ring.
7. Arrange the jars in a boiling water canner and process for about 15 minutes.

8. Take the jars out of the water canner and place them onto a wood surface several inches apart to cool completely.

9. After cooling, press the top of each jar's lid with your finger to ensure that the seal is tight.

10. Canned pear sauce can be stored in the refrigerator for up to 2–3 weeks.

Per serving: Calories: 36kcal; Fat: 0.1g; Carbs: 9.6g; Protein: 0.2g

3. Blueberry Jam

Preparation time: 10 minutes
Cooking time: 18 minutes
Servings: 40
Ingredients:

- 7 cups fresh blueberries
- 1 cup unsweetened apple juice
- 1 package of no-sugar added pectin
- 1 ½ tsp. liquid stevia

Directions:

1. Add blueberries, apple juice, and pectin into a heavy-bottomed saucepan. Stir to combine.

2. Add the stevia and mix well.

3. Heat and then cook over medium heat until boiling, stirring continuously.

4. Boil for about 3 minutes.

5. Remove the pan of jam from heat and immediately skim off foam from the top.

6. Divide the jam into 5 (1/2-pint) hot, sterilized jars, leaving about ½-inch space from the top.

7. Slide a small knife around the insides of each jar to remove air bubbles.

8. Remove any traces of food from the jar rims with a clean, moist kitchen towel.

9. Close each jar with a lid and screw on the ring.

10. Arrange the jars in a boiling water canner and process for about 10 minutes.

11. Take the jars out of the water canner and place them onto a wood surface several inches apart to cool completely.

12. After cooling, press the top of each jar's lid with your finger to ensure that the seal is tight.

13. The canned jam can be preserved in the pantry for up to 1 year.

Per serving: Calories: 17kcal; Fat: 0.1g; Carbs: 4.4g; Protein: 0.2g

4. Raspberry Jelly

Preparation time: 10 minutes
Cooking time: 16 minutes
Servings: 48
Ingredients:

- 4 cups fresh raspberries, crushed
- 1 cup water
- 4 ½ tbsp. no sugar added pectin

Directions:

1. Add crushed raspberries, water, and pectin into a heavy-bottomed stainless-steel saucepan. Stir to combine well.

2. Heat then cook over medium heat until boiling, stirring continuously.

3. Boil for about 1 minute.

4. Remove the saucepan of jelly from the heat and immediately skim off foam from the top.

5. Divide the jelly into 6 (1/2 pint) hot, sterilized jars, leaving about ½-inch space from the top.

6. Slide a small knife around the insides of each jar to remove air bubbles.

7. Remove all traces of food from the edges of the jar with a clean, moist kitchen towel.

8. Close each jar with a lid and screw on the ring.

9. Arrange the jars in a boiling water canner and process for about 10 minutes.

10. Take the jars out of the water canner and place them onto a wood surface several inches apart to cool completely.

11. After cooling, press the top of each jar's lid with your finger to ensure that the seal is tight.

12. The canned jelly can be preserved in the pantry for up to 1 year.

Per serving: Calories: 5kcal; Fat: 0.1g; Carbs: 1.2g; Protein: 0.1g

5. Strawberry & Lemon Concentrate

Preparation time: 15 minutes
Cooking time: 20 minutes
Servings: 56
Ingredients:

- 3 cups fresh strawberries
- 2 cups erythritol
- 2 cups fresh lemon juice

Directions:

1. Place hulled strawberries into a blender. Pulse on high until smooth.

2. Add pureed strawberries, erythritol, and lemon juice into a heavy-bottomed stainless-steel saucepan over medium-high heat. Cook for about 3–5 minutes, stirring continuously.

3. Remove the pan of the strawberry mixture from heat and immediately skim off foam from the top.

4. Divide the strawberry mixture into 7 (1/2-pint) hot, sterilized jars, leaving about ½-inch space from the top.

5. Slide a small knife around the insides of each jar to remove air bubbles.

6. Clean all the traces of food from the jar rims with a clean, moist kitchen towel.

7. Close each jar with a lid and screw on the ring.

8. Arrange the jars in a boiling water canner and process for about 15 minutes.

9. Take the jars out of the water canner and place them onto a wood surface several inches apart to cool completely.

10. After cooling, press the top of each jar's lid with your finger to ensure that the seal is tight.

11. You can store the canned preserves in the refrigerator for up to 3 weeks.

Per serving: Calories: 5kcal; Fat: 0.1g; Carbs: 0.8g; Protein: 0.1g

6. Pickled Beets

Preparation time: 15 minutes
Cooking time: 60 minutes
Servings: 24
Ingredients:

- 3 pounds beets, trimmed
- 1 tsp. all spice berries
- 6 whole cloves
- 1 cinnamon stick
- 2 cups apple cider vinegar
- ¼ tsp. stevia extract

Directions:

1. Cook the beets in a saucepan of boiling water for about 20–25 minutes.

2. Drain the beets, reserving 1 cup of cooking liquid.

3. Set the beets aside to cool.

4. Remove the skin of the beets and then cut them into slices.

5. Tie all of the spices in a cheesecloth.

6. Add vinegar, reserved cooking liquid, stevia, and spice bag into a large nonreactive saucepan over medium-high heat. Cook until boiling.

7. Next, set the heat to low and cook for about 15 minutes.

8. Divide the beet slices into 3 (1-pint) hot, sterilized jars.

9. Next, add pickling liquid to each jar, leaving about ½-inch space from the top.

10. Slide a small knife around the insides of each jar to remove air bubbles.

11. Clean all the traces of food from the jar rims with a clean, moist kitchen towel. Close each jar with a lid and screw on the ring.

12. Arrange the jars in a boiling water canner and process for about 15 minutes.

13. Pull the jars out of the water canner and place them onto a wood surface several inches apart to cool completely.

14. After cooling, press the top of each jar's lid with your finger to ensure that the seal is tight.

15. Place the jars in refrigerator for up to 1 month.

Per serving: Calories: 29kcal; Fat: 0.1g; Carbs: 5.9g; Protein: 1g

7. Hot Sauce

Preparation time: 15 minutes
Cooking time: 55 minutes
Servings: 64
Ingredients:

- 2 tbsp. pickling spices
- 1 ½ cups hot pepper; stemmed, seeded, and chopped
- 64 ounces canned-no-sugar added tomatoes
- 4 cups white vinegar
- 1 teaspoon pickling salt

Directions:

1. Tie the pickling spices into a cheesecloth.

2. Add spice bag and remaining ingredients into a large nonreactive saucepan over medium-high heat and cook until boiling.

3. Next, set the heat to low and cook for about 20 minutes.

4. Press the mixture through a food mill.

5. Return the liquid into the same saucepan and allow it to boil.

6. Cook for about 15 minutes.

7. Divide the sauce into 8 (1/2-pint) hot, sterilized jars, leaving about ½-inch space from the top.

8. Slide a small knife around the insides of each jar to remove air bubbles.

9. Clean all the traces of food from the jar rims with a clean, moist kitchen towel.

10. Close each jar with a lid and screw on the ring.

11. Arrange the jars in a boiling water canner and process for about 10 minutes.

12. Take the jars out of the water canner and place them onto a wood surface several inches apart to cool completely.

13. After cooling, press the top of each jar's lid with your finger to ensure that the seal is tight.

14. The canned sauce can be preserved in the pantry for up to 1 month.

Per serving: Calories: 9kcal; Fat: 0.1g; Carbs: 1.4g; Protein: 0.3g

8. Canned Apple Slices

Preparation time: 15 minutes
Cooking time: 30 minutes
Servings: 32
Ingredients:

- 1 tsp. citric acid

- 5 pounds apples, peeled and cut into slices
- 2 cups water
- 1 tsp. ground cinnamon

Directions:

1. Place the citric acid into a nonreactive saucepan.
2. Add apple slices and water. Mix well.
3. Place the pan over medium-high heat and cook until boiling.
4. Boil for about 5 minutes.
5. Divide the apple slices into the bottom of 4 (1-pint) hot, sterilized jars.
6. Add cooking liquid to each jar, leaving about ½-inch space from the top.
7. Sprinkle cinnamon into each jar.
8. Slide a small knife around the insides of each jar to remove air bubbles.
9. Remove all traces of food from the edges of the jar with a clean, moist kitchen towel.
10. Close each jar with a lid and screw on the ring.
11. Arrange the jars in a boiling water canner and process for about 20 minutes.
12. Take the jars out of the water canner and place them onto a wood surface several inches apart to cool completely.
13. After cooling, press the top of each jar's lid with your finger to ensure that the seal is tight.
14. You can preserve these canned apples in a refrigerator for up to 1 month.

Per serving: Calories: 18kcal; Fat: 0.1g; Carbs: 4.9g; Protein: 0.1g

9. Diced Tomatoes

Preparation time: 15 minutes
Cooking time: 45 minutes
Servings: 36
Ingredients:

- 15 pounds tomatoes
- 9 tbsp. bottled lemon juice

Directions:

1. Cut a small "X" in the bottom of each tomato with a sharp knife.
2. Add the tomatoes into a large stainless steel saucepan of water— Cook for about 1 minute.
3. Transfer the tomatoes into a huge bowl of ice water with a slotted spoon.
4. Remove the skin of the tomatoes with a sharp paring knife.
5. Next, roughly chop the tomatoes.
6. Add chopped tomatoes with lemon juice into a heavy-bottomed saucepan over medium-high heat. Bring it to a boil.
7. Cook for 5 minutes.
8. Divide the lemon juice into the bottom of 9 (1-pint) hot, sterilized jars.
9. Next, pack each jar with tomatoes, leaving a ½-inch space from the top.
10. Slide a small knife around the insides of each jar to remove air bubbles.
11. Remove all traces of food from the edges of the jar of jars with a clean, moist kitchen towel.
12. Close each jar with a lid and screw on the ring.
13. Arrange the jars in a boiling water canner and process for about 35 minutes.
14. Take the jars out of the water canner and place them onto a wood surface several inches apart to cool completely.
15. After cooling, press the top of each jar's lid with your finger to ensure that the seal is tight.
16. These canned tomatoes can be preserved in the refrigerator for up 18 months.

Per serving: Calories: 35kcal; Fat: 0.4g; Carbs: 7.4g; Protein: 1.7g

10. Apple Sauce

Preparation time: 15 minutes
Cooking time: 20 minutes
Servings: 4 pints
Ingredients:

- 20 big apples
- 4 cups of water
- 2 1/2 cups of sugar

Directions:

1. Wash apples, quarters, and core; remove any blemishes or any other impurities. If you work in larger lots, drop apples in lemon water; see on acidifying fruit.
2. Upon preparing all apples, drain if necessary and place in a large cooking pot. Add the four cups of water and cook until apples are soft over medium-high heat.
3. Press a colander to remove peels. Return to the saucepan and add 2 1/2 cups of sugar. Bring the mixture to a boil until the sugar dissolves completely.
4. Pack into boiling jars, leaving 1/2 inch of headspace. Wipe the surface with the glass. Screw the lids and rings.
5. Run for 25 minutes in a boiling water bath: both pints and quarts.

Per serving: Calories: 70kcal; Fat: 0g; Carbs: 27g; Protein: 0g

Jams, And Marmalades Recipes

11. Clementine Marmalade

Preparation time: 15 minutes
Cooking time: 26 minutes
Servings: 40
Ingredients:

- ½ lemon
- 8 whole Clementines
- 2 cups water
- 3½ cups sugar

Directions:

1. Squeeze the lemon halves, reserving the juice in a cup.
2. In a cheesecloth, tie the lemon seeds.
3. In a nonreactive saucepan, add clementines, water, squeezed lemon halves, and the bundle of lemon seeds over medium-high heat and simmer, covered for about 2–3 hours.
4. Remove the saucepan of clementine mixture from the heat and set aside overnight.
5. Discard the bundle of lemon seeds.
6. With a slotted spoon, remove the fruit from liquid and transfer into a bowl.
7. Cut the clementines in half and scoop pulp and seeds.
8. Through a strainer, strain the pulp in the same pan by pressing with the back of a spoon.
9. Reserve all peels.
10. In the pan, add the sugar and lemon juice over medium-low heat and cook for about 2–3 minutes, stirring continuously.
11. Meanwhile, cut the clementine peel into fine very thin slices.

12. In the pan, add the peel slices and cook for about 5–10 minutes, stirring occasionally.
13. Remove the saucepan of marmalade from heat and immediately skim off foam from the top.
14. Set aside for about 10–15 minutes.
15. In 5 (½-pint) hot sterilized jars, divide the marmalade, leaving about ½-inch space from the top.
16. Slide a small knife around the insides of each jar to remove air bubbles.
17. Close each jar with a lid and screw on the ring.
18. Arrange the jars in a boiling water canner and process for about 10 minutes.
19. Remove the jars from water canner and place onto a wood surface several inches apart to cool completely.
20. After cooling with your finger, press the top of each jar's lid to ensure that the seal is tight.
21. The canned marmalade can be stored in the pantry for up to 1 year.

Per serving: Calories: 73kcal; Fat: 0g; Carbs: 19.3g; Protein: 0.1g

12. Orange & Carrot Marmalade

Preparation time: 15 minutes
Cooking time: 35 minutes
Servings: 48
Ingredients:

- 3 cups sugar
- 4½ teaspoons pectin
- 3 medium navel oranges
- 1/8 teaspoon baking soda
- 2½ cups water
- 2 cups carrots, peeled and shredded finely
- ½ cup golden raisins, chopped roughly

- 3 tablespoons fresh lemon juice
- 3 teaspoons calcium water
- ¾ teaspoon ground cinnamon
- ¼ teaspoon unsalted butter

Directions:

1. In a bowl, add sugar and pectin and mix well. Set aside.
2. Remove the rind of oranges and cut in quarters.
3. Scrape away the white from oranges.
4. Cut the orange rind into small pieces.
5. In a nonreactive saucepan, add orange rind, baking soda, and water over high heat and cook until boiling.
6. Now set the heat to low and cook, covered for about 15 minutes.
7. Meanwhile, chop the oranges roughly and remove any seeds.
8. Transfer oranges into a food processor and pulse until orange pieces are chopped.
9. In the pan of orange rind mixture, add oranges and carrots and bring to a gentle boil.
10. Simmer, covered for about 10 minutes.
11. Remove the saucepan of orange mixture from the heat and transfer 6 cups of mixture into a bowl.
12. In the same pan, add 6 cups of orange mixture, raisins, lemon juice, calcium water, cinnamon, and butter, and cook until boiling.
13. Stir in pectin mixture and again bring to a full rolling boil, stirring continuously.
14. Boil for about 1 minute.
15. Remove the saucepan of marmalade from heat and immediately skim off foam from the top.
16. In 6 (½-pint) hot sterilized jars, divide the marmalade, leaving about ½-inch space from the top.

17. Slide a small knife around the insides of each jar to remove air bubbles.
18. Close each jar with a lid and screw on the ring.
19. Arrange the jars in a boiling water canner and process for about 10 minutes.
20. Remove the jars from water canner and place onto a wood surface several inches apart to cool completely.
21. After cooling with your finger, press the top of each jar's lid to ensure that the seal is tight.
22. You can store the canned marmalade in the pantry for up to 1 year.

Per serving: Calories: 60kcal; Fat: 0g; Carbs: 15.7g; Protein: 0.2g

13. Apple Marmalade

Preparation time: 15 minutes
Cooking time: 40 minutes
Servings: 48
Ingredients:

- 6 cups apples; peeled, cored, and sliced
- 1 cup water
- 1 tablespoon fresh lemon juice
- 1 (2-ounce) package of fruit pectin
- 4 cups white sugar
- 1 lemon, sliced thinly
- 1 teaspoon ground cinnamon

Directions:

1. In a nonreactive saucepan, add chopped apples, water, and lemon juice and bring to a gentle simmer.
2. Cover the saucepan and cook for about 15 minutes, stirring occasionally.
3. Stir in fruit pectin and bring to a full boil, stirring continuously.
4. Add sugar, lemon slices, and cinnamon, and again, bring to a full boil, stirring continuously.

5. Boil for about 1 minute, stirring continuously.
6. In 6 (½-pint) hot sterilized jars, divide the marmalade, leaving about ½-inch space from the top.
7. Slide a small knife around the insides of each jar to remove air bubbles.
8. Close each jar with a lid and screw on the ring.
9. Arrange the jars in a boiling water canner and process for about 10 minutes.
10. Remove the jars from the water canner and place them onto a wood surface several inches apart to cool completely.
11. After cooling with your finger, press the top of each jar's lid to ensure that the seal is tight.
12. The canned marmalade can be stored in the pantry for up to 1 year.

Per serving: Calories: 85kcal; Fat: 0.1g; Carbs: 22.1g; Protein: 0.1g

14. Grapefruit-Lemon Marmalade

Preparation time: 20 minutes
Cooking time: 60 minutes
Servings: 4 pints
Ingredients:

- 3 clean grapefruits
- 2 clean medium lemons
- 4 cup water
- 5 cup sugar, granulated

Directions:

1. Cut the grapefruits and lemons into quarters, then slice thinly. Place the fruits and water in a large, heavy-bottomed pot or saucepan. Bring to a boil and cook for about 30 minutes, or until the rind is tender.
2. Reduce heat and add the sugar, stirring constantly, until the sugar is dissolved completely. Add ginger and increase

heat, cook until it reaches setting point 220 F.

3. Transfer marmalade to hot sterilized jars, leaving 1/4-inch headspace. Cover tightly with a lid.
4. Place the jars in a hot water bath. Process for 10 minutes. Cool completely at room temperature.
5. Store in a cool, dark place. Keep refrigerated once opened.

Per serving: Calories: 50kcal; Fat: 0g; Carbs: 13g; Protein: 2g

15. Grapefruit Marmalade

Preparation time: 20 minutes
Cooking time: 35minutes
Servings: 20
Ingredients:

- 4 ruby red grapefruits
- 3 cups white sugar

Directions:

1. With a zester, remove the zest of 2 grapefruits into ribbons.
2. With a sharp paring knife, cut the thin strips of peel from the remaining grapefruits.
3. Reserve the zest ribbons and peel strips.
4. Now peel off all remaining outer white parts of the fruit and discard it.
5. Cut the grapefruits into wheels and remove any seeds.
6. In a nonreactive saucepan, add grapefruit wheels, peel strips, and sugar over medium-high heat and cook until boiling, stirring continuously.
7. With a potato masher, mash the fruit completely.
8. Now set the heat to low and cook for about 4–5 minutes, stirring and skimming off foam from the top occasionally.

9. Cook for about 10 minutes, stirring occasionally.
10. Stir in the zest ribbons and cook for about 5 minutes, stirring occasionally.
11. In 2 (5-ounce) hot sterilized jars, divide the marmalade, leaving about ½-inch space from the top.
12. Slide a small knife around the insides of each jar to remove air bubbles.
13. Remove all traces of food from the edges of the jar of jars with a clean, moist kitchen towel.
14. Close each jar with a lid and screw on the ring.
15. Arrange the jars in a boiling water canner and process for about 10 minutes.
16. Remove the jars from the water canner and place them onto a wood surface several inches apart to cool completely.
17. After cooling with your finger, press the top of each jar's lid to ensure that the seal is tight.
18. The canned marmalade can be stored in the pantry for up to 1 year.

Per serving: Calories: 121kcal; Fat: 0g; Carbs: 32.1g; Protein: 0.2g

16. Cherry Marmalade

Preparation time: 20 minutes
Cooking time: 30 minutes
Servings: 4 pints
Ingredients:

- 4 tbsps. lime
- 4 cup cherries
- 2/3 cup peeled and chopped orange
- 3-1/2 cup sugar

Directions:

1. Take a large pan and mix cherries, oranges, and juice in it. Make them boil at medium heat. Low the flame and add cove with gentle boiling with frequent

stirring for 20 minutes. Keep boiling with slow stirring.

2. Now boil hard with frequent stirring as the mixture gets gel-like, for about 30 minutes. Remove the flame.

3. Pour the hot marmalade into sterilized jars. Remove the air bubble by adding more marmalade. Seal them with lids.

Per serving: Calories: 56kcal; Fat: 0g; Carbs: 13g; Protein: 1g

17. Three-Citrus Marmalade

Preparation time: 20 minutes
Cooking time: 45 minutes
Servings: 4 pints
Ingredients:

- 3 large lemons
- 6 cup sugar
- 4 medium navel oranges
- 2 pink grapefruit
- 4 cup poached zest liquid

Directions:

1. Wash the fruit thoroughly and let them dry. Use the peeler to remove the zest from the fruit. Cut the zest into strips by using fine confetti. Mix the zest in the pot along with 6 cups of water. Make them boil at a reduced flame and allow them to simmer for 30 minutes.

2. As the zest cooks, cut the white pith off the fruit and separate their membranes.

3. Drain the zest and save the liquid or cooking.

4. Take a large stainless-steel pot, add zest in it with citrus fruit, 6 cups of sugar, 4 cups of liquid from the zest, and a cheesecloth roll. Boil them and cook instantly as the mixture gets heated to 220 degrees.

5. Stir them before removing the flame for helping the zest to become spread evenly throughout the marmalade.

6. Pour out hot marmalade into the sterilized jars. Remove the air bubble and cover them with lids.

7. Process the jars in a boiling water canner for about 10 minutes. Allow them to cool.

Per serving: Calories: 30kcal; Fat: 0g; Carbs: 8g; Protein: 0g

18. Ginger Marmalade

Preparation time: 15 minutes
Cooking time: 42 minutes
Servings: 40
Ingredients:

- 3½ cups fresh ginger, peeled
- 4 cups water
- 5 cups white sugar
- 1 (3-ounce) pouch liquid pectin

Directions:

1. Cut half of the peeled ginger into cubes and then shred the remaining.

2. In a nonreactive saucepan, add ginger and water over medium heat and cook until boiling.

3. Now set the heat to low and cook, covered for about 1¼ hours. (You can add more water if needed).

4. Remove the saucepan of the ginger mixture from heat and through a fine-mesh strainer, drain the mixture.

5. In a bowl, add about ½ cup of ginger water and cooked ginger and refrigerate for at least 4 hours or overnight.

6. In a large, heavy-bottomed pot, add ginger mixture and sugar over medium-high heat and cook until boiling, stirring continuously.

7. Boil for about 1 minute, stirring continuously.

8. Add the liquid pectin then stir to combine.

9. Now set the heat to low and cook for about 7 minutes, skimming foam from the top of the marmalade.

10. In 5 (½-pint) hot sterilized jars, divide the marmalade, leaving about ½-inch space from the top.

11. Slide a small knife around the insides of each jar to remove air bubbles.

12. Remove all traces of food from the edges of the jar of jars with a clean, moist kitchen towel.

13. Close each jar with a lid and screw on the ring.

14. Arrange the jars in a boiling water canner and process for about 10 minutes.

15. Remove the jars from the water canner and place them onto a wood surface several inches apart to cool completely.

16. After cooling with your finger, press the top of each jar's lid to ensure that the seal is tight.

17. You can store the canned marmalade in the pantry for up to 1 year.

Per serving: Calories: 121kcal; Fat: 0.5g; Carbs: 30.5g; Protein: 0.7g

19. Strawberry Lemon Marmalade

Preparation time: 20 minutes
Cooking time: 20 minutes
Servings: 4 pints
Ingredients:

- 6 cup sugar
- 1 tbsp. lime
- 1/4 cup peeled and sliced lemons
- 6 tbsps. classic pectin
- 4 cup crushed strawberries

Directions:

1. Get the canners prepared. Heat jars with simmering water. Don't boil them. Wash the lids with hot soapy water.

2. Mix the lemon peels with water in a pan. Cover the pan. Boil the mixture at medium flame and let them boil for about 5 minutes until the peel gets softened. Drain the liquid.

3. Now include the lime and strawberries to lemon peel and mix them. Slowly stir the pectin. Heat the mixture at a high flame with occasional stirring.

4. Include sugar and stir until it dissolves. Make the mixture to get boiled for one minute with constant stirring. Remove the flame and skim off the foam if required.

5. Pour the jam into sterilized jars with a ladle. Cover them with lids and seal them.

6. Process the jars in a boiling water canner for about 10 minutes. Remove the jars and allows them to cool.

Per serving: Calories: 31.5kcal; Fat: 0g; Carbs: 8.1g; Protein: 0.2g

20.   Lemon Marmalade

Preparation time: 15 minutes
Cooking time: 4 hours 30 minutes
Servings: 48
Ingredients:

- 10 large lemons
- 4 cups water
- 4 cups sugar

Directions:

1. With a vegetable peeler, slice the yellow part of the lemon peel into strips.

2. Cut the lemon strips into 1 1/8-inch strips.

3. With a sharp knife, cut off any remaining white pith from lemons.

4. Cut the peeled lemons into ¼-inch-thick slices crosswise.

5. In a nonreactive saucepan, add the chopped lemons, peel strips, and water and refrigerate, covered for 4 hours.

6. Place the saucepan of lemon mixture over high heat and cook until boiling, stirring frequently.

7. Now set the heat to low and cook, covered for about 1 hour.

8. Add sugar and increase the heat to medium-high.

9. Cook for about 3–5 minutes or until sugar is dissolved, stirring continuously.

10. Now set the heat to low and cook, uncovered for about 45–60 minutes, stirring frequently.

11. In 3 (1-pint) hot sterilized jars, divide the marmalade, leaving about ½-inch space from the top.

12. Slide a small knife around the insides of each jar to remove air bubbles.

13. Remove all traces of food from the edges of the jar of jars with a clean, moist kitchen towel.

14. Close each jar with a lid and screw on the ring.

15. Arrange the jars in a boiling water canner and process for about 10 minutes.

16. Remove the jars from the water canner and place them onto a wood surface several inches apart to cool completely.

17. After cooling with your finger, press the top of each jar's lid to ensure that the seal is tight.

18. The canned marmalade can be stored in the pantry for up to 1 year.

Per serving: Calories: 63kcal; Fat: 0g; Carbs: 17g; Protein: 0g

21. Tangerine Marmalade

Preparation time: 20 minutes
Cooking time: 20 minutes
Servings: 4 pints
Ingredients:

- 1/2 tsp. vanilla extract
- 5-1/2 cup sugar
- 12 oz. tangerines
- 3 lbs. kumquats
- 1/2 cup vanilla bean

Directions:

1. Cut the fruits in half and remove the flesh and skin. Cut them into thin slices. This will make 2 cups of the kumquat rinds.

2. Use a fine mesh peeler to remove the zest of tangerines, be careful about the thin skin of tangerines.

3. Cut the peel of tangerines and divide the fruit into two. Put the segments of tangerine in a bowl. Collect the pulp of fruit in a separate bowl.

4. Mix the slices of kumquat with its juice, zests of tangerine, the pulp of tangerines, sugar, and water. Boil them, reduce the heat from medium to low and cook the mixture for about 15 minutes. Remove the flame.

5. Take a large pot containing water and boil it. Put the jars in it along with the lids. Pour the hot jam into these sterilized jars. Cover them with lids tightly and allow them to get cooled.

Per serving: Calories: 30kcal; Fat: 0g; Carbs: 7g; Protein: 0g

22. Onion Marmalade

Preparation time: 15 minutes
Cooking time: 21 minutes
Servings: 48
Ingredients:

- 6 cups sweet onions, cut into ¼-inch slices widthwise
- 2 teaspoons fresh garlic, minced
- 1 cup apple juice
- ½ cup cider vinegar
- ¼ teaspoon ground mustard
- 1 teaspoon red pepper flakes, crushed
- 1 teaspoon salt
- ½ teaspoon ground black pepper
- 3 tablespoons low-sugar pectin
- ½ teaspoon butter
- 1 cup honey
- ½ cup brown sugar

Directions:

1. In a nonreactive saucepan, add onion slices, garlic, apple juice, vinegar, mustard, red pepper flakes, salt, and black pepper.
2. Slowly, add in the pectin, stirring continuously.
3. Add in the butter and stir to combine.
4. Place the saucepan of the onion mixture over high heat and cook until boiling, stirring continuously.
5. Add honey and sugar and again, bring to a full boil.
6. Boil for about 1 minute.
7. Remove the saucepan of marmalade from heat and immediately skim off foam from the top.
8. In 6 (½-pint) hot sterilized jars, divide the marmalade, leaving about ½-inch space from the top.
9. Slide a small knife around the insides of each jar to remove air bubbles.
10. Remove all traces of food from the edges of the jar of jars with a clean, moist kitchen towel.
11. Close each jar with a lid and screw on the ring.
12. Arrange the jars in a boiling water canner and process for about 10 minutes.
13. Remove the jars from the water canner and place them onto a wood surface several inches apart to cool completely.
14. After cooling with your finger, press the top of each jar's lid to ensure that the seal is tight.
15. The canned marmalade can be stored in the pantry for up to 1 year.

Per serving: Calories: 37kcal; Fat: 0.1g; Carbs: 9.3g; Protein: 0.2g

23.   Lime Marmalade

Preparation time: 15 minutes
Cooking time: 1 hour 17 minutes
Servings: 64
Ingredients:

- 2¼ pounds limes
- 7 cups water
- 3½ pounds sugar

Directions:

1. With a sharp paring knife, cut the limes into very thin slices.
2. Retain any juice from limes and then remove the seeds.
3. In a glass bowl, add lime slices, any reserved juice, and water and refrigerate them, covered overnight.
4. In a nonreactive saucepan, add lime mixture over medium-high heat and cook until boiling.
5. Now set the heat to low and cook, covered for about 30–45 minutes.
6. Add the sugar and increase the heat to medium-high.
7. Cook for about 3–5 minutes or until sugar is dissolved, stirring continuously.
8. Boil the mixture for about 12 minutes.

9. Remove the saucepan of marmalade from heat and set aside for about 5 minutes.

10. In 8 (½-pint) hot sterilized jars, divide the marmalade, leaving about ½-inch space from the top.

11. Slide a small knife around the insides of each jar to remove air bubbles.

12. Remove all traces of food from the edges of the jar of jars with a clean, moist kitchen towel.

13. Close each jar with a lid and screw on the ring.

14. Arrange the jars in a boiling water canner and process for about 10 minutes.

15. Remove the jars from the water canner and place them onto a wood surface several inches apart to cool completely.

16. After cooling with your finger, press the top of each jar's lid to ensure that the seal is tight.

17. The canned marmalade can be stored in the pantry for up to 1 year.

Per serving: Calories: 98kcal; Fat: 0g; Carbs: 26.5g; Protein: 0.1g

24. **Kumquat Marmalade**

Preparation time: 15 minutes
Cooking time: 21 minutes
Servings: 56
Ingredients:

- 1¾ pounds kumquats, halved and seeded
- 1 cup water
- 1 (1¾-ounce) package powdered fruit pectin
- 6½ cups sugar

Directions:

1. Place kumquat in a food processor and pulse until roughly chopped.

2. In a Dutch oven, add chopped kumquats, water and pectin, and stir to combine.

3. Place the pan of kumquat over high heat and cook until boiling, stirring continuously.

4. Stir in sugar and cook until boiling, stirring continuously.

5. Boil for about 1 minute.

6. Remove the pan of marmalade from heat and immediately skim off foam from the top.

7. In 7 (½-pint) hot sterilized jars, divide the marmalade, leaving about ½-inch space from the top.

8. Slide a small knife around the insides of each jar to remove air bubbles.

9. Remove all traces of food from the edges of the jar of jars with a clean, moist kitchen towel.

10. Close each jar with a lid and screw on the ring.

11. Arrange the jars in a boiling water canner and process for about 10 minutes.

12. Remove the jars from the water canner and place them onto a wood surface several inches apart to cool completely.

13. After cooling with your finger, press the top of each jar's lid to ensure that the seal is tight.

14. The canned marmalade can be stored in the pantry for up to 1 year.

Per serving: Calories: 97kcal; Fat: 0.1g; Carbs: 26.6g; Protein: 0.3g

Sauces Recipes

25. Cherry BBQ Sauce

Preparation time: 15 minutes
Cooking time: 1 hour 20 minutes
Servings: 40
Ingredients:

- pounds fresh sweet cherries, pitted
- 1 cup onion, chopped
- 3 garlic cloves, minced
- 1 cup apple cider vinegar
- ¾ cup honey
- 3 teaspoons salt
- 2 teaspoons Worcestershire sauce
- 2 teaspoons natural liquid smoke
- 2 teaspoons red chili powder
- 1–2 teaspoons cayenne powder

Directions:

1. In a nonreactive saucepan, add all ingredients over medium-high heat and cook until boiling, stirring continuously.
2. Now adjust the heat to medium-low and cook, covered for about 15 minutes, stirring occasionally.
3. Uncover the saucepan and cook for about 20–25 minutes, stirring occasionally.
4. Remove the saucepan of sauce from heat and with an immersion blender, blend until smooth.
5. Return the pan over low heat and cook for about 10–15 minutes, stirring occasionally.
6. In 5 (½-pint) hot sterilized jars, divide the sauce, leaving about ½-inch space from the top.
7. Slide a small knife around the insides of each jar to remove air bubbles.
8. Remove all traces of food from the edges of the jar of jars with a clean, moist kitchen towel.
9. Close each jar with a lid and screw on the ring.
10. Arrange the jars in a boiling water canner and process for about 20 minutes.
11. Remove the jars from water canner and place onto a wood surface several inches apart to cool completely.
12. After cooling with your finger, press the top of each jar's lid to ensure that the seal is tight.
13. The canned sauce can be stored in the refrigerator for up to 1 year.

Per serving: Calories: 62kcal; Fat: 0.1g; Carbs: 15.3g; Protein: 0.2g

26. Pear Caramel Sauce

Preparation time: 15 minutes
Cooking time: 40 minutes
Servings: 32
Ingredients:

- 2 pounds ripe pears, cored and cut into pieces
- 2 teaspoons vanilla bean paste
- 1 teaspoon sea salt
- 1¾ cups water, divided
- 3 cups granulated sugar

Directions:

1. In a blender, add chopped pears, vanilla bean paste, salt, and ¼ cup of water and pulse until smooth.
2. Transfer the pear puree into a bowl and set aside.
3. In a heavy-bottomed saucepan, add sugar and remaining water over medium-high heat and simmer for about 15–20 minutes, swirling the pan often.

4. Remove the saucepan of sugar syrup from heat and stir in the pear puree.

5. Return the saucepan over medium-low heat and cook for about 5–10 minutes or until the temperature of caramel sauce reaches between 215°F–225°F, stirring continuously.

6. In 4 (½-pint) hot sterilized jars, divide the sauce, leaving about ½-inch space from the top.

7. Slide a small knife around the insides of each jar to remove air bubbles.

8. Remove all traces of food from the edges of the jar of jars with a clean, moist kitchen towel.

9. Close each jar with a lid and screw on the ring.

10. Arrange the jars in a boiling water canner and process for about 10 minutes.

11. Remove the jars from water canner and place onto a wood surface several inches apart to cool completely.

12. After cooling with your finger, press the top of each jar's lid to ensure that the seal is tight.

13. The canned sauce can be stored in the refrigerator for up to 1 year.

Per serving: Calories: 87kcal; Fat: 0g; Carbs: 23.1g; Protein: 0.1g

27. Chocolate Sauce

Preparation time: 10 minutes
Cooking time: 35 minutes
Servings: 48
Ingredients:

- 3 cups sugar
- 1½ cups water
- 1½ cups Dutch-processed cocoa powder
- 2 tablespoons light corn syrup
- 1 tablespoon vanilla extract
- ¼ teaspoon salt

Directions:

1. In a heavy-bottomed stainless-steel saucepan, add sugar and water over medium heat and cook until boiling.

2. Add the cocoa powder, corn syrup, vanilla extract, and salt and with a wire whisk, beat until well combined.

3. Cook for about 14–15 minutes, stirring frequently.

4. In 3 (1-pint) hot sterilized jars, divide the sauce, leaving about ½-inch space from the top.

5. Slide a small knife around the insides of each jar to remove air bubbles.

6. Remove all traces of food from the edges of the jar of jars with a clean, moist kitchen towel.

7. Close each jar with a lid and screw on the ring.

8. Arrange the jars in a boiling water canner and process for about 15 minutes.

9. Remove the jars from water canner and place onto a wood surface several inches apart to cool completely.

10. After cooling with your finger, press the top of each jar's lid to ensure that the seal is tight.

11. The canned sauce can be stored in the refrigerator for up to 1 month.

Per serving: Calories: 56kcal; Fat: 0.4g; Carbs: 14.6g; Protein: 0.5g

28. Blueberry Sauce

Preparation time: 10 minutes
Cooking time: 20 minutes
Servings: 32
Ingredients:

- 4 cups fresh blueberries
- 3 cups granulated sugar
- 1 tablespoon fresh lemon juice

- 2 teaspoons fresh lemon zest
- 3 ounces liquid fruit pectin

Directions:

1. In a stainless-steel saucepan, add blueberries over medium heat and with a potato masher; crush them lightly.
2. In the pan, add the sugar, lemon juice, lemon zest, and berries. Stir to combine.
3. Turn heat to high and bring to a full, rolling boil, stirring continuously.
4. Stir in pectin and boil for about 1 minute, stirring continuously.
5. Remove the saucepan of sauce from heat and immediately skim off foam from the top.
6. In 2 (1-pint) hot sterilized jars, divide the sauce, leaving about ½-inch space from the top.
7. Slide a small knife around the insides of each jar to remove air bubbles.
8. Remove all traces of food from the edges of the jar of jars with a clean, moist kitchen towel.
9. Close each jar with a lid and screw on the ring.
10. Arrange the jars in a boiling water canner and process for about 10 minutes.
11. Remove the jars from water canner and place onto a wood surface several inches apart to cool completely.
12. After cooling with your finger, press the top of each jar's lid to ensure that the seal is tight.

Per serving: Calories: 98kcal; Fat: 0.1g; Carbs: 24.8g; Protein: 0.1g

29. Chipotle BBQ Sauce

Preparation time: 15 minutes
Cooking time: 1 hour 10 minutes

Servings: 48
Ingredients:

- 1 tablespoon olive oil
- ¼ cup onion, chopped finely
- 2 garlic cloves, minced
- 2 cups tomato sauce
- 1½ (12-ounce) cans tomato paste
- 1¾ ounces canned chipotle peppers in adobo sauce
- 1 cup apple cider vinegar
- ½ cup honey
- ½ cup brown sugar
- 1 teaspoon dry mustard
- ½ teaspoons pickling salt
- ½ teaspoon ground black pepper

Directions:

1. In a nonreactive saucepan, heat olive oil over medium heat and sauté the onion and garlic for about 2–3 minutes.
2. Add in the remaining ingredients then cook until boiling.
3. Now set the heat to low and cook for about 15–20 minutes, stirring occasionally.
4. Remove the saucepan of sauce from heat and with an immersion blender, blend until smooth.
5. Return the pan over low heat and cook for about 20–25 minutes, stirring occasionally.
6. In 6 (½-pint) hot sterilized jars, divide the sauce, leaving about ½-inch space from the top.
7. Slide a small knife around the insides of each jar to remove air bubbles.
8. Remove all traces of food from the edges of the jar of jars with a clean, moist kitchen towel.
9. Close each jar with a lid and screw on the ring.

10. Arrange the jars in a boiling water canner and process for about 20 minutes.

11. Remove the jars from water canner and place onto a wood surface several inches apart to cool completely.

12. After cooling with your finger, press the top of each jar's lid to ensure that the seal is tight.

13. The canned sauce can be stored in the refrigerator for up to 1 year.

Per serving: Calories: 60kcal; Fat: 0g; Carbs: 15g; Protein: 0g

30. **Canned BBQ Sauce**

Preparation time: 15 minutes
Cooking time: 1 hour & 20 minutes
Servings: 3 pints
Ingredients:

- 1 tbsp. hot pepper flakes
- 3 chopped garlic cloves
- 2 cups chopped onions
- 21 chopped tomatoes
- 1½ cups of brown sugar, packed lightly
- 1 tbsp. celery seeds
- 1/3 cup lemon juice
- 1 cup white vinegar
- 1½ tbsp. ground nutmeg or mace
- 2 tbsp. salt
- 1 tsp. ground ginger
- 1 tsp. cinnamon
- 1 tbsp. dry mustard

Directions:

1. Combine the tomatoes with the celery seeds, pepper flakes, garlic, and onions in a large steel saucepan.

2. Boil on high heat while stirring constantly. Lower the heat and cover the pan. Gently boil for about ½ an hour until the veggies have softened.

3. Transfer the mixture in batches to a sieve over a glass bowl. Discard the solids.

4. Return the pulp and liquid to the saucepan. Add the brown sugar, cinnamon, ginger, mustard, mace, salt, lemon juice, and vinegar.

5. Let it boil again on medium-high heat and stir occasionally.

6. Reduce the heat. Allow it to boil for about ½ an hour while you frequently stir until the mixture is thicker and about the consistency of bottled BBQ sauce gently.

7. Heat the jars you will be using in simmering hot water until you are ready for them. Do not allow them to boil. Wash the lids in soapy, warm water. Set the bands aside.

8. Ladle the hot sauce into jars. Leave ½ an inch open at the top. Rinse the rims and tighten the lids. Arrange the jars in the canner with boiling water. Process for about 20 minutes, as adjusted for altitude.

Per serving: Calories: 60kcal; Fat: 0g; Carbs: 15g; Protein: 0g

31. Cranberry Sauce

Preparation time: 15 minutes
Cooking time: 55 minutes
Servings: 4 pints
Ingredients:

- 4 cups of sugar, granulated
- 4 x 12-oz. bags of cranberries, fresh
- 1 fresh orange, juiced, + add water to make 4 cups liquid total
- Zest from 1 orange

Directions:

1. Combine water, zest, orange juice, and sugar in a large stockpot on high heat. Bring to boil.

2. Add cranberries. Return to boil—lower heat. Boil gently for about 10 minutes. Cranberries will pop open.

3. Pour into a sieve over a heat-safe bowl until all left is a paste with twigs and seeds from orange zest and cranberries.

4. Pour into hot, sterile canning jars. Leave 1/4" of headspace. Wipe rims and place lids on jars. Screw on until fingertip tight.

5. Place jars in canner. Cover using hot water. Bring to boil. Process for 15 minutes. Turn heat off.

6. Remove cover from canner. Leave jars inside for about five minutes and transfer to towel or rack to cool, undisturbed, overnight.

7. Wipe jars down and label them.

8. Store in a cool place for as long as 12 months.

Per serving: Calories: 110kcal; Fat: 0g; Carbs: 25g; Protein: 0g

32. Fresh Summer Tomato Sauce

Preparation time: 15 minutes
Cooking time: 30 minutes
Servings: 8 jars
Ingredients:

- 2 tbsps. extra-virgin olive oil
- 3 cloves garlic, minced
- 1 red onion, chopped
- 3 pounds tomatoes, halved
- A pinch of red pepper flakes
- 1/2 teaspoon chopped thyme
- 1 tsp chopped oregano
- 1 tsp chopped basil
- 1 tbsp. chopped parsley
- A pinch of sea salt
- A pinch of pepper

Directions:

1. Preheat a nonstick pan into a medium heat then add in oil.

2. Sauté onion and garlic for about 3 minutes or until fragrant.

3. Stir in tomatoes, red pepper flakes, thyme, oregano, basil, parsley, salt, and black pepper and lower the heat. Cover and simmer for about 30 minutes.

4. Remove the pan from the heat and purée the sauce until smooth in a food processor. Fill sterilized jars halfway with the mixture and close them tightly.

5. Allow cooling before freezing after processing in a hot water bath for about 5 minutes.

Per serving: Calories: 70kcal; Fat: 4g; Carbs: 6g; Protein: 3g

33. Homemade Pizza Sauce

Preparation time: 15 minutes
Cooking time: 1 hour & 20 minutes
Servings: 4 pints
Ingredients:

- 2 tbsp. chopped parsley
- 28 ripe tomatoes
- 1 tsp. celery seed
- 2 yellow onions
- 3 tbsp. olive oil
- 1 tsp. black pepper
- 1 tbsp. oregano
- 1 tbsp. dry basil
- 2 tbsp. lemon juice
- 1 tsp. dry rosemary
- 4 garlic cloves
- 2 tsp. kosher salt
- 1 tbsp. white sugar

Directions:

1. Peel the tomatoes. Blanch for 2-3 minutes in boiling water so that they are easier to peel. Puree them in a

blender or food processor. Mince the onions and garlic cloves.

2. Sauté the onions and garlic in a large saucepan with olive oil for about 3-4 minutes until tender and fragrant.

3. Add the tomato puree. Bring to a boil on medium-high heat. Reduce the heat to low then let simmer for 45 minutes. Once the sauce thickens, put it into jars.

4. Boil the jars for approximately 25 minutes in a water bath. Let cool completely before storing.

Per serving: Calories: 40kcal; Fat: 3g; Carbs: 3g; Protein: 1g

34. Homemade Spaghetti Sweet Sauce

Preparation time: 15 minutes
Cooking time: 4 hours
Servings: 8 pints
Ingredients:

- 4 large onions, cut into wedges
- 4 large green peppers
- 25 pounds tomatoes
- 1/4 cup canola oil
- 3 cups tomato paste
- 2 tsps. dried basil
- 8 garlic cloves, minced
- 2 tsps. dried parsley flakes
- 4 tsps. dried oregano
- 2 tsps. Worcestershire sauce
- 1/4 cup salt
- 2/3 cup sugar
- 2 bay leaves
- 1 cup fresh lemon juice
- 2 tsps. red pepper flakes

Directions:
1. Boil water, add in tomatoes, let boil for about 1 minute, and then plunge them into iced water. Peel off the skin and add to a stockpot.

2. Pulse together onions and green peppers in a food processor until chopped and add to the stockpot. Stir in the remaining ingredients, except lemon juice, and add in water.

3. Cook for about 4 hours and discard the bay leaves. Stir in fresh lemon juice then divide among sterile jars.

4. Seal and process in a hot water bath for about 30 minutes. Remove, let cool and then store in the fridge.

Per serving: Calories: 54kcal; Fat: 1g; Carbs: 12g; Protein: 3g

35. Homemade Tomato Sauce

Preparation time: 15 minutes
Cooking time: 50 minutes
Servings: 4 jars
Ingredients:

- 8 lb. ripe tomatoes
- 1 tsp sea salt
- 4 tbsp. bottled or jarred lemon juice

Directions:
1. Rinse and clean the tomatoes. Remove their seeds and skins. Put the peeled or pureed tomatoes into a pot with the salt and then bring it to a boil.

2. In each jar, add 1 tablespoon of lemon juice and then transfer the tomato sauce into them. Boil the jars for at least 45 minutes.

3. After 45 minutes, remove the jars from the boiling water and let them cool. Store in a cool, dark place afterward.

Per serving: Calories: 86kcal; Fat: 2g; Carbs: 16g; Protein: 4g

36. Lemon Strawberry Sauce

Preparation time: 15 minutes
Cooking time: 15 minutes

Servings: 2 pints
Ingredients:

- ¼ cup lemon juice
- 2 lb. strawberries
- 4 cups granulated sugar

Directions:

1. In a sizable bowl, use a potato masher to crush the strawberries in batches until you have 3 cups of mashed berries. Leave strawberries more intact if you prefer more chunkiness.
2. In a heavy-bottomed, nonreactive pot, mix the strawberries, sugar, and lemon juice. Stir over low heat until the sugar is dissolved, then increase the heat to high and boil for 15 minutes as you stir occasionally.
3. Spoon the sauce into a prepared jar. Use a funnel to transfer the sauce, leaving some headspace safely.
4. Rinse the rims of the jars with a dampened, clean, lint-free cloth or paper towel and once again with a dry towel to remove any sauce or liquid from the rim of the jar.
5. Arrange the canning lid on the jar and twist the canning ring on until it's just-snug on the jar.
6. Carefully transfer the jars into the water bath using the canning tongs and place the lid on the canning pot. Start the timer and process in the water bath for 10 minutes.

Per serving: Calories: 5kcal; Fat: 0g; Carbs: 1g; Protein: 0g

Chutneys Recipes

37. Plum Chutney

Preparation time: 15 minutes
Cooking time: 1 hour 05 minutes

Servings: 24
Ingredients:

- 4 cups plums, chopped
- 1 cup onion, minced
- 2 teaspoons fresh ginger, grated
- ¾ cup raisins
- 2 cups brown sugar
- 1½ cups apple cider vinegar
- 2 teaspoons lemon zest, grated
- 2 teaspoons sea salt
- 1 teaspoon ground cinnamon
- ½ teaspoon ground cloves
- ½ teaspoon mustard seeds
- ¼ teaspoon red chili flakes

Directions:

1. In a nonreactive saucepan, add all ingredients over high heat and cook until boiling, stirring continuously.
2. Now adjust the heat to medium and cook, covered for about 40–45 minutes, stirring often.
3. In 3 (½-pint) hot sterilized jars, divide the chutney, leaving about ½-inch space from the top.
4. Slide a small knife around the insides of each jar to remove air bubbles.
5. Close each jar with a lid and screw on the ring.
6. Arrange the jars in a boiling water canner and process for about 15 minutes.
7. Remove the jars from water canner and place onto a wood surface several inches apart to cool completely.
8. After cooling with your finger, press the top of each jar's lid to ensure that the seal is tight.
9. The canned chutney can be stored in the refrigerator for up to 1 month.

Per serving: Calories: 71kcal; Fat: 0.1g; Carbs: 17.6g; Protein: 0.3g

38.   Plum Tomato Chutney

Preparation time: 15 minutes
Cooking time: 15 minutes
Servings: 4-quart pints
Ingredients:

- 4 tomatoes, chopped
- 6 plums, seeded and chopped
- 2 green chilies, chopped
- 4 tablespoons fresh ginger, grated
- 1 teaspoon lemon zest
- Juice of 1 lemon
- 2 bay leaves
- Pinch of salt
- 1/2 cup plus 2 tablespoons brown sugar
- 2 teaspoons vinegar
- Pinch black pepper
- 4 tsps. vegetable oil

Directions

1. Heat the oil in a deep saucepan. Add the bay leaves, ginger and green chilies, and stir. Add the tomatoes, plums. Add the salt, zest, lemon juice and vinegar. Stir in the sugar and pepper, cover, and cook for 3 minutes.
2. Spoon the chutney into sterilized jars, leaving a 1/2 inch headspace. Wipe the edge of the jar rim clean and add the lid. Process these in a boiling water bath for 10 minutes.

Per serving: Calories: 70kcal; Fat: 0g; Carbs: 31g; Protein: 1g

39.   Apple Chutney

Preparation time: 15 minutes
Cooking time: 1½ hours 10 minutes
Servings: 56
Ingredients:

- 2 tablespoons olive oil
- 1 onion, chopped finely
- 1 tsp. coarse salt
- 2 lbs. cider apples, cored and cut into pieces
- ½ cup raisins
- 2 tablespoons crystallized ginger
- 2 teaspoon mustard seed, roughly ground
- 1 teaspoon ground cinnamon
- ½ teaspoon ground cardamom
- ½ teaspoon curry powder
- ½ teaspoon red chili flakes
- ¼ teaspoon cayenne pepper
- ¼ teaspoon ground allspice
- 12 whole cloves
- 1 cup apple cider vinegar
- ½ cup brown sugar

Directions:

1. In a heavy-bottomed saucepan, heat the oil over medium-high heat and cook the onions and salt for about 10–12 minutes, stirring frequently.
2. Add in the apples and cook for about 10–12 minutes, stirring frequently.
3. Stir in the raisins, ginger, and spices and cook for about 2 minutes, stirring frequently.
4. Add in the vinegar and brown sugar then cook until boiling.
5. Now set the heat to low and cook, covered for about 45–60 minutes, stirring occasionally.
6. In 7 (½-pint) hot sterilized jars, divide the chutney, leaving about ½-inch space from the top.
7. Slide a small knife around the insides of each jar to remove air bubbles.
8. Close each jar with a lid and screw on the ring.
9. Arrange the jars in a boiling water canner and process for about 10 minutes.

10. Remove the jars from water canner and place onto a wood surface several inches apart to cool completely.
11. After cooling with your finger, press the top of each jar's lid to ensure that the seal is tight.
12. The canned chutney can be stored in the refrigerator for up to 1 month.

Per serving: Calories: 20kcal; Fat: 0.6g; Carbs: 3.7g; Protein: 0.1g

40. Cranberry Chutney

Preparation time: 15 minutes
Cooking time: 50 minutes
Servings: 48
Ingredients:

- 3 cups fresh cranberries
- 1¼ cups red onion, chopped finely
- 1¼ cups dried pineapple, chopped
- 2 tablespoons fresh ginger root, chopped
- 3 garlic cloves, chopped finely
- 1 teaspoon orange zest, grated
- 1 cup apple cider vinegar
- ¼ cup fresh orange juice
- 1½ cups sugar
- 1 cup golden raisins
- 1 cup water
- 1 teaspoon dry mustard
- 1 teaspoon ground cinnamon
- ¾ teaspoon ground cloves
- ½ teaspoon cayenne pepper

Directions:

1. In a large stainless-steel saucepan, add cranberries, onions, pineapple, ginger root, garlic, orange zest, vinegar, and orange juice over medium heat and cook until boiling, stirring occasionally.

2. Now set the heat to low and cook, covered for about 15 minutes, stirring occasionally.
3. Add in the remaining ingredients then cook, uncovered for about 15 minutes, stirring occasionally.
4. In 6 (½-pint) hot sterilized jars, divide the cranberry chutney, leaving about ½-inch space from the top.
5. Slide a small knife around the insides of each jar to remove air bubbles.
6. Close each jar with a lid and screw on the ring.
7. Arrange the jars in a boiling water canner and process for about 15 minutes.
8. Remove the jars from water canner and place onto a wood surface several inches apart to cool completely.
9. After cooling with your finger, press the top of each jar's lid to ensure that the seal is tight.
10. The canned chutney can be stored in the refrigerator for up to 1 month.

Per serving: Calories: 42kcal; Fat: 0.1g; Carbs: 10.5g; Protein: 0.2g

41. Peach Chutney

Preparation time: 20 minutes
Cooking time: 1 hour 05 minutes
Servings: 64
Ingredients:

- 4 pounds yellow peaches, pitted and quartered
- 1 medium yellow onion, minced
- 1 tablespoon fresh ginger, grated
- 2 cups golden raisins
- 1¾ cups red wine vinegar
- 1½ cups honey
- 2 tablespoons fresh lemon juice
- 1–2 teaspoons lemon zest, grated

- 1 tablespoon mustard seeds
- 1½ teaspoons sea salt
- ½ teaspoon red chili flakes

Directions:

1. In a large, heat-proof bowl, place the peach quarters and cover them with boiling water.
2. Cover the bowl and set aside for about 2–3 minutes.
3. Drain the peach quarters completely and remove the skin.
4. Then chop the peach quarters into small pieces.
5. In a large, nonreactive saucepan, add the peaches and remaining ingredients over high heat.
6. Now adjust the heat to medium-low and simmer for about 45 minutes, stirring occasionally.
7. In 8 (½-pint) hot sterilized jars, divide the chutney, leaving about ½-inch space from the top.
8. Slide a small knife around the insides of each jar to remove air bubbles.
9. Close each jar with a lid and screw on the ring.
10. Arrange the jars in a boiling water canner and process for about 15 minutes.
11. Remove the jars from water canner and place onto a wood surface several inches apart to cool completely.
12. After cooling with your finger, press the top of each jar's lid to ensure that the seal is tight.
13. The canned chutney can be stored in the refrigerator for up to 1 month.

Per serving: Calories: 45kcal; Fat: 0.1g; Carbs: 11.4g; Protein: 0.3g

42. Curried Apple Chutney

Preparation time: 15 minutes

Cooking time: 15 minutes
Servings: 10 pints
Ingredients:

- 2 quarts apples, peeled, cored and chopped
- 2 pounds raisins
- 4 cups brown sugar
- 1 cup onion, chopped
- 1 cup sweet pepper, chopped
- 3 tbsps. mustard seed
- 2 tbsps. ground ginger
- 2 tsps. allspice
- 2 tsps. curry powder
- 2 tsps. salt
- 2 hot red peppers, chopped
- 1 clove garlic, minced
- 4 cups vinegar

Directions:

1. In a large saucepan, mix all of the ingredients together, and then bring to a boil
2. Simmer for 1 hour.
3. Spoon the chutney into sterilized jars, leaving a 1/2 inch headspace. Wipe the jars' edge rim clean and add the lid.
4. Process jars in a water bath for 10 minutes.

Per serving: Calories: 23kcal; Fat: 0g; Carbs: 11g; Protein: 0g

43. Indian Apple Chutney

Preparation time: 14 minutes
Cooking time: 20 minutes
Servings: 6 pint jars
Ingredients:

- 2 pounds of apples (medium in size)
- 1 cup of diced onions (finely diced)
- Allspice, two teaspoons

- Ginger, ground or fresh, about two tablespoons
- Raisins, about 7 cups or two pounds
- Red bell pepper, chopped finely, about one cup
- mustard seeds, about three tablespoons
- Curry powder, about two teaspoons
- Pickling salt, two teaspoons
- 1 clove of garlic, crushed
- 2 hot peppers, seeds removed and diced finely
- 4 cups of malt vinegar
- Brown sugar, about 4 cups (or less, if you prefer less sugar)

Directions:

1. To prepare, wash, and scrub the apples, then peel, core, and slice. Place the apples in a large cooking pot and cover with water. Wash and slice the onions, removing all the skin, and add to the cooking pot.
2. Repeat the same process with the peppers and add them into the pot with the onions and apples. Pour the remaining ingredients into the cooking pot, including the malt vinegar, and bring the contents to a boil. Once this point is reached, cook for about 2 minutes, then reduce to a simmer and stir often.
3. Continue this process till the apples are tender, which can take up to one hour. Place the mixture into sterilized jars and adjust to allow for one inch of space at the top.
4. Clean down the rims of the jars before scooping the contents of the chutney into the jars. Place the lids on tightly and process in a water bath canner for 10-11 minutes.

5. Allow the jars to cool on a wire rack or cloth overnight, then store in a pantry or fruit cellar for up to one month.

Per serving: Calories: 47kcal; Fat: 0g; Carbs: 11.1g; Protein: 0g

44.   **Cantaloupe Chutney**

Preparation time: 15 minutes
Cooking time: 1 hour & 30 minutes
Servings: 4 pints
Ingredients:

- 3 medium cantaloupes
- 1 pound of dried apricots
- 1 fresh hot chili
- 2 cups of raisins
- 1 tsp. ground cloves
- 1 tsp. ground nutmeg
- 2 tbsps. salt
- 2 tbsps. mustard seed
- 1/4 cup fresh ginger, chopped
- 3 cloves garlic
- 4-1/2 cups apple cider vinegar
- 2-1/4 cups brown sugar
- 4 onions
- 1/2 cup orange juice
- 2 tbsps. orange zest
- cinnamon

Directions:

1. Thinly slice the apricots and put them into a large bowl. Chop the ginger and garlic thinly and add to the dish. Stir in chili, seed, and dice, and add to the pot.
2. Add raisins, cloves, cinnamon, nutmeg, and mustard seeds. Mix together and set aside. Mix the vinegar and sugar in a non-reactive pot or kettle; bring to boil over medium heat.
3. Add mixture to the pot in a bowl and return to a moderate simmer. Keep

simmer for 45 minutes. Do not deck the pot.

4. Meanwhile chop the onions and place them in a bowl. Peel and seed the Cantaloupes. Split the fruit into cubes of ½ inches. Add onions. In a cup, add orange juice and zest; mix well.

5. Once the vinegar mixture has been cooked for 45 minutes, add the cantaloupe mixture to the bowl, bring it back to a cooler, and start cooking for another 45 minutes or until thickened at the simmer.

6. Pour into hot glasses, clean the rims, screw the lids and rings together. Boiling water bath process: pints and quarts 10 minutes in both.

Per serving: Calories: 54kcal; Fat: 0g; Carbs: 14g; Protein: 1g

45. **Raisin Pear Chutney**

Preparation time: 2 hours 15 minutes
Cooking time: 15 minutes
Servings: 2 pints
Ingredients:

- 2 cups cider vinegar
- 1¼ cups packed brown sugar
- 3 lbs. unpeeled ripe pears, diced
- 1 medium onion, chopped
- 1 cup raisins
- 2 teaspoons ground cinnamon
- 1 teaspoon ground cloves
- 1 garlic clove, minced
- ½-1 teaspoon cayenne pepper

Directions:

1. In a saucepan, bring brown sugar and vinegar to a boil.
2. Stir in the remaining ingredients and return to a boil.

3. Reduce heat to low and leave chutney to simmer, uncovered, for about 2 hours or until desired consistency is reached.

4. Scoop the heated mixture into hot sterilized pint jars, allowing a 14-inch headspace. Remove any air bubbles and, if required, correct the headspace with a hot mixture. Wipe the rims cleanly. Screw on bands until fingertip tight and place tops on jars.

5. Place jars into the canner with boiling water, ensuring that they are completely covered with water. Let boil for 15 minutes. Remove jars and cool.

Per serving: Calories: 152kcal; Fat: 0g; Carbs: 40g; Protein: 1g

46. **Vinegary Peach Chutney**

Preparation time: 25 minutes
Cooking time: 60 minutes
Servings: 5 pint jars
Ingredients:

- 5 pounds (2.3 kg) yellow peaches, or nectarines, peeled, pitted, and cut into 1/2-inch dice
- 2 cups sugar
- 11/2 cups apple cider vinegar
- 1 cup chopped sweet onion
- 3/4 cup raisins
- 2 or 3 jalapeño peppers, diced
- 1 sweet banana pepper, or 1/2 yellow bell pepper, diced
- 3 tablespoons mustard seed
- 2 tablespoons grated fresh ginger
- 2 garlic cloves, minced
- 1 teaspoon garam masala
- 1/2 teaspoon ground turmeric

Directions:

1. Set a hot water bath. Bring the jars in it to keep warm. Clean the lids and rings in hot, soapy water, and set aside.

2. In a deep pot or a preserving pot set over medium heat, combine the peaches, sugar, cider vinegar, onion, raisins, jalapeños, banana pepper, mustard seed, ginger, garlic, garam masala, and turmeric. Slowly bring to a boil, stirring frequently. Reduce the heat to low. Parboil for 1 hour, or until very thick.

3. Ladle the chutney into the prepared jars, leaving 1/4 inch of headspace. Use a nonmetallic utensil to free any air bubbles. Clean the rims and seal with the lids and rings.

4. Set the jars in a hot water bath for 10 minutes. Set off the heat and let the jars rest in the water bath.

5. Carefully detach the jars from the hot water canner. Set aside to cool for 12 hours.

6. Check the lids for proper seals. Detach the rings, wipe the jars, label and date them, and transfer to a cupboard or pantry.

7. For the best flavor, allow the chutney to cure for 3 to 4 weeks before serving. Properly secured jars will last in the cupboard for 12 months. Once opened, refrigerate and consume within 6 weeks.

Per serving: Calories: 58kcal; Fat: 1g; Carbs: 12g; Protein: 0g

Vegetable Recipes

47. Chunky Zucchini Pickles

Preparation time: 15 minutes
Cooking time: 35 minutes
Servings: 4

Ingredients:

- 14 cups of unpeeled zucchini (I peeled half of them because this zucchini was huge and the skin was tougher than smaller zucchini)
- 6 cups finely chopped onions
- ¼ cup pickling or canning salt
- 3 cups granulated sugar
- 4 tablespoons Clear Jel (I have never seen this in stores, but you can purchase it online, I used 2 tbsp. corn starch, instead)
- ¼ cup dry mustard
- tablespoon ground ginger
- 1 teaspoon ground turmeric
- 1/2 cup water
- cups white vinegar
- 1 red bell pepper, chopped in fine bites

Directions:

1. Combine the onions and zucchini in a large stainless steel or glass bowl. Sprinkle with pickling salt, cover, and allow to stand at room temperature for 1 hour.

2. Transfer to a colander set over a sink, and drain with care. Note: I also rinsed part of the mixture because I've done it in the past with pickles, but it says DRAIN, not rinse. They still seemed salty.

3. Prepare for water bath canning. Sterilize your jars in the oven at 250 °F for 30 minutes.

4. Combine the sugar, Clear Jel, or corn starch, mustard, ginger, and turmeric in a large stainless steel saucepan. Stir dry the ingredients well. Gradually blend in water. Add vinegar and red pepper.

5. Bring to a boil over medium-high heat, frequently stirring to dissolve sugar

and prevent lumps from forming. Reduce the heat and boil gently, frequently stirring, until the mixture thickens for about 6 minutes. Add the zucchini mixture and return to a boil.

6. Ladle the hot zucchini mixture into hot sterilized jars, leaving right 1/2 headspace. Add extra hot zucchini mixture to adjust headspace and remove air bubbles.

7. Wipe the rim with a damp towel. Place rings and snaps on each jar, screwing bands down until they are fingertip tight.

8. Place the jars in a canner, making sure they are completely covered with water. Bring to a full rolling boil and process for 10 minutes. When time is completed, turn off the heat, remove the canner lid and wait 6 minutes before removing jars to a folded clean towel on the counter.

9. Check the seals, label, and store. Refrigerate any unsealed jars.

Per serving: Calories: 126kcal; Fat: 0.42g; Carbs: 29.68g; Protein: 1.4g

48. Pickled Brussels Sprouts

Preparation time: 5 minutes
Cooking time: 10 minutes
Servings: 4
Ingredients:

- 3 lbs. fresh Brussels sprouts, halved
- A medium sweet red pepper, finely chopped
- 6 garlic cloves, halved
- 1 medium onion, thinly sliced
- A teaspoon of red pepper flakes, crushed
- 1 tablespoon celery seeds
- 1 tablespoon whole peppercorns

- A tablespoon of canning salt
- ½ cup sugar
- 2 ½ cups white vinegar
- 2 ½ cups water

Directions:

1. Fill a Dutch oven three-fourths full with water; bring to a boil.

2. Add Brussels sprouts in batches, cook, and uncover for 4 minutes until tender-crisp.

3. With a slotted spoon, remove and drop into ice water. Drain and pat dry.

4. Pack Brussels sprouts into six hot 1-pint jars.

5. Divide garlic and pepper flakes among jars.

6. In a large saucepan, bring all remaining ingredients to a boil.

7. Carefully scoop the hot liquid over the Brussels sprouts, leaving a ¼- inch space on the top. Remove air bubbles and, if needed, adjust headspace by adding a hot mixture. Wipe the rims with care. Place tops on your jars and screw on bands until fingertip tight.

8. Place the jars into a canner with simmering water, making sure they are completely covered with water. Let boil for 10 minutes. Remove jars and cool.

Per serving: Calories: 256kcal; Fat: 1.69g; Carbs: 49.72g; Protein: 12.74g

49. Mustard Pickled Vegetables

Preparation time: 15 minutes
Cooking time: 15 minutes
Servings: 4
Ingredients:

- 1 head cauliflower
- 20 small green tomatoes
- 3 green bell peppers
- 4 cups pickled onions

- 2 pickling cucumbers
- 1 cup sugar
- ¾ cup flour
- ½ cup dry mustard
- 1 tablespoon turmeric
- 7 cups apple cider vinegar
- 7 cups water
- 1 cup pickling salt

Directions:

1. Wash all the veggies and chop them.
2. Toss the vegetables in a large nonreactive bowl or pot with salt.
3. Pour a quart of water over all of them and let this stand overnight.
4. Drain, cover with boiling water, and let it stand for 10 minutes. Drain.
5. Combine the sugar, flour, spices, vinegar, and 3 cups of water, then cook until thick.
6. Mix in the veggies then cook until tender-crisp.
7. Pack into pint jars, dividing liquid evenly and leaving ½ inch of headspace.
8. Wipe the rims, screw-on lids, and rings.
9. Finish the canning process in a boiling water bath for 15 minutes.

Per serving: Calories: 271kcal; Fat: 3.2g; Carbs: 108.88g; Protein: 12.32g

50. Tarragon Pickled Green Beans

Preparation time: 15 minutes
Cooking time: 2 Hours
Servings: 5
Ingredients:

- 6 garlic cloves, thinly sliced
- 36 whole peppercorns, crushed
- 3 lbs. green beans, washed and trimmed to 4 inches
- 6 sprigs fresh tarragon (can be substituted with 12 basil sprigs)
- 3 ½ cups of white wine vinegar, or just white vinegar
- 3 ½ cups of water
- 2 tablespoons pickling salt or Kosher salt

Directions:

1. Process the lids.
2. Then, divide the garlic and peppercorns into 6-pint jars.
3. Pack the green beans into the jars tightly and add sprigs of tarragon/basil
4. Heat the water, vinegar, and salt to boil at medium heat. Pour over the green beans in your jars, and give it a ½ inch headspace.
5. Process for 5 minutes in boiling water. Remove and let cool. You should hear the ping as it cools.

Per serving: Calories: 107kcal; Fat: 1.43g; Carbs: 15.8g; Protein: 3.55g

51. Pickled Curry Cauliflower

Preparation time: 5 minutes
Cooking time: 45 minutes
Servings: 4
Ingredients:

- 1 ½ tablespoon canning salt
- 4 cups vinegar
- 3 cups water
- 3 teaspoons cumin seeds
- 3 teaspoons turmeric
- 3 teaspoons curry powder
- 5 lbs. cauliflower
- 6 Serrano peppers

Directions:

1. With a 4-quart kettle, combine the water, salt, and vinegar. Bring to a simmer over low heat then whisk to

help dissolve the salt. Keep hot until ready to use.

2. Pack jars with cauliflower. Add ½ teaspoon of cumin seeds, turmeric, curry flower, and 1 Serrano pepper into each jar.
3. Pour hot brine into the jars, leaving ½ inch headspace.
4. Process for 12 minutes.
5. Remove from water, and let cool for 12 hours.

Per serving: Calories: 213kcal; Fat: 2.26g; Carbs: 34.06g; Protein: 11.76g

52. Spicy Dill Pickles

Preparation time: 15 minutes
Cooking time: 1 Hour
Servings: 5
Ingredients:

- ½ teaspoon red pepper flakes
- 10 garlic cloves, peeled and smashed
- 5 teaspoons dill seed, separated
- 2 tablespoons canning salt
- 3 tablespoons honey
- 4 cups water
- 1cup white vinegar
- 3 cups apple cider vinegar
- 11 lbs. cucumber

Directions:

1. Combine both kinds of vinegar, honey, salt, and water. Bring to a boil and lower to low heat.
2. Cut ½ inch off each end of the cucumbers and discard. Slice ¼ inch slices and set aside. If you are not using fresh cucumber, soak in ice water for 2 hours first.
3. Add one smashed garlic clove and one hot pepper or ½ red pepper flakes to each jar. Pack cucumbers in, and give it

a ½ inch headspace. Add ½ teaspoon of dill seed on top.

4. Pour brine over, giving the same headspace.
5. Process jars in boiling water for 10 minutes.
6. Remove and let cool naturally for 12 hours.
7. Store in a cold dry place for two weeks before consumption or storage.

Per serving: Calories: 284kcal; Fat: 1.64g; Carbs: 67.43g; Protein: 7.48g

53. Spiced Beets

Preparation time: 5 minutes
Cooking time: 60 minutes
Servings: 4
Ingredients:

- ¼ teaspoon salt
- ¾ teaspoon allspice
- ¾ teaspoon cloves
- ¼ stick cinnamon
- ¼ piece mace
- 1 ½ teaspoon celery seed
- 2 cups cider vinegar, 5% acidity
- 1 cup sugar
- 2 pints beets

Directions:

1. Sterilize a quart jar for 15 minutes. Remove your jar from the water and pour in the vinegar mix. Fix the lid and set it aside for 2 weeks.
2. Remove the spice bag. Cook fresh beets until tender but firm, and let cool. Peel the beets. Heat the vinegar and add ½ cup of the beet liquid. Add the beets and simmer for 15 minutes.
3. Pack into sterile jars, being sure the vinegar covers the beets. Remove air bubbles and adjust the lids. Process for 10 minutes in a boiling water bath.

Per serving: Calories: 144kcal; Fat: 0.29g; Carbs: 30.54g; Protein: 0.82g

54. Spicy Carrots

Preparation time: 5 minutes
Cooking time: 60 minutes
Servings: 4
Ingredients:

- ¼ teaspoon salt
- ¾ teaspoon allspice
- ¾ teaspoon cloves
- ¼ stick cinnamon
- ¼ piece mace
- 1 ½ teaspoon celery seed
- 2 cups cider vinegar, 5% acidity
- 1 cup sugar
- 2 pints carrots

Directions:

1. Tie the salt and the spices in a thin cloth bag. Boil the vinegar, sugar, and spices for 15 minutes. Sterilize a quart jar for about 15 minutes in boiling water. Remove your jar from the water and pour in the vinegar mix. Fix the lid and set it aside for 2 weeks.
2. Remove the spice bag. Cook fresh carrots until tender but firm, and let cool. Heat the vinegar and add ½ cup of the carrot liquid. Add the carrots and simmer for 15 minutes.
3. Pack into sterile jars, being sure the vinegar covers the carrots. Remove air bubbles and adjust the lids. Process for 10 minutes in a boiling water bath.

Per serving: Calories: 134kcal; Fat: 0.26g; Carbs: 28.51g; Protein: 0.33g

55. Sweet and Sour Fennel

Preparation time: 5 minutes
Cooking time: 30 minutes
Servings: 2-3 pint jars

Ingredients:

- 1 lb. fennel bulbs
- 3 tbsp. chopped fresh chives
- ⅓ cup olive oil
- 1 tbsp. salt
- ½ cup Turbinado/raw cane sugar
- 3 cups of water
- 2 cups white wine vinegar

Directions:

1. Prepare your jars by properly sterilizing them in warm water.
2. Core and slice your fennel and rinse it well under running water.
3. In a large pan, combine the salt, vinegar, and water. Bring the liquid to a boil before adding the rest of the ingredients. Allow the mixture to boil again for 3 minutes.
4. Using a slotted spoon, remove the fennel pieces from the mixture and place them into your jars. Pour the liquid over the fennel pieces, ensuring there is enough headspace.
5. Prepare and place the lids as the process steps direct.
6. Have your water bath canner ready and fill it halfway with water. Set the canner on high heat and bring it to a boil. Carefully place the jars in the water, making sure that everything is covered completely. Bring the canner back up to a boil and place the lid on top. As soon as it is boiling, continue process for 15 minutes.
7. When finished, remove and cool the jars as instructed. However, place the cooled jars in a dark and cool area for a week before consuming them.

Per serving: Calories: 214kcal; Fat: 14.45g; Carbs: 17.57g; Protein: 1.18g

56. Crisp Okra

Preparation time: 15 minutes
Cooking time: 45 minutes
Servings: 3-pint jars
Ingredients:

- 1 ½ lb. fresh okra
- 3 dried red chili peppers
- 3 tsp dried dill
- 2 cups water
- ½ cup apple cider vinegar
- ½ cup white vinegar
- 2 tbsp. salt

Directions:

1. Wash and rinse your okra thoroughly before placing them in your sterilized jars.
2. Place an equal amount of okra, chili, and dill in each of the jars.
3. Combine the salt, vinegar, and water in a small saucepan and bring it to a boil.
4. Fill each jar halfway with the heated liquid, leaving a good headroom.
5. Prepare the jars for proper sealing according to the processing Instructions.
6. Have your water canner ready and fill halfway with water. Allow water to boil before placing the jars on the rack. Be sure to leave enough space around the jars and enough water to cover them.
7. Bring the water to a rolling boil, cover, and start the 10-minute processing time.
8. Follow the cooling period as recommended.

Per serving: Calories: 76kcal; Fat: 0.59g; Carbs: 16.24g; Protein: 3.36g

57. Tasty Pickled Cauliflower

Preparation time: 30 minutes
Cooking time: 10 minutes
Servings: 12
Ingredients:

- 2-1/2 lbs. cauliflower florets
- quart white wine vinegar
- 2 thinly sliced onions, medium
- 1/2 tablespoon red pepper flakes, hot
- 2 cups sugar

Directions:

1. Boil a pot of water over high heat then add 1/4 cup pickling salt.
2. Add the florets and bring to a boil for 3 minutes, then drain.
3. Combine vinegar, onions, pepper flakes, and sugar in a medium pot, nonreactive while swirling until sugar is dissolved.
4. Boil over low-medium heat gently for about 5 minutes, then remove from heat.
5. Pack florets and onions into hot jars and cover with the vinegar solution. Make sure pepper flakes are evenly distributed. Leave 1/2 -inch headspace.
6. Wipe the rims of the jars then set lids and rings ensuring fingertip tightness.
7. Place the jars in boiling water and process for about 10 minutes.

Per serving: Calories: 249kcal; Fat: 0.5g; Carbs: 56g; Protein: 8g

58. Pickled Jalapenos

Preparation time: 50 minutes
Cooking time: 10 minutes
Servings: 2
Ingredients:

- 3-1/2 cups white vinegar
- 1 cup of water
- 1 tablespoon pickling salt
- 1-1/2 lbs. jalapenos peppers, washed and stems cut off

Directions:

1. In a saucepan, mix the vinegar, water, and salt. Bring to a boil for about 5 minutes.
2. Place peppers into the hot jars, then add hot brine into the jars using a ladle. Leave 1/2-inch headspace.
3. Remove air bubbles using non-metal utensils and add more brine but maintain headspace.
4. Wipe the jar rims using a clean damp cloth.
5. Place the jars in boiling water and let them process for about 10 minutes.

Per serving: Calories: 765kcal; Fat: 7g; Carbs: 50g; Protein: 16g

59. Canned Garlic Dill Pickles

Preparation time: 45 minutes
Cooking time: 15 minutes
Servings: 15

Ingredients:

- 3 lbs. onions
- 20 lbs. sliced pickling cucumbers, whole or speared
- 22 cups water
- 10 cups white vinegar
- 1-1/3 cup pickling salt
- 45 garlic cloves, peeled
- 1 sprig of fresh dill
- 45 peppercorns

Directions:

1. Layer the onions and cucumber in a bowl, large, then cover with salt. Top them with ice cubes then cover and refrigerate for about 2 hours.
2. Drain well and rinse well. Use a colander to rinse and drain.
3. Combine water, vinegar, and pickling salt then boil.

4. Add 3 garlic cloves and 1 fresh dill sprig to each hot quart jar then fill with onions and cucumbers.
5. Ladle the hot vinegar mixture to the hot jar and leave 1/2-inch headspace.
6. Release any air bubbles then wipe jar rims. Place lids and rings on.
7. Place the jars in boiling water and process them for about 10 minutes following the manufacturer's guide.

Per serving: Calories: 175kcal; Fat: 0.8g; Carbs: 29.9g; Protein: 5.6g

60. Canned Pumpkin

Preparation time: 35 minutes
Cooking time: 60 minutes
Servings: 3-quart jars
Ingredients:

- 1 lb. Pie pumpkins
- Water

Directions:

1. Start by cutting out the stem as if you want to use the pumpkin to curve, then cut it into 4 equal wedges.
2. Scrape out the seeds, then use a knife to peel the pumpkin. Slice the pumpkin into 1-inch cubes.
3. After this, place the pumpkin cubes in a large pot and water until the pumpkin is just covered.
4. Bring the pumpkin and water to boil for 2 minutes. Carefully transfer the pumpkin pieces into jars making sure you avoid smashing them.
5. Fill each jar with the cooking liquid leaving 1-inch headspace. Wipe the jar rims with a clean damp piece of cloth.
6. After this, place the lids and rings on the jars and place them in the pressure canner.

7. Process the jars in boiling water for 60 minutes for quart jars and 55 minutes for pint jars.

Per serving: Calories: 151kcal; Fat: 5.37g; Carbs: 8g; Protein: 17.63g

PRESSURE CANNING

Meat Recipes

61. Beef Meatballs

Preparation time: 20 minutes
Cooking time: 1 hour 30 minutes
Servings: 16
Ingredients:

- 6 pounds of ground beef
- 6 cups soft breadcrumbs
- 6 large eggs
- 1½ cups water
- 1 cup onion, chopped finely
- 1 tablespoon salt
- ¼ teaspoon ground black pepper
- 8 cups hot chicken broth

Directions:

1. In a glass bowl, add all ingredients (except for broth) and mix until just combined.
2. Set aside for about 15–30 minutes.
3. Preheat your oven to 425°F.
4. Lightly grease 2 shallow baking dishes.
5. Make 1-inch balls from the mixture.
6. Arrange the meatballs onto the prepared baking dishes in a single layer.
7. Bake for approximately 15 minutes.
8. In 8 (1-pint) hot sterilized jars, divide the meatballs.
9. Now pack each jar with hot broth, leaving 1-inch space from the top.
10. Run a knife around the insides of each jar to remove any air bubbles.
11. Remove all traces of food from the edges of the jar of jars with a clean, moist kitchen towel.
12. Close each jar with a lid and screw on the ring.
13. Carefully place the jars in the pressure canner and process at 10 pounds pressure for about 75 minutes.
14. Remove the jars from the pressure canner and place them onto a wood surface several inches apart to cool completely.
15. After cooling with your finger, press the top of each jar's lid to ensure that the seal is tight.
16. Store these canning jars in a cool, dark place.

Per serving: Calories: 525kcal; Fat: 15.3g; Carbs: 30.4g; Protein: 61.9g

62. Beef in Wine Sauce

Preparation time: 20 minutes
Cooking time: 2 hours 25 minutes
Servings: 6
Ingredients:

- 1 tablespoon vegetable oil
- 2 pounds of beef stew meat, cut into 1-inch cubes
- 1 cup carrot, peeled and shredded
- ¾ cup onion, sliced
- 1 large apple; peeled, cored, and shredded
- 2 garlic cloves, minced
- ¾ cup water
- ½ cup red wine
- 2 beef bouillon cubes
- 2 bay leaves
- 1 teaspoon salt

Directions:

1. In a cast-iron wok, heat vegetable oil over medium-high heat and sear beef

cubes in 2 batches for about 4–5 minutes.

2. Add in the remaining ingredients then stir to combine well.

3. Now adjust the heat to high and bring to a full rolling boil.

4. Now set the heat to low and cook, covered for about 1 hour, stirring occasionally.

5. Remove the wok of the meat mixture from heat and discard the bay leaves.

6. In 3 (1-pint) hot sterilized jars, divide the beef mixture, leaving about 1-inch space from the top.

7. Run a knife around the insides of each jar to remove any air bubbles.

8. Remove all traces of food from the edges of the jar of jars with a clean, moist kitchen towel.

9. Close each jar with a lid and screw on the ring.

10. Carefully place the jars in the pressure canner and process at 10 pounds pressure for about 75 minutes.

11. Remove the jars from the pressure canner and place them onto a wood surface several inches apart to cool completely.

12. After cooling with your finger, press the top of each jar's lid to ensure that the seal is tight.

13. Store these canning jars in a cool, dark place.

Per serving: Calories: 354kcal; Fat: 11.9g; Carbs: 9.4g; Protein: 46.5g

63. Smoky Meatloaf

Preparation time: 20 minutes
Time: 1 hour 20 minutes
Servings: 16
Ingredients:

- ¼ of French bread loaf

- 5 pounds of ground beef
- 1 onion, chopped
- 4 large eggs
- 1½ cups ketchup
- 2 tablespoons Worcestershire sauce
- ¾ cup brown sugar
- 2 tablespoons salt
- 1 tablespoon powdered smoke
- 1 tablespoon sage
- 1 tablespoon garlic powder
- ½ tablespoon onion salt
- ½ tablespoon ground black pepper

Directions:

1. Add bread loaf into a food processor and process until crumbed.

2. In a large glass bowl, add bread crumbs and remaining ingredients and mix until well combined.

3. In 8 (1-pint) hot sterilized jars, divide the beef mixture, leaving about 1-inch space from the top.

4. Run a knife around the insides of each jar to remove any air bubbles.

5. Remove all traces of food from the edges of the jar of jars with a clean, moist kitchen towel.

6. Close each jar with a lid and screw on the ring.

7. Carefully place the jars in the pressure canner and process at 10 pounds pressure for about 75 minutes.

8. Remove the jars from the pressure canner and place them onto a wood surface several inches apart to cool completely.

9. After cooling with your finger, press the top of each jar's lid to ensure that the seal is tight.

10. Store these canning jars in a cool, dark place.

Per serving: Calories: 347kcal; Fat: 10.3g; Carbs: 16.3g; Protein: 45.5g

64. Canned Ham

Preparation time: 5 minutes
Cooking time: 25 minutes
Servings: 4
Ingredients:

- 19 lbs. ham, cut into ½- inch chunks

Directions:

1. Heat a lightly greased large cast-iron skillet over medium-high heat and sear ham chunks in 8 batches for about 3–5 minutes.
2. In 10 (1-pint) hot sterilized jars, divide the ham chunks.
3. Now pack each jar with hot water, leaving a 1-inch space from the top.
4. Run a knife around the insides of each jar to remove any air bubbles.
5. Remove all traces of food from the edges of the jar of jars with a clean, moist kitchen towel.
6. Close each jar with a lid and screw on the ring.
7. Carefully place the jars in the pressure canner and process at 11 pounds pressure for about 75 minutes.
8. Remove each jar from the pressure canner and place them onto a wood surface several inches apart to cool completely.
9. After cooling, press the top of each jar's lid with your finger to ensure a tight seal.
10. Store these canning jars in a cool, dark place.

Per serving: Calories: 220kcal; Fat: 7.33g; Carbs: 2.09g; Protein: 36.41g

65. Pot Roast in a Jar

Preparation time: 5 minutes

Cooking time: 50 minutes
Servings: 6
Ingredients:

- 2 lbs. stewing beef, cut into chunks
- 1 cup chopped onions
- 2 teaspoons dried thyme
- 2 minced garlic cloves
- 2 bay leaves
- 1 cup beef broth
- 1 cup dry red wine
- 2 teaspoons salt
- 1 teaspoon black pepper
- 1 cup chopped carrots
- 1 cup diced potatoes
- ½ cup chopped celery

Directions:

1. Sterilize the jars in a pressure canner. Allow the jars to cool.
2. Place the beef in a pot and add the onions, thyme, garlic, bay leaves, broth, and wine. Season with salt and black pepper.
3. Seal the lid then turn on the heat. Bring to a boil for 10 minutes and allow to simmer for 10 minutes.
4. Add the vegetables and simmer for another 5 minutes. Turn off the heat.
5. Transfer the mixture to sterilized jars.
6. Remove the air bubbles and close the lid.
7. Place the jars in the pressure canner and process them for 25 minutes.

Per serving: Calories: 249kcal; Fat: 6.2g; Carbs: 12.75g; Protein: 34.45g

66. Canned Chipotle Beef

Preparation time: 5 minutes
Cooking time: 48 minutes
Servings: 6
Ingredients:

- 2 lbs. beef brisket, cut into chunks
- 2 teaspoons of salt
- 8 minced garlic cloves
- 2 cups chopped onion
- 2 teaspoons oregano
- ½ cup coriander
- 2 chipotle chilies
- 4 cups beef broth

Directions:
1. Sterilize the jars in a pressure canner. Allow the jars to cool.
2. Place the beef in a pot and season with salt. Turn on the heat and sear all sides for 3 minutes. Stir in the garlic and onion. Cook for another minute. Add in the rest of the ingredients.
3. Seal the lid and allow the meat to simmer for 20 minutes on medium heat. Turn off the heat and allow the mixture to cool slightly.
4. Transfer the mixture to the jars.
5. Remove the air bubbles and close the lid.
6. Transfer the jars to the pressure canner and process for 25 minutes.

Per serving: Calories: 158kcal; Fat: 5.87g; Carbs: 19.06g; Protein: 7.26g

67.   Canned Meatballs

Preparation time: 5 minutes
Cooking time: 30 minutes
Servings: 5
Ingredients:

- 2 lbs. ground meat
- Herbs (your choice)
- 2 teaspoons salt
- 2 cups tomato juice

Directions:
1. Sterilize the jars in a pressure canner. Allow the jars to cool.

2. Put the meat in a bowl then stir in the herbs and salt. Mix until well combined.
3. Boil enough water in a saucepan. Make balls out of the ground meat mixture and gently drop them into the boiling water. Let them cook for 5 minutes, then strain the meatballs.
4. Gently pack the meatballs inside the sterilized jars. Add enough tomato juice to completely cover the meatballs. Leave an inch of headspace.
5. Remove the air bubbles and close the lid.
6. Place all jars in your pressure canner and process for 25 minutes.

Per serving: Calories: 217kcal; Fat: 7.13g; Carbs: 3.33g; Protein: 35.78g

68.   Meat Chunks

Preparation time: 5 minutes
Cooking time: 1 hour and 30 minutes
Servings: 7
Ingredients:

- Salt (1 teaspoon for each quart jar)
- Preferred meat, fresh, chilled, cut into chunks/strips
- meat broth, boiling/tomato juice/water

Directions:
1. Remove any excess fat from your chilled, high-quality meat. If using wild meats, soak first in brine water (5 quarts water plus 5 tablespoons salt) to remove the strong flavors. Discard the large bones after rinsing.
2. Roast or stew your meat chunks until they are rare (you may also brown them with a little fat). Add the cooked meat to clean and hot mason jars filled with salt (1 teaspoon). Pour your preferred liquid into it, leaving an inch of headspace.

3. If choosing to raw pack, fill each jar with 1 teaspoon of salt first before adding your raw meat chunks, letting an inch of headspace remain and without adding any liquid.

4. Get rid of air bubbles and secure the lids on the jars. Put them in the pressure canner for 1 hour and 15 minutes (pints) or 1 hour and 30 minutes (quarts).

Per serving: Calories: 95kcal; Fat: 3.11g; Carbs: 0g; Protein: 15.58g

69. Chopped meat

Preparation time: 5 minutes
Cooking time: 1 Hour and 30 minutes
Servings: 2
Ingredients:

- 2 preferred meat types, fresh, chilled, chopped/ground
- Salt (1 teaspoon for each quart jar)
- 2 cups meat broth
- ¼ cup tomato juice
- 1/8 cup water

Directions:

1. Chop the chilled fresh meat into small chunks. If using venison, grind after mixing with one cup of pork fat (high quality) to every three to four cups of venison. If using sausage (freshly made), combine with cayenne pepper and salt.

2. Shape into meatballs or patties. If using cased sausage, chop into three to 4-inch links.

3. Cook the meat until light brown. If using ground meat, sauté without shaping.

4. Add the cooked meat to clean and hot mason jars, each filled with salt (1 teaspoon).

5. Boil the meat broth. Pour the meat broth, tomato juice, or water into the jars until filled up to one inch from the top.

6. Remove air bubbles before adjusting the lids, then process in the pressure canner for one hour and fifteen minutes (pints) or one hour and thirty minutes (quarts).

Per serving: Calories: 141kcal; Fat: 4.23g; Carbs: 11.98g; Protein: 14.74g

70. Pulled Pork

Preparation time: 5 minutes
Cooking time: 90 minutes
Servings: 2
Ingredients:

- 3-5 lbs. pork rear (barbecued or slow-cooked. It needs to be tender enough to be pulled apart or shredded)
- 1quart beef stock or water
- 1-pint jar or homemade barbecue sauce (this is optional)

Directions:

1. This recipe is designed for 3 to 5-pint jars. Sterilize your jars and keep them in simmering hot water until it is time for them to be used.

2. Fill your pressure canner with water and let it simmer

3. Place the beef stock in a stainless steel pot of hot water and let it boil. Remove it from the heat.

4. Place your hot jars on a towel and use a canning funnel to fill every jar with the pulled pork—the jars should be three-quarters full.

5. Add a quarter cup of the barbecue sauce to every jar—if you would like that flavor. If not, fill the jars with the stock or water, leaving one inch of headspace.

6. Remove the air bubbles with a rubber spatula and use a cloth or paper towel to clean the rims of the jars.

7. Extract all lids from the hot water and place them on the rims of the jars. Add the rings to the tops of every jar and turn the seal until they are finger tight.

8. Place the jars in the canning rack—which should be at the bottom of the canner.

9. Follow the venting and sealing instructions provided by the manufacturer's manual.

10. Processing time for this recipe is 75 minutes for pint jars at ten pounds of pressure and 90 minutes for quart jars.

11. Once the processing time is completed, turn off the heat then allow the pressure to return to zero on its own.

12. Wait until the lid lock falls off—if you have a lid lock.

13. Wait for a couple of minutes before you attempt to remove the gauge or the regulator.

14. Remove the canner's lid and wait for ten minutes before removing the jars. Place all jars on a clean towel and leave them undisturbed for 12 to 24 hours. Do not touch the jars until the following day.

15. An hour after removing the jars, they will make a 'ping' or a popping sound. This means the glass is cooling, and the lids react to being sucked into the jars. This means the sealing process is taking place.

16. After 24 hours, check the lids for sealing. Place the sealed jars in a dry, cool storage area and reprocess any jars that did not seal properly. If you don't want to reprocess them, you can consume the pork within 24 to 72 hours.

Per serving: Calories: 149kcal; Fat: 11.89g; Carbs: 0.34g; Protein: 9.38g

Poultry Recipes

71. Chicken Marsala

Preparation time: 15 minutes
Cooking time: 1 hour 45 minutes
Servings: 20
Ingredients:

- 6 pounds boneless, skinless chicken, cut into bite-sized pieces
- Salt and ground black pepper, as needed
- 2-3 tablespoons olive oil
- 1 medium onion chopped
- 1 teaspoon garlic, chopped
- 1 teaspoon dried oregano
- 2 cups dry Marsala wine
- 8 cups chicken broth
- 5 cups mushrooms, sliced

Directions:

1. Rub the chicken pieces with salt and black pepper generously.

2. In a cast-iron wok, heat olive oil over medium-high heat and sear the chicken pieces in 4 batches for about 3–5 minutes.

3. Transfer each cooked chicken batch to a colander to drain excess grease.

4. In the same wok, add the onion then sauté for about 3–4 minutes.

5. Add in the garlic and oregano and sauté for about 1 minute.

6. Stir in the wine and boil for about 1 minute.

7. Stir in the broth and cook until boiling.

8. Now set the heat to low and cook for about 3–5 minutes.

9. In 10 (1-pint) hot sterilized jars, divide the chicken pieces and mushrooms.

10. Now pack each jar with a hot cooking mixture, leaving 1-inch space from the top.

11. Run a knife around the insides of each jar to remove any air bubbles.

12. Remove all traces of food from the edges of the jar of jars with a clean, moist kitchen towel.

13. Close each jar with a lid and screw on the ring.

14. Carefully place the jars in the pressure canner and process at 11 pounds pressure for about 75 minutes.

15. Remove the jars from the pressure canner and place them onto a wood surface several inches apart to cool completely.

16. After cooling with your finger, press the top of each jar's lid to ensure that the seal is tight.

17. Store these canning jars in a cool, dark place.

Per serving: Calories: 259kcal; Fat: 6.1g; Carbs: 2.2g; Protein: 42g

72. Sweet & Sour Chicken

Preparation time: 15 minutes
Cooking time: 1 hour 20 minutes
Servings: 20
Ingredients:

- 3 (20-ounce) cans of pineapple chunks
- 1¼ cup white vinegar
- ½ cup water
- 1/3 cup soy sauce
- ¼ cup ketchup
- ¾ cup brown sugar
- 1 teaspoon ginger powder
- 4½ pounds boneless, skinless chicken breasts, cut into 1-inch bite-sized pieces

- 3 large bell peppers (red and green), seeded and chopped
- 2 medium onions, chopped

Directions:

1. Drain the cans of pineapple, reserving the juice in a bowl.

2. In a nonreactive saucepan, add 2½ cups of reserved pineapple juice, vinegar, water, soy sauce, ketchup, brown sugar, and ginger powder over medium-high heat and cook until boiling, stirring continuously.

3. In 10 (1-pint) hot sterilized jars, divide the chicken pieces, onions, bell peppers, and pineapple.

4. Now pack each jar with hot cooking liquid, leaving 1-inch space from the top.

5. Run a knife around the insides of each jar to remove any air bubbles.

6. Remove all traces of food from the edges of the jar of jars with a clean, moist kitchen towel.

7. Close each jar with a lid and screw on the ring.

8. Carefully place the jars in the pressure canner and process at 11 pounds pressure for about 75 minutes.

9. Remove the jars from the pressure canner and place them onto a wood surface several inches apart to cool completely.

10. After cooling with your finger, press the top of each jar's lid to ensure that the seal is tight.

11. Store these canning jars in a cool, dark place.

Per serving: Calories: 276kcal; Fat: 7.7g; Carbs: 20.2g; Protein: 30.6g

73. Canned Chicken

Preparation time: 30 minutes

Cooking time: 2 hours
Servings: 8-pint jars
Ingredients:

- 18 medium boneless and skinless chicken breasts
- 1 ½ tablespoon of salt
- 4 ½ cups of water
- Butter or Olive Oil for frying in a skillet

Directions:

1. Cook each side of the chicken in a skillet with some butter or olive oil, for about 8-10 minutes. Remove from heat when the chicken is white and cooked all the way through. If you poke it with a fork, the juices run clear.
2. In each pint jar place a ½ teaspoon of salt and 2 chicken breasts.
3. Fill the jar with water, and process for 70 minutes at 10 pounds of pressure for the weighted gauge of the pressure canner or 11 pounds if the pressure canner has a dial gauge.
4. Remove jars, and let cool until it is room temperature, which may take about a day.

Per serving: Calories: 509kcal; Fat: 55.09g; Carbs: 0g Protein: 5.06g

74. Mexican Turkey Soup

Preparation time: 20 minutes
Cooking time: 1 hour and 30 minutes
Servings: 8-quart jars or 16-pint jars
Cooking time:

- 6 cups of cooked turkey, chopped
- 2 cups of chopped onions
- 8 ounces can of Mexican green chilies, chopped and drained
- ¼ cup of taco seasoning mix, packed
- 28 ounces of crushed tomatoes with the juices

- 16 cups of turkey or chicken broth
- 3 cups of corn
- 1 ½ tablespoon of extra virgin olive oil

Directions:

1. In a large stockpot, warm olive oil on medium-high heat. Sauté the onions until tender and fragrant, about 2 minutes on medium-high heat. Reduce heat to medium-low.
2. Add taco seasoning and the chilies. Cook and stir for another 3 minutes, add in the tomatoes and the broth. Bring to a boil, and then add the corn and the turkey.
3. Reduce heat to low then let simmer for 10 minutes.
4. Ladle equally into the jars.
5. Process pints at 10 pounds for 75 minutes and quarts at 10 pounds for 90 minutes for the weighted gauge of the pressure canner or 11 pounds if the pressure canner has a dial gauge.
6. Remove jars, and let cool until it is at room temperature. This may take about a day.

Per serving: Calories: 1079kcal; Fat: 76.84g; Carbs: 30.08g; Protein: 63.66g;

75. Ground Turkey

Preparation time: 10 minutes
Cooking time: 2 hours 25 minutes
Servings: 16
Ingredients:

- 4 pounds of ground turkey
- 4 teaspoons salt

Directions:

1. In a large pan of water, add ground turkey and cook until boiling.
2. Now set the heat to low and cook for about 5 minutes.
3. Drain the meat completely.

4. In 4 (1-pint) hot sterilized jars, divide the ground turkey and salt.

5. Now pack each jar with hot water, leaving a 1-inch space from the top.

6. Run a knife around the insides of each jar to remove any air bubbles.

7. Remove all traces of food from the edges of the jar of jars with a clean, moist kitchen towel.

8. Close each jar with a lid and screw on the ring.

9. Carefully place the jars in the pressure canner and process at 10 pounds pressure for about 75 minutes.

10. Remove the jars from the pressure canner and place them onto a wood surface several inches apart to cool completely.

11. After cooling with your finger, press the top of each jar's lid to ensure that the seal is tight.

12. Store these canning jars in a cool, dark place.

Per serving: Calories: 221kcal; Fat: 12.5g; Carbs: 0g; Protein: 31g

76. Pressure Canned Turkey pieces

Preparation time: 10 – 20 minutes
Cooking time: 65 minutes
Servings: 5 Pints
Ingredients:

- 5 lbs. turkey
- boiling water

Directions:

1. Use a method of choice to cook the turkey meat until it is 2/3 cooked.

2. Pack the turkey pieces in the sterilized jars, then add water or stock leaving 1-inch headspace.

3. Remove the air bubbles then wipe the rims with a damp cloth.

4. Put the lids and the rings on the jars. Transfer the jars to the pressure canner and process them at 10 pounds pressure for 65 minutes if the turkey had bones and for 75 minutes if without bones.

5. Wait for the pressure canner to depressurize to zero before removing the jars.

6. Place the jars on a cooling rack for 24 hours then store them in a cool dry place.

Per serving: Calories: 262kcal; Fat: 10.1g; Carbs: 40g; Protein: 25g

77. Pressure Canned Chicken Breast

Preparation time: 10 – 20 minutes
Cooking time: 75 minutes
Servings: 5 Pints
Ingredients:

- 5 lbs. chicken breast
- salt

Directions:

1. Cut the chicken into small pieces that will fit into the jars. Place the chicken in the sterilized jars leaving 1-inch headspace.

2. Add a ½ tablespoon of salt to each jar. (You may add water, but chicken makes its juice.)

3. Get rid of the air bubbles and wipe the jar rims with a damp cloth.

4. Put the lids and the rings on the jars. Transfer the jars to the pressure canner and process them at 10 pounds pressure for 75 minutes.

5. Wait for the pressure canner to depressurize to zero before removing the jars.

6. Place the jars on a cooling rack for 24 hours then store them in a cool dry place.

Per serving: Calories: 120kcal; Fat: 2.5g; Carbs: 2.5g; Protein: 25g

78. Chicken Cacciatore

Preparation time: 10 – 20 minutes
Cooking time: 20 minutes
Servings: 8
Ingredients:

- 3 tbsps. olive oil
- 8 boneless and skinless chicken breasts, cubed
- 12 boneless and skinless chicken thighs, cubed
- 1 tbsp. dried oregano
- 1 tbsp. dried basil
- 1 tsp. dried thyme
- 1 tsp. dried rosemary, crushed
- 1 tsp. coarse sea salt
- ½ tsp. ground black pepper
- 1 cup red wine
- 4 cups diced tomatoes, with their juice
- 4 cups tomato juice
- 2 cups sliced white mushrooms
- 3 cups coarsely chopped sweet onion
- 1 chopped red bell pepper
- 1 chopped celery stalk
- 6 minced garlic cloves
- ¾ cup tomato paste
- 1 tbsp. granulated sugar

Directions:

1. Combine the oil, chicken breasts, and thighs in a heavy-bottomed stockpot. To coat the chicken, thoroughly combine all of the ingredients. Cook the chicken for 3 minutes over medium-high heat, stirring often.
2. Add the seasonings, thyme, oregano, basil, and rosemary.
3. Mix evenly and cook for an additional 3 minutes.
4. Add the red wine and cook for 5 minutes while covered.
5. Add the tomatoes, celery, onion, mushrooms, bell pepper, tomato juice, and garlic.
6. Mix well then allow to boil for 5 minutes.
7. Stir in the sugar and tomato paste, cook for another five minutes, and then remove from the fire.
8. Fill each hot jar ¾ full with the chicken and veggies.
9. Add the hot tomato sauce over the mixture, leaving some space.
10. Remove any air bubbles and add more sauce if necessary.
11. Rinse the rim of each jar with a warm washcloth dipped in distilled white vinegar, then tighten the lids.
12. Arrange the jars in the pressure canner with the lids on.
13. Allow the canner to vent for 10 minutes then close the vent and continue heating to attain 10 PSI for a weighted gauge and 11 PSI for a dial gauge.
14. Can the quart jars for 1 hour 30 minutes and pint jars for 1 hour 15 minutes.

Per serving: Calories: 701kcal; Fat: 43.8g; Carbs: 42.14g; Protein: 37.12g

79. Whole Chicken

Preparation time: 10 – 20 minutes
Cooking time: 20 minutes
Servings: 3
Ingredients:

- 1 tsp. salt in each quart
- 32 cups water
- 1 whole chicken, cut into pieces
- 3 bay leaves
- 6 cups chopped carrots

- 3 cups diced Roma tomatoes
- 2 cups celery, chopped
- 2 cups diced onions
- 8 chopped garlic cloves
- 1 tbsp. dried basil
- 1 tbsp. coarse sea salt (optional)
- 2 tsp. ground black pepper

Directions:

1. Chill the chicken meat for 6 to 12 hours before canning (either with or without the bones). Soak the meat (either with or without the bones) in a mixture of water and salt (1 tbsp. per quart) for one hour, then rinse.
2. Discard any excess fat on the meat before slicing it into one-inch chunks.
3. Boil the meat chunks until almost done. Meanwhile, fill your clean and hot mason jars with salt (1 tsp. per quart). Add the boiled meat and hot liquid, making sure to leave a quarter of an inch of headspace.
4. If choosing to raw pack chicken, place in clean and hot mason jars, packing them in loosely and leaving 1¼-inch of headspace. For each quart, add one tsp. of salt (no liquids).
5. Get rid of air bubbles before adjusting the lids on the jars, process in the pressure canner for 1 hr and 15 minutes (for pint jars) or 1 hour and 30 minutes (for quart jars).

Per serving: Calories: 104kcal; Fat: 4.1g; Carbs: 16.3g; Protein: 1.3g

80. Chicken with Garlic

Preparation time: 10 – 20 minutes
Cooking time: 90 minutes
Servings: 3
Ingredients:

- 1 crushed garlic clove

- 3 skinless boneless chicken breasts
- ½ tsp. sea salt
- ½ tsp. black pepper
- water, as needed

Directions:

1. Put part of the garlic clove at the bottom of each sanitized quart jar.
2. Add chicken pieces, pushing them down to pack tightly.
3. Add salt and pepper, and then fill the jar with water, allowing 1 inch of headspace.
4. Carefully slide a rubber spatula down the interior sides of the jars, removing air pockets. Do not skip this step, or your jars may not seal. Wipe the rims of the jars.
5. Process in a pressure canner for 90 minutes at 10 PSI, adjusting for altitude with the lids on.

Per serving: Calories: 233.1kcal; Fat: 8.3g; Carbs: 8.6g; Protein: 27.9g

81. Pineapple Chicken

Preparation time: 10 – 20 minutes
Cooking time: 90 minutes
Servings: 6
Ingredients:

- 3 cups pineapple juice
- ¾ cup brown sugar
- 1¼ cups apple cider vinegar
- 6 tbsps. soy sauce
- 4 tbsps. tomato paste
- 1 tsp. ground ginger
- 4 minced garlic cloves
- 5 lbs. chopped boneless and skinless chicken
- 2 diced onions
- 3 diced bell peppers
- 1 diced pineapple

- crushed chili pepper, to taste

Directions:

1. In a sizable saucepan, bring to a boil pineapple juice, sugar, vinegar, soy sauce, tomato paste, ginger, and garlic, stirring frequently.
2. Boil till the sugar dissolves and until the mixture is smooth.
3. In your jars, layer chicken, onions, peppers, and pineapple. If you're using crushed chili, add them now.
4. Put the sauce over the contents of the jars.
5. Wipe the rims of the jars, put the lids on, and process in a pressure canner at 11 PSI for 90 minutes, adjusting for altitude.

Per serving: Calories: 391kcal; Fat: 3.5g; Carbs: 32.6g; Protein: 19.5g

Fish Recipes

82. Fish

Preparation time: 20 minutes
Cooking time: 1 hour and 30 minutes
Servings: 5 pints
Cooking time:

- 5 pounds tuna or salmon
- 5-pint sized mason jars with lids and rings
- Canning salt
- Lemon juice
- 1 jalapeño pepper

Directions:

1. Place 1 slice of jalapeño pepper into each jar.
2. Fill jars with meat to 1/2 inch from the top.
3. Add 1/4 tsp. canning salt and 1 tsp. lemon juice per pint.

4. Use a knife to jiggle meat and remove any air pockets.
5. Wipe rim of jar clean.
6. Heat lids in hot water for 3 minutes; place lids on jars and tighten rings slightly.
7. Place jars in the canner then fill with water to the jar rings.
8. Close and lock pressure canner and bring to a boil over high heat, then add cooking weight to the top.
9. After 20 minutes, turn heat to medium and cook for 75 minutes.
10. Turn off heat and leave canner alone until it has cooled completely to room temperature.
11. After canner has cooled, remove jars from the canner and check for sealing.
12. If jars have sealed, store for up to 2 years; if not, use meat right away.

Per serving: Calories: 700kcal; Fat: 32.56g; Carbs: 1.51g; Protein: 93.79g

83. Pressure Canned Shrimps

Preparation time: 10 – 20 minutes
Cooking time: 45 minutes
Servings: 10
Ingredients:

- 10 lbs. shrimps
- ¼ cup salt
- 1 cup vinegar

Directions:

1. Remove the heads immediately, then chill until ready to preserve them.
2. Wash the shrimps and drain them well.
3. Add a gallon of water to a pot, add salt and vinegar. Bring to a boil, then cook shrimps for 10 minutes.
4. Remove the shrimps from the cooking liquid with a slotted spoon, then rinse in cold water and drain. Peel the

shrimps while packing them in the sterilized jars.

5. Add a gallon of water with 3 tbsp. salt and bring it to a boil. Add the brine to the jars and remove the air bubbles. Add more brine if necessary.

6. Wipe the jar rims with a cloth damped in vinegar. Place the lids and the rings.

7. Process at 10 pounds pressure for 45 minutes.

8. Wait for the pressure canner to depressurize to zero before removing the jars.

9. Place the jars on a cooling rack undisturbed then store in a cool dry place.

Per serving: Calories: 100kcal; Fat: 2g; Carbs: 1g; Protein: 15g

84. Canned Oysters

Preparation time: 10 minutes
Cooking time: 85 minutes
Servings: 6
Ingredients:

- 5 lbs. oysters
- salt
- water

Directions:

1. Wash the oysters in clean water, then heat them in an oven at 400°F for 7 minutes to open.

2. Cool them in ice-cold water. Remove the meat, placing it in water containing salt.

3. Drain the meat and pack in the jars, leaving a 1-inch headspace. Add 1/2 tbsp. of salt in each half-pint jar and add water maintaining the headspace.

4. Wipe the jar rims, then place the lids and the rings.

5. Can for 75 minutes at 10 pounds.

6. Wait for the pressure canner to depressurize to zero before removing the jars from the canner.

7. Place the jars on a cooling rack undisturbed, then store in a cool dry place.

Per serving: Calories: 68kcal; Fat: 3g; Carbs: 0g; Protein: 7g

85. Pressure Canned Salmon

Preparation time: 10 – 20 minutes
Cooking time: 100 minutes
Servings: 6
Ingredients:

- 5 lbs. salmon
- salt

Directions:

1. Eviscerate the salmon immediately after catching it and clean it thoroughly with clean water.

2. Chill it until you are ready to pressure can it. Remove the tail, the head, and the fins. Split the fish lengthwise then cut into small pieces that perfectly fit into your jars.

3. Pack the fish in sterilized jars leaving a 1-inch headspace. Add a tbsp. of salt in each jar if you desire.

4. Rinse the jar rims with a damp paper towel, then place the lids and the rings on the jar.

5. Pressure-can the jars in the pressure canner at 11 pounds pressure for 100 minutes.

6. Wait for the pressure canner to depressurize to zero before removing the jars.

7. Transfer the jars to a cooling rack for 24 hours before storing them in a cool dry place.

Per serving: Calories: 121kcal; Fat: 5.4g; Carbs: 0g; Protein: 17g

86. Pressure Canned Tuna

Preparation time: 10 – 20 minutes
Cooking time: 100 minutes
Servings: 6
Ingredients:

- 5 lbs. tuna
- salt

Directions:

1. Use a sharp kitchen knife to peel off the skin, then scrape the surface to remove the blood vessels.
2. Cut the fish lengthwise, then into pieces that fit into a pint jar.
3. Add salt in each jar.
4. If you have precooked the tuna, add the fish, some vegetable oil, and a tbsp. of salt per pint jar.
5. Clean the rims and place the lids and the rings on the jars.
6. Process at 10 pounds pressure for 100 minutes.
7. Wait for the pressure canner to depressurize to zero before removing the jars.
8. Transfer the jars to a cooling rack for 24 hours, then store them in a cool dry place.

Per serving: Calories: 191kcal; Fat: 1.4g; Carbs: 0g; Protein: 42g

87. Fish Chowder

Preparation time: 10 – 20 minutes
Cooking time: 30 minutes
Servings: 8
Ingredients:

- ¾ cup chopped onion
- 3 tbsps. butter
- ½ cup chopped celery
- 2 cups diced potatoes
- 1 tsp. garlic powder
- 2 cups chicken broth
- 2 diced carrots
- 1 tsp black pepper
- 1 tsp salt
- 32 oz. canned fish
- 1 tsp. dried dill weed
- 15 oz. canned creamed corn
- 12 oz. canned evaporated milk
- ½ lb. shredded cheddar cheese

Directions:

1. Melt the butter in a huge pot over medium heat.
2. Cook the celery, onion, and garlic powder for 5 minutes in the melted butter.
3. Stir in carrots, potatoes, salt, broth, pepper, and dill.
4. Boil, then reduce the heat to low.
5. Cover and simmer for 20 minutes.
6. Stir in milk, cheese, corn, and fish.
7. Cook until cheese melts.
8. Fill jars with fish chowder to ½ inch from the top.
9. Put the jars in the canner then fill with water up to the jar rings.
10. Close and lock the pressure canner and bring to a boil over high heat, then add cooking weight to the top.
11. After 20 minutes, turn the heat to medium and cook for 75 minutes.
12. Turn off the heat then leave the canner alone until it has cooled completely to room temperature.
13. After the canner has cooled, remove the jars from the canner and check for sealing.
14. If the jars have sealed, store for up to 2 years; if not, use it right away.

Per serving: Calories: 249.0kcal; Fat: 8.1g; Carbs: 14.5g; Protein: 26.5g

88. Fish Rice Casserole

Preparation time: 10 – 20 minutes
Cooking time: 30 minutes
Servings: 4
Ingredients:

- 14 oz. fish
- 2 cups cooked rice, divided
- 1 egg
- ¼ cup milk
- ¼ tsp. salt
- ¼ tsp. pepper
- 2 tbsps. butter

Directions:

1. Grease an 8-inch baking dish.
2. Preheat the oven to 375°F.
3. Drain the fish, saving the juice to use later.
4. Spread 1 cup of the rice in the baking dish.
5. Spread the fish over the rice, flaking it finely.
6. Pour the reserved fish juice over the fish.
7. Spread the remaining 1 cup of rice over the top.
8. Mix the egg, milk, salt, and pepper in a bowl.
9. Transfer the egg mixture evenly over the casserole.
10. Dot with butter.
11. Bake until heated through and golden, about 30 minutes.
12. Fill the jars with fish and rice casserole.
13. Put the jars in the canner then fill with water to the jar rings.
14. Close and lock the pressure canner and bring to a boil over high heat, then add cooking weight to the top.
15. After 20 minutes, turn the heat to medium and cook for 75 minutes.
16. Turn off the heat and leave the canner alone until it has cooled completely to room temperature.
17. After the canner has cooled, remove jars from the canner and check for sealing.

Per serving: Calories: 209.6kcal; Fat: 5.0g; Carbs: 18.8g; Protein: 21.1g

89. Pressure Canned Whole Clams

Preparation time: 10 minutes
Cooking time: 10 minutes
Servings: 7 pints
Ingredients:

- 5 lbs. Clam
- 3 tbsps. salt
- 2 tbsps. lemon juice

Directions:

1. Keep the clams cold in ice until you are ready to pressure can them.
2. Scrub the shells then stream them over water for 5 minutes. Open the clams and remove the meat. Save the juices.
3. Add a gallon of water to a mixing bowl then add (at most) 3 tbsps. of salt. Wash the clam meat in the salted water.
4. Add water to a shallow saucepan, then add lemon juice. Bring the water to boil. Add the clam meat and boil for 2 minutes.
5. Heat the reserved clam juices until boiling.
6. Drain the meat and pack it loosely into the jars leaving a 1-inch headspace. Pour the hot clam juice over the meat, then remove the bubbles.
7. You may add boiling water if you run out of the clam juice.
8. Process the sealed and cleaned jars at 10 pounds of pressure for 60 minutes.

9. Wait for the pressure canner to depressurize to zero before removing the jars.
10. Place the jars on a cooling rack for 12-24 hours undisturbed, and then store in a cool dry place.

Per serving: Calories: 148kcal; Fat: 2g; Carbs: 5.1g; Protein: 25.5g

90. Canned Spicy mackerel

Preparation time: 10 minutes
Cooking time: 100 minutes
Servings: 1 pint
Ingredients:

- Pickling spices
- 1 tsp Sea salt
- 1 lb. Whole mackerel

Directions:
1. Remove the head, tail, fins, and scales. The bones will soften.
2. Cut into 3 ½ inch pieces, then pack into jar. Add ½ tsp salt or pickling spice per jar.
3. Do not add any liquid.
4. Process the jar at 10 pounds pressure (weighted gauge) or 11 pounds pressure (dial gauge) for 100 minutes.
5. Let it cool naturally for 12 hours before removal and storage.

Per serving: Calories: 293kcal; Fat: 15.15g; Carbs: 25.03g; Protein: 14.96g

91. Canned Olive Oil Tuna

Preparation time: 5 minutes
Cooking time: 120 minutes
Servings: 6 half-pints
Ingredients:

- 4 tbsps. olive oil
- 3 tsps. kosher salt
- 2 ½ lbs. boneless skinless tuna (Bluefin or yellowfin)

Directions:
1. Wash tuna and discard connective tissue.
2. Cut into 2 ½ by 3-inch chunks, pack into jars, leaving 1 inch headspace.
3. Sprinkle ½ tsp kosher salt into each jar and pour olive oil in, leaving ¾ inch headspace.
4. Make sure the oil penetrates deep into the content.
5. Process jars at 11 pounds pressure for 1hr 40 minutes.
6. Let it cool before removal and storage.

Per serving: Calories: 289kcal; Fat: 10.26g; Carbs: 0g; Protein: 46.12g

92. Canned River Fish

Preparation time: 10 minutes
Cooking time: 125 minutes
Servings: 4 pints
Ingredients:

- 8 lbs. Trout
- 16 peppercorns, optional
- 4 tsps. canning salt

Directions:
1. Process your trout by cutting off the heads, tails, and fins. Discard those.
2. Pack the jars with 4 peppercorns and fish, leaving a 1 inch headspace, then add ½ tbsp. salt into each jar.
3. Process the jars under 11 pounds pressure for 1 hour 45 minutes.
4. Let them cool before removal and storage.

Per serving: Calories: 336kcal; Fat: 14.99g; Carbs: 0g; Protein: 47.11g

93. Simple Canned Salmon

Preparation time: 20 minutes (+ 1 hour to brine)

Cooking time: 1 hour 40 minutes
Servings: 4 pints
Ingredients:

- 2 pounds salmon fillets, skin-on or skinless
- 1 cup Diamond Crystal kosher salt
- 1 gallon water

Directions:

1. If you caught your own salmon, gut it within 2 hours of being caught. Remove the head, tail, and scales, but leave the skin on. Wash the fish and remove any blood. Keep the fish clean and refrigerated or on ice until you are ready to process it.
2. In a large food-safe container, dissolve the salt in the water to make a brine (it should dissolve without needing to heat the water).
3. Cut the salmon into 3-inch pieces, add to the brine, and refrigerate for 1 hour.
4. Prep 4-pint jars and your pressure canner according to the instructions in Pressure Canning, Step-by-Step.
5. Drain the fish and pack it into the hot jars, skin-side facing the glass, leaving 1 inch of headspace.
6. Remove any air bubbles, wipe the jar rims, secure the lids and rings finger-tight, and load the jars into the pressure canner. For 1 hour 40 minutes, process the jars at 10 pounds of pressure, adjusting for altitude.
7. Switch off the heat then let the pressure drop naturally.
8. Remove the lid and cool the jars in the canner for 5 minutes.
9. Take out the jars and cool further.
10. Inspect the lid seals after 24 hours.

Per serving: Calories: 358kcal; Fat: 13.31g; Carbs: 0g; Protein: 59.72g

94.   Canned Shad

Preparation time: 10 minutes
Cooking time: 120 minutes
Servings: 6 half-pints
Ingredients:

- 3 tsp kosher salt
- 2 ½ lbs. boneless skinless shad
- 1 gallon Water

Directions:

1. Make the brine by dissolving 1 cup salt in 1-gallon water.
2. Cut the fish into jar-length pieces. Let it soak for 1 hour, then drain for 10 minutes.
3. Pack the fish into jars, leaving a 1 inch headspace.
4. Process the jars at 10 pounds pressure for 1hr 40 minutes.
5. Let it cool for 12 hours before removal and storage.

Per serving: Calories: 249kcal; Fat: 7.67g; Carbs: 0g; Protein: 42.32g

Vegetable Recipes

95.   Pressure Canned Asparagus

Preparation time: 35 minutes
Cooking time: 50 minutes
Servings: 9-quart jars
Ingredients:

- 10 pounds asparagus
- Canning salt
- Boiling water

Directions:

1. First, bring the water to a boil using a pot over high heat.
2. Trim the asparagus so that they fit in the jars. Pack them in the jars, add 1/2

tablespoon of salt and the boiling water leaving 1-inch headspace.

3. Wipe the jar rims, place the lids, place the rings, and use your hands to tighten.

4. After this, put the jars in the pressure canner and process at 10 pounds for a minimum of 30 minutes for pints and at least 40 minutes for quarts.

5. Allow the pressure canner to depressurize before removing the jars.

Per serving: Calories: 52kcal; Fat: 1g; Carbs: 55g; Protein: 2g

96. Pressure Canned Plain Beets

Preparation time: 35 minutes
Cooking time: 55 minutes
Servings: 3-quart jars
Ingredients:

- 1 pound beets
- Water
- Pickling salt

Directions:

1. Trim the tops of the beets leaving an inch-long top. Also, leave the roots on the beets.

2. Wash the beets thoroughly with clean water, then put them in a pot.

3. Cover the beets with water and bring to boil for 15–25 minutes or until the skin can come out easily.

4. Remove the beets from the hot water then let them cool a little bit so that you can hold them. They should be at least warm when being put in the jar.

5. Trim the remaining stem and roots then peel the beets.

6. Slice the beets into large slices leaving the small ones whole. Put the beets in jars and leave a 1-inch headspace.

7. Add a 1/2 tablespoon of salt to each jar, then add boiling water to each jar.

8. Remove any bubbles in the jar and wipe the rims with a clean piece of cloth.

9. Put on the lids and the rings. Process the jars at 10 pounds for 30 minutes.

10. Let the pressure canner depressurize to zero before removing the jars.

Per serving: Calories: 52kcal; Fat: 1g; Carbs: 55g; Protein: 2g

97. Canned Sweet Potatoes

Preparation time: 35 minutes
Cooking time: 115 minutes
Servings: 10-quart jars
Ingredients:

- 10 pounds sweet potatoes
- Water
- 1–1/2 cup brown sugar
- 3 cups water

Directions:

1. Add the whole sweet potatoes into a stockpot, then add water until they are covered. Bring to a boil for 15 minutes.

2. Remove the sweet potatoes from the water and let them cool so that they are easy to peel.

3. Cut them into large chunks and pack them in the clean jars leaving a half-inch headspace.

4. Bring to boil 3 cups of water and add 1–1/2 cups of brown sugar until the sugar has dissolved.

5. Add boiled water to some of the jars and simple brown sugar syrup to others but maintain the headspace. Remove the bubble and add more hot water if necessary.

6. Clean the jar rims and place the lids and rings on. After this, place the jars in the canner and process at 10 pounds for 90 minutes for quart jars and 65 minutes for pint jars.

7. Let the pressure drop so that you can remove the jars from the canner.

Per serving: Calories: 200kcal; Fat: 8g; Carbs: 8g; Protein: 6g

98. Canned Broccoli

Preparation time: 35 minutes
Cooking time: 35 minutes
Servings: 4-pint jars
Ingredients:

- 4 pounds fresh broccoli
- Canning salt
- Water

Directions:

1. Soak and thoroughly wash the broccoli to remove all the dirt that could be in the head.
2. Cut the head into 2-inch pieces and discard the stems. You can also can the stems if you desire.
3. Place the broccoli in boiling water and let it boil for 3 minutes.
4. Use a slotted spoon to pack the broccoli in sterilized jars and add the hot water to each jar leaving 1-inch headspace. Release any air bubbles in each jar and add water if necessary.
5. Add 1 tablespoon of canning salt to each jar and wipe the rims with a clean towel. Place the lids and rings, then transfer the jars to the pressure canner.
6. Process the jars at 10 pounds for 30 minutes. Let the canner depressurize before removing the jars.
7. Let the jars rest overnight to store them in a cool dry place.

Per serving: Calories: 275kcal; Fat: 20g; Carbs: 8g; Protein: 20g

99. Canning Turnips

Preparation time: 35 minutes
Cooking time: 40 minutes
Servings: 12-pint jars
Ingredients:

- 10 pounds turnips
- Water

Directions:

1. Peel the turnips then dice them into small pieces.
2. Add the turnips to a stockpot and add cold water until just covered. Drain the water to get rid of dirt and debris.
3. Cover with water once more and bring them to boil over medium-high heat. Diminish the heat and let simmer for 5 minutes.
4. Utilize a slotted spoon to transfer the hot turnips to the sterilized jars. Fill the jar with the cooking liquid leaving 1-inch headspace. Add a half tablespoon of pickling salt.
5. Remove any air bubbles and add the cooking liquid if necessary. Wipe the pint jars and place the lids and rings.
6. Fill the pressure canner with the jars, and process them at 10 pounds for 30 minutes.
7. Allow the canner to depressurize to zero before removing the jars.

Per serving: Calories: 198kcal; Fat: 12g; Carbs: 20g; Protein: 5g

100. Pressure Canned Caramelized Onions

Preparation time: 35 minutes
Cooking time: 12 hours and 10 minutes
Servings: 6-pint jars
Ingredients:

- 6 pounds onions
- 2 butter sticks
- Water

Directions:

1. Peel the onions and also slice them into ¼-inch slices.

2. Melt 1 stick of butter in the stockpot over high heat and add the diced onions.

3. Slice another stick of butter over the onions. Cook on high for an hour until the butter has melted and the onions are sweating a little bit.

4. Reduce the heat and cook for 10 hours or overnight while stirring occasionally. The onions should be golden brown and well caramelized.

5. Ladle the onions in the sterilized hot jars then remove any air bubbles. Also, wipe the jar rims with a damp clean cloth.

6. Place the lid and rings on the jars and process them at 10 pounds pressure for 70 minutes.

7. Remove the pressure canner from heat then let its pressure reduce to zero before removing the jars.

Per serving: Calories: 198kcal; Fat: 12g; Carbs: 20g; Protein: 5g

101. **Canned Fiddleheads**

Preparation time: 35 minutes
Cooking time: 30 minutes
Servings: 1-pint jar
Ingredients:

- 2 cups fiddleheads
- ½ cup water
- ½ cup white vinegar
- 1 tablespoon salt
- ½ tablespoon peppercorns
- ½ tablespoon fennel
- ½ tablespoon coriander
- 1 sprig thyme
- 3 garlic cloves

Directions:

1. Trim off the cut ends and boil the fiddleheads for 10 minutes in salted water.

2. Strain the fiddleheads and rinse them with clean water. Pack the fiddleheads in the jars and leave a 1-inch headspace.

3. Add the spices directly to each jar on top of the fiddleheads.

4. Boil water, vinegar, and salt in a saucepan and pour over the fiddleheads.

5. Wipe the rims, then place the lids and the rings on the jars. After this, place the jars in the pressure canner and process at 10 pounds pressure for 10 minutes.

Per serving: Calories: 340kcal; Fat: 23g; Carbs: 8g; Protein: 28g

102. **Glazed Sweet Carrots**

Preparation time: 15 minutes
Cooking time: 70 minutes
Servings: 16 pints
Ingredients:

- 8 cups of brown sugar
- 10 pounds carrots
- 4 cups of orange juice
- 8 cups of water, filtered

Directions:

1. Wash carrots and drain them.

2. Combine orange juice, brown sugar, and water in a large-sized saucepan.

3. Heat on medium heat and stir till sugar dissolves.

4. Keep the mixture hot.

5. Place the raw carrots in the sterilized, hot jars.

6. Leave an inch of headspace.

7. Fill the jars with the hot syrup, still leaving an inch of headspace.

8. Tap the jars to remove any air bubbles.

9. Wipe the jar rims and screw on the lids.

10. Process the jars in a pressure canner for 1/2 hour under 10 pounds of pressure.
11. Store in a cool, dry area.

Per serving: Calories: 185kcal; Fat: 12g; Carbs: 4g; Protein: 11g

103. Pressure Canned Carrots

Preparation time: 20 minutes
Cooking time: 25 minutes
Servings: 7
Ingredients:

- 2 ½ pounds carrots
- 1 tablespoon salt
- 1 cup water

Directions:

1. Wash the carrots and trim them. Peel the carrots and wash them again, if you desire.
2. Slice the carrots into pieces according to your preferences.
3. Pack the carrots in the jars, leaving 1-inch headspace.
4. Add ½ tablespoon of salt to each jar, then add boiling water to each jar.
5. Rinse the jar rims with a clean, damp towel, and place the lids on the jars.
6. Arrange the jars in the pressure canner and process them for 25 minutes at 10 pounds of pressure.
7. Let the canner rest and depressurize before removing the jars.

Per serving: Calories: 340kcal; Fat: 15g; Carbs: 18g; Protein: 30g

104. Pressure Canned Potatoes

Preparation time: 15 minutes
Cooking time: 50 minutes
Servings: 7
Ingredients:

- 6 pounds cubed white potatoes
- Canning salt

Directions:

1. Wash the jars thoroughly, then place them in a cold oven. Heat it to 250°F.
2. Boil water in a pot. Also, add 4 inches of water to the pressure canner and place it over medium heat.
3. Add some salt to each jar, then fill with potatoes, leaving 1-inch headspace. Pour the boiling water into each jar, then use a canning knife to remove the air bubbles from the jars.
4. Rinse the jar rims and place the lids and rings on the jars.
5. Arrange the jars in the pressure canner and secure the lid according to the manufacturer's instructions.
6. Process the jars at 10 pounds for 40 minutes for quart jars and 35 minutes for pint jars.
7. Turn off the heat then let the canner depressurize before removing the jars. Place the jars on a towel, undisturbed, for 24 hours.
8. Store in a cool, dry place.

Per serving: Calories: 340kcal; Fat: 15g; Carbs: 18g; Protein: 30g

105. Pressure Canned Tomatoes

Preparation time: 30 minutes
Cooking time: 1 hour and 30 minutes
Servings: 6
Ingredients:

- 9 pounds ripe peeled and halved tomatoes
- 1 tablespoon lemon juice
- 1 tablespoon salt

Directions:

1. Pack the tomatoes in the sterilized jars while pressing them down so that the space between the tomato pieces is filled with their juices.
2. Leave a ½-inch headspace.

3. Add a tablespoon of lemon juice and ½ tablespoons of salt to each jar.

4. Rinse the rims and place the lids and the rings on the jars.

5. They can be in the pressure canner for 90 minutes at 10 pounds of pressure.

6. Wait for the pressure canner to depressurize to remove the jars.

7. Let the jars to cool, and then store them in a cool, dry place.

Per serving: Calories: 354kcal; Fat: 14g; Carbs: 16g; Protein: 26g

106. **Marinated Mushrooms**

Preparation time: 30 minutes
Cooking time: 35 minutes
Servings: 9 pints
Ingredients:

- ¼ cup pimiento, diced
- ½ cup lemon juice, bottled
- 1 tablespoon basil leaves, dried
- 2 ½ cups white vinegar, 5%
- ½ cup onions, chopped finely
- 7 pounds mushrooms, small, whole
- 2 cups oil, olive/salad
- 1 tablespoon oregano leaves
- 1 tablespoon pickling/canning salt
- 25 pieces black peppercorns
- Water
- Garlic clove

Directions:

1. Make sure your mushrooms are very fresh, still unopened, and have caps with a diameter of less than 1 ¼ inches.

2. Wash the mushrooms before cutting the stems, but leave a quarter of an inch still attached to their caps. Put in a saucepan then cover with water and lemon juice. Heat until boiling, and then simmer for 5 minutes before draining.

3. Add the vinegar, salt, basil, oregano, and olive oil to a saucepan. Stir to combine as you also add the pimiento and onions. Heat the mixture until boiling.

4. Meanwhile, fill each of your clean and hot mason jars (half-pint) with garlic cloves (1/4 portion) and peppercorns (2 to 3 pieces)

5. Add the cooked mushrooms and the hot liquid mixture, making sure to leave half an inch of headspace.

6. Take out any air bubbles before adjusting the lids.

7. Place the jars in the pressure canner and process for 20 minutes.

Per serving: Calories: 451kcal; Fat: 48.25g; Carbs: 2.97g; Protein: 0.49g

107. **Cucumber Slices**

Preparation time: 40 minutes
Cooking time: 20 minutes
Servings: 5 pints
Ingredients:

- 3-1/2 lb. pickling cucumbers
- 4 cups cider vinegar
- 3 cups Splenda
- 1 tbsp. canning salt
- 1 cup water
- 1 tbsp. mustard seed
- 1 tbsp. whole allspice
- 1 tbsp. celery seed
- 4 1-inch cinnamon sticks

Directions:

1. Remove the blossom end of the cucumbers and wash them.

2. Cut the cucumbers into 1/4-inch pieces, then pour boiling water over them. Let stand for 10 minutes.

3. Drain the hot water and pour running cold water on the cucumbers. Drain the cucumber slices thoroughly.

4. Mix all other ingredients except cinnamon sticks in a stockpot and allow it to boil. Add the cucumber slices and return to boil.

5. Place a cinnamon stick in each sterilized jar, then, using a slotted spoon, fill the jars with the hot cucumber pieces leaving a 1/2-inch headspace.

6. Remove any air bubbles then wipe the rims with a clean damp paper towel. Process the jars in the pressure canner at 10 pounds pressure for 10 minutes.

Per serving: Calories: 17kcal; Fat: 0.2g; Carbs: 3.1g; Protein: 0.8g

Soups, Stews and Broth Recipes

108. Mexican Beef and Sweet Potato Soup

Preparation time: 90 minutes
Cooking time: 80 minutes
Servings: 8-pint (500 ml) jars
Ingredients:

- 1 tbsp. vegetable oil
- 2-1/2 quarts beef broth
- 2-1/2 lbs. beef chuck roast, trimmed of fat & slice into one-inch dices
- 4 La Roma Tomatoes, seeded & sliced
- 1 medium sweet potato, peeled & sliced
- 8 1-inch diameter carrots, peeled & cut into 1/4-inch rounds
- 1 cup frozen/fresh whole kernel corn
- 1 large onion, sliced
- 2 jalapeño peppers, stemmed, seeded, & thinly sliced
- 2 Poblano peppers, stemmed, seeded & sliced
- 1 tbsp. salt
- 6 cloves garlic, minced
- 1/2 tbsp. ground black pepper
- 1/2 tbsp. chili powder

Directions:

1. Pour 1/2 tbsp. vegetable oil in a 6-quart pot and place over low-medium heat. Add half of the beef cubes. Fry and stir to turn brown. Move beef into a small bowl. Do the same with the remaining 1/2 tbsp. oil and beef. Transfer all the meat to the pot and add broth. Reduce heat and allow to it boil. Simmer covered until beef is soft.

2. Add sweet potatoes, carrots, tomatoes, onions, corn, garlic, jalapeno peppers, Poblano peppers, salt, black pepper, and chili powder to beef mixture in the pot. Cover and leave it to boil for five minutes.

3. Ladle the vegetables and beef into the canning jars by filling each halfway. Pour hot broth to every jar and leave one-inch headspace. Remove air bubbles, wipe jar rims, adjust lids, and screw band.

4. Set the filled jars in a pressure canner at 11 pounds pressure for dial-gauge or 10 pounds for the weighted-gauge canner. Process the heat jars for seventy-five minutes, adjusting for altitude. Switch off the heat and let pressure drop naturally. Remove the lid and cool the jars in the canner for five minutes. Take out the jars and cool. Inspect lids seal after twenty-four hours.

Per serving: Calories: 377 kcal; Fat: 6g; Carbs: 6.2g; Protein: 3g

109. Canned Chili Con Carne

Preparation time: 20 minutes
Cooking time: 60 minutes
Servings: 9 half pint jars
Ingredients:

- 3 cups pinto bean
- 51/2 cups water
- 5 tbsps. salt, divided
- 3 lbs. ground beef
- 11/2 cups chopped onion
- 1 cup chopped pepper
- 1 tbsp. black pepper
- 6 tbsps. Chili powder
- 8 cups crushed tomatoes

Directions:

1. Set the beans in a 2-quart saucepan, then add cold water 2-3 inches above the beans. Cover and refrigerate for about 12-18 hours to soak. Now drain the beans and discard the water.
2. Place the beans in a saucepot with 5 1/2 cups of water. Season with 2 tbsp. salt and set to a boil for about 25 minutes.
3. Simmer for about 30 minutes. **Meanwhile**, sauté the beef with onions and pepper (optional) in a skillet, then drain the fat off. Add 3 tbsp. salt and the remaining ingredients together with cooked beans and simmer for about 5 minutes. Make sure not to thicken the mixture.
4. Scoop hot chili stew into hot pint jars. Leave a 1-inch headspace. Do not use quart jars.
5. If needed, remove the air bubbles, adjusting the headspace.
6. Clean the rims of the jars using a clean, damp paper towel.
7. Now apply the 2-piece metal caps.
8. Process the pint jars in a pressure canner for about 75 minutes at 11 pounds pressure if using a dial-gauge canner, or a 10 pounds pressure if using a weighted-gauge canner.

Per serving: Calories: 556kcal; Fat: 11.4g; Carbs: 51g; Protein: 61.9g

110. Pea Soup with Carrot

Preparation time: 20 minutes
Cooking time: 1 hour 30 minutes
Servings: 6 pint jars
Ingredients:

- 6 quarts dried split peas
- 6 quarts water
- 41/2 cups diced carrots
- 3 cups chopped onion
- 3 cups cooked and diced ham
- 1/2 tsp. allspice
- salt and black pepper, to taste

Directions:

1. Mix the split peas and water in a large pot and boil.
2. Simmer for 1 hour while covered or until peas are soft. Mash the peas, if desired, with a potato masher.
3. Mix in the remaining ingredients and simmer for 30 minutes. Adjust the consistency of the soup by adding boiling water or broth if needed.
4. Add hot soup into hot jars, leaving 1-inch headspace. Following the "Pressure Canning" directions, process quarts for 90 minutes and pints for 75 minutes at 10 psi, adjusting the psi as necessary for your altitude according to the altitude adjustment directions.

Per serving: Calories: 118.7kcal; Fat: 2.6g; Carbs: 18.7g; Protein: 6.0g

111. Thick Beef Bone Broth

Preparation time: 20 minutes
Cooking time: 16 hour

Servings: 4 pint jars

Ingredients:

- 4 pounds (2 kg) meaty beef bones
- 2 quarts. (2 L) water
- 2 tablespoons (30 mL) unfiltered apple cider vinegar (5% acidity)
- 2 teaspoons (10 mL) salt
- 3 garlic cloves, crushed
- 2 bay leaves
- 1 large onion, quartered

Directions:

1. Preheat oven to 400°F (200°C). Bring beef bones to a large roasting pan. Bake at 400°F (200°C) for 30 minutes. Remove bones from the oven. Reduce oven temperature to 225 deg. F (107 deg. C). Add bones and pan drippings to a large stainless steel or enameled Dutch oven. Stir in water and remaining ingredients. Cover and bake at 225F (107C) for 8 hours.

2. Reduce oven temperature to 180°F (90°C), and bake 8 more hours. Remove bones from broth. Spill broth through a fine wire-mesh strainer into 2-quarts. (2-L) glass measure or large bowl; discard solids. Skim fat, and add water, if needed, until broth measures 2 quarts. (2 L). Place broth in a large Dutch oven; bring to a simmer.

3. Set hot broth into a hot jar, leaving 1-inch (2.5-cm) headspace. Detach air bubbles. Wipe jar rim. Center lid on jar. Apply band, and adjust to fingertip-tight. Bring jar on rack in a pressure canner containing 2 inches (5 cm) of simmering water (180°F90°C). Repeat until all jars are filled.

4. Bring lid on canner, and turn to locked position. Change heat to medium-high. Vent steam for 10 minutes. Bring the counter weight or weighted gauge on vent; bring pressure to 10 pounds (psi)

for a weighted-gauge canner or 11 pounds (psi) for a dial-gauge canner.

5. Perform 1-pt. (500-mL) jars for 20 minutes or 1-quarts. (1-L) jars for 25 minutes. Set off heat; cool canner to zero pressure. Set stand 5 more minutes before removing lid.

6. Cool jars in canner 10 minutes. Detach jars and cool.

Per serving: Calories: 412kcal; Fat: 20.9g; Carbs: 10.4g; Protein: 43.8g

112. Potato and Leek Soup

Preparation time: 20 minutes
Cooking time: 30 minutes
Servings: 7 pint jars
Ingredients:

- 6 cubed potatoes
- 4 cups stock, chicken or beef
- 5 lbs. sliced leeks

Directions:

1. Layer leaks at the bottom of each jar. Place a layer of potatoes on top of the leeks, followed by another layer of the sliced leeks.

2. Boil the chicken or beef stock before pouring into the jars. Make sure to leave about an inch of space at the top of each jar.

3. Attach the lids to the jars and process in a pressure canner using 11 pounds for 60 minutes.

Per serving: Calories: 462kcal; Fat: 2.34g; Carbs: 101.1g; Protein: 14.26g

113. Canned Turkey Stock

Preparation time: 20 minutes
Cooking time: 30 minutes
Servings: 1 pint jar
Ingredients:

- turkey bones, meat removed

- water, to cover
- salt, to taste
- 1 bay leaf

Directions:

1. Place the bones with enough water to cover the bones in a pressure cooker.
2. Add the bay leaf and cook on high pressure for about 30 minutes until the remaining meat falls off from the bones.
3. Sieve the stock into a sizable bowl and discard loosened meat from bones. Refrigerate the stock overnight.
4. Discard the Fat by skimming, and then reheat the stock in a saucepot.
5. Pour the stock into quart jars leaving a 1-inch headspace.
6. Clean the rims of the jars using a clean, damp paper towel.
7. Apply the 2-piece metal caps.
8. Process the quart jars in a pressure canner for 25 minutes at 11 pounds pressure if using a dial-gauge canner, or a 10 pounds pressure if using a weighted-gauge canner.

Per serving: Calories: 20kcal; Fat: 0g; Carbs: 1g; Protein: 4g

114. Late Season Garden Stew

Preparation time: 20 minutes
Cooking time: 1 hour and 30 minutes
Servings: 6 pint jars
Ingredients:

- 8 cups water or stock
- 1 tablespoon dried thyme
- 1/2 tablespoon dried marjoram
- 2 tablespoons dried parsley
- 4 pounds (1.8 kg) cubed beast
- 4 to 6 cups cubed root vegetables
- 2 cups carrot rounds
- 3 cups finely chopped onion

- 6 cloves garlic, crushed and minced

Directions:

1. In a stockpot, combine water or stock, thyme, marjoram, and parsley, and set to a boil.
2. Set the meat and vegetables into your jars.
3. Spill the hot liquid over the layered meat and vegetables. Add more water if needed. Leave 1 to 11/2-inches of headspace.
4. Lid your jars and process them in your pressure canner for 90 minutes at 10 PSI. Be sure to adjust for altitude.

Per serving: Calories: 627kcal; Fat: 29.2g; Carbs: 11.2g; Protein: 80.9g

115. Split Pea Soup

Preparation time: 20 minutes
Cooking time: 90 minutes
Servings: 2 pint jars
Ingredients:

- 1 lb. yellow, dry split peas
- 2 quarts water
- 4 tsps. lime juice
- 3/4 cups sliced carrots
- 1 cup chopped onions
- 2 minced garlic cloves
- 1/2 tsp. cayenne pepper
- 1 tsp. cumin seed and coriander
- 1 tsp. salt

Directions:

1. Allow the water with split peas in it to come to a boil in a large stockpot. Let it gently simmer without covering until the peas become soft; this will take about an hour.
2. Add the other ingredients and allow it to continue simmering for 30 minutes more. Check the consistency and thin out the water if necessary.

3. Ladle it into the jars and leave a headspace of 1 inch. Put cap on and seal. Put it in a canner with hot water of 2-3 inches and allow a processing time of 90 minutes at high pressure.

Per serving: Calories: 158kcal; Fat: 2.8g; Carbs: 26g; Protein: 8.3g

116. Tomato Soup with Celery

Preparation time: 20 minutes
Cooking time: 80 minutes
Servings: 8 pint jars
Ingredients:

- 6 sliced onions
- 1 bunch sliced celery
- 5-quarts tomato juice
- 1 cup sugar
- 1/4 cup salt
- 1 cup butter
- 1 cup flour

Directions:

1. Add chopped celery and onions to a large pot with a little amount of water to prevent them from burning. Place pot over medium heat. Bring to a boil. While boiling, add tomatoes to the pot and cook to become softened. Pour the combination all through a strainer and then return to the pot. Add salt and sugar.

2. Combine flour and butter. Mix evenly and add 2 cups of cold juice until well blended. Add flour and butter mixture to warm juice (before it is hot to prevent flour lumps). Stir well. The flour can turn lumpy if it reaches a boil, so only heat to hot and turn off the heater before boiling. It will keep thickening as it cools.

3. Ladle hot soup into each canning jar. Remember to leave a one-inch headspace. Use a spatula to free air bubbles, then use a clean cloth to wipe jar rims. After that, adjust lids and screw band.

4. Bring the filled jars in a pressure canner at 11 pounds pressure for dial-gauge or 10 pounds for the weighted-gauge canner. Perform heat jars for 25 minutes, adjusting for altitude. Switch off the heat then let the pressure drop naturally. Detach the lid and cool the jars in the canner for three minutes. Take out the jars and cool. Inspect lids seal after twenty-four hours.

Per serving: Calories: 126.9kcal; Fat: 9.3g; Carbs: 10.1g; Protein: 2.5g

117. Venison and Tomato Chili

Preparation time: 20 minutes
Cooking time: 30 minutes
Servings: 8 half pint jars
Ingredients:

- 6 lbs. chopped venison
- 6 cups canned tomatoes
- 1/2 cup chili powder
- 2 cups chopped onions
- 41/2 tsp. salt
- 1 tsp. cumin seeds
- 2 minced jalapeno peppers
- 2 minced garlic cloves

Directions:

1. Sterilize the jars.
2. Brown the meat in a skillet in batches and then transfer it into a pot.
3. Stir fry the garlic and onions in a skillet and add it to the pot with the remaining ingredients.
4. Bring to a boil and then cook for 20 minutes at reduced heat.
5. Ladle the mix immediately into the sterilized jars, leaving one inch of headspace.

6. Free of any air bubbles and clean the rims.

7. Secure the jars with the lid and apply the bands, making sure that it is tightened.

8. Process the jars for 75 at 10 pounds pressure in a pressure canner.

9. Remove and allow to cool then label the jars.

Per serving: Calories: 150.3kcal; Fat: 2.7g; Carbs: 5.2g; Protein: 26.1g

118. American Chicken Stock

Preparation time: 20 minutes
Cooking time: 30 minutes
Servings: 1 pint jar
Ingredients:

- chicken bones
- water, to cover

Directions:

1. Place bones in a pressure cooker and add water to cover.

2. Cook on high pressure for about 30 minutes until the remaining meat falls off the bones.

3. Sieve the stock into a huge bowl and discard the loosened meat from the bones. Refrigerate the stock overnight.

4. Skim off and discard the fat, then reheat the stock in a saucepot.

5. Pour the stock into 1-liter US quart jars, leaving a 1-inch headspace.

6. Clean the rims of the jars using a paper towel, dampened and clean.

7. Apply the 2-piece metal caps.

8. Can the quart jars in a pressure canner for 25 minutes.

Per serving: Calories: 17kcal; Fat: 0g; Carbs: 2g; Protein: 2g

119. Squash Soup with Chili

Preparation time: 20 minutes

Cooking time: 30 minutes
Servings: 3 pint jars
Ingredients:

- 8 cups chicken or vegetable broth
- 1/2 tsp. ground red pepper
- 3 minced garlic cloves
- 2 minced Thai chilies
- 1 quartered lemongrass stalk
- 1 grated ginger
- 11/2 lbs. cubed butternut
- 2 tbsps. sugar
- 2 tsps. salt
- 1 tsp. lime zest
- 2 tbsps. lime juice
- 4 chopped shallots
- 1 chopped red bell pepper
- 1/2 cup coconut milk
- 2 tbsps. red onion slivers
- 1 tbsp. chopped cilantro
- lime wedges

Directions:

1. Boil the broth in a 6-qt (6-L) stainless steel or enameled Dutch oven. Stir in ground red pepper and the next 4 ingredients; cover, reduce heat, and simmer for 20 minutes, stirring occasionally.

2. Remove lemongrass. Add squash and the next 6 ingredients. Simmer for 5 minutes as you stir.

3. Set hot soup into a hot jar, leaving 1-inch (2.5cm) headspace.

4. Remove air bubbles. Wipe jar rim. Center lid on jar. Apply band and adjust to fingertip tight. Set jar on rack in a pressure canner containing 2 inches (5cm) of simmering water 180°F (82°C).

5. Repeat until all jars are filled.

6. Tighten the lid on the canner and switch to the locked position.

7. Set the heat to medium-high. Vent steam for 10 minutes. Set the counterweight or weighted gauge on vent; bring pressure to 10 pounds (psi) for a weighted-gauge canner or 11 pounds (psi) for a dial-gauge canner.

8. Perform 1-pint jars for 1 hour and 15 minutes or 1-quart jars for 1 hour and 30 minutes.

9. Cool jars in canner for 10 minutes. Remove jars and cool.

10. Serve with lime wedges.

Per serving: Calories: 110.9kcal; Fat: 2.3g; Carbs: 18.3g; Protein: 5.6g

120. **Polish Cabbage Roll Soup**

Preparation time: 20 minutes
Cooking time: 60 minutes
Servings: 6 pint jars
Ingredients:

- 3 pounds (1.4 kg) ground beef
- 6 cups shredded cabbage
- 11/2 cups shredded carrots
- 2 medium onions, finely chopped
- 6 cloves garlic, minced
- 12 cups tomato juice
- 3 tablespoons brown sugar
- 11/2 cups white vinegar
- 2 tablespoons dried oregano
- 2 tablespoons dried basil
- Salt and pepper, to taste

Directions:

1. Layer meat, cabbage, carrots, onion, and garlic in equal parts across your jars.

2. In a large stockpot, combine tomato juice, sugar, vinegar, salt, pepper, and herbs. Heat this mixture to a simmer for 10 minutes.

3. Top the ingredients in the jars with your canning liquid. If needed, add more water, leaving 1 inch of headroom.

4. Process in a pressure canner at 11 PSI for 90 minutes. Be sure to adjust for altitude.

Per serving: Calories: 110.9kcal; Fat: 2.3g; Carbs: 18.3g; Protein: 5.6g

Conclusion

Canning is a widely used way of preserving food that has been around for quite some time. Compared to purchasing food from a grocery store that has additives, this is a far better and more cost-effective choice. Preserving food by putting it in a can, heating it to a certain temperature for a certain amount of time, and then storing it away from light is known as canning. In this experiment, we autoclaved the food in the can for thirty minutes. After a week, the color, aroma, taste, and texture of the canned beef curry that was produced are examined, where the odor generates a horrible stench while the color goes to light grey. The overall acceptability of the canned meat curry is also rated. Both the flavor and general acceptability are diminished compared to the fresh beef curry. The flavor becomes less pleasant. The accuracy of the outcome may be affected because of some errors that occurred during this experiment. While carrying out this experiment, several preventative measures have to be carried out to cut down on the number of mistakes that occur. These measures also need to be taken to make sure that quality characteristics like color and texture are not compromised. Because of this, one may conclude that the beef curry's texture and sensory qualities improve in direct proportion to the length of time it is heated.

Book 7:

DEHYDRATOR COOKBOOK FOR PREPPERS

1200 Days of Easy and Affordable Homemade Recipes to Dehydrate Fruit, Meat, Vegetables, Bread, Herbs.
An Essential Guide to Be Totally Prepared for Any Emergency

Jonathan Henry

Introduction

Some people ask: "Why bother dehydrating your food?" Food is abundant anyway, and dehydrating individual ingredients takes a long time. For some people, fresh food is always better than dried ones; the latter is readily available in most supermarkets.

First off, there's a difference between dehydrated and dried food.

Dehydrating or desiccating food (terms that can be used interchangeably) entails the application of gentle heat to gradually remove 30% to 75% moisture from individual ingredients. Traditional methods include air-drying, smoking, or sun-drying. These methods take some time, dramatically changing the appearance, color, shape, texture, and more importantly, the taste of the original ingredients.

Aromas and flavors intensify too. In some cases, fermentation (due to the remaining moisture within) is encouraged to further improve the taste of the food, as with the case of cured meat (e.g., bacon) and salted fish (e.g., bacalhau or cured cod.)

Commercial or large-scale food processing uses either drum-drying (using lightly heated drums to tumble-dry viscous food, e.g., mashed potato or oatmeal) or spray-drying (spraying liquid in a container with circulating hot air to produce powder or fine flakes, e.g., instant coffee or powdered milk.)

Today, processing food using dehydrators or conventional ovens are becoming common. These are easier to handle and considerably speed up the drying process, especially on a small or minute (home use) scale.

The lifespan of dehydrated food depends greatly on the quality and moisture content of the original ingredient. Some may need further treatment to prevent premature decay, such as chilling, freezing, or steeping in oil.

On the other hand, most items labeled as "dried food" are usually freeze-dried.

Also called cryodesiccation and lyophilization, freeze-drying is a form of dehydration that uses sub-zero temperatures to draw out moisture from food. Once frozen, pressure is applied gradually. This turns frozen moisture into gas. Ingredients undergo light processing (e.g., cleaning, rinsing, curing, etc.), freezing, primary drying, and second drying, which removes almost 90% to 99% of their moisture.

When processed correctly, freeze-dried food may be stored at room temperature for years, even without refrigeration. The reduced moisture content inhibits food-degrading enzymes and microorganisms' actions, growth, and spread.

Freeze-dried ingredients are easier to reconstitute (rehydrate) because the process leaves microscopic pores inside the food when ice crystals form and evaporate. Ingredients retain most of their original color, shape, and taste. The texture is compromised, though.

To avoid confusion, it focuses on how to dehydrate or desiccate ingredients using a conventional oven or a dehydrator.

Let's get started!

The Wonder of Dehydrating

A dried item means that its water content has been decreased to a minimum level or, more precisely, 10 percent or less. A constant level of heat used in dehydration evaporates moisture from the food, and the air circulating around it absorbs the moisture. Although the process changes the food's appearance, its nutritional value remains unchanged.

Dehydration is a super-easy and inexpensive way to preserve food for extended periods by maintaining the same nutritional value without using unnatural preservatives compared to other complicated and extensive methods. As an additional benefit, it's a big space-saver for stacking our pantries and making delightful meals and innovative snacks.

Dehydrating food is not difficult, but there are a few things you need to know before you try it for yourself. Below is a collection of tips to help you get the most out of your food dehydration:

- Always start with high-quality ingredients – choose ripe, unbruised fruits and vegetables and fresh meats.
- Prepare your food items in the way you want them to be served. For example, if you want to make apple chips, you need to slice the apple – you won't be able to dehydrate a whole apple and then slice it.
- Always wash your produce before preparing it for dehydration – this applies to fruits, vegetables, and herbs.
- If you want to keep fruits and vegetables from browning, brush them with lemon juice. Blanching or lightly steaming vegetables may also help.
- Maintain a stable temperature in your food dehydrator between 130°F and 140°F with constant air circulation.

- Once your food is properly dried, you should store it in an airtight container immediately after it has cooled. Store your containers in a cool, dark location.
- Check your stored food periodically to ensure it is still dry – the food may spoil if it is exposed to moisture.

The fundamental reason for dehydrating foods is preservation, preventing them from rotting and extending their life. By reducing moisture in foods, we create an unsuitable environment for microorganisms, the sole causes of decay and rotting. Proper storage ensures that it is safe from heat and moisture found in the air, hence lengthening its shelf life.

Food dehydration or drying involves the different methods or processes of removing the moisture content (water) from the food you want to keep for prolonged use.

The moisture content is removed so that microorganisms (enzymes) that cause the spoilage or decaying are prevented, thus increasing the shelf life of seasonally abundant fruits or vegetables. The food is dried using hot, dry air.

The actual dehydration is simple, with all the preliminaries along the way. Temperature, airflow, and time are three ingredients.

Water will migrate from a region where it is more concentrated to somewhere where it is less concentrated on the premise that there is a means for that migration. At higher temperatures, the air can retain more humidity than it does at lower temperatures. For an extreme example, just 17 percent relative humidity at 72 degrees would provide the amount of moisture required to provide a relative humidity of 80 percent at a temperature of 30 degrees. And the colder the air, the quicker and more deeply it can suck moisture out of the food you dehydrate.

A Winding stream is required to evacuate dampness-loaded air and convey a lower mugginess in the outside air. In present-day dehydrators, this is practiced with a fan with experience, you'll build up an eye for this, yet until your eye is created, here are a few different ways to test whether organic products are sufficiently dry. Take a bit of the natural product, and tear it fifty-fifty. Crush it as hard as possible close to the torn edge. On the off chance that it shows no proof of dampness close to the tear, it is finished. Another sign for most organic products (aside from prunes, dates, and raisins) is that they don't remain together. The last test is to take a few pieces while still hot from the dehydrator and put them in a fixed sack, (for example, a zipper sandwich pack) at that point pop the pack in the cooler. Return an hour and check whether there is a buildup within the pack. In the event that there is, the organic product should be dried longer. On the off chance that there's no buildup, it is finished; however, it should likewise be possible through a "smokestack impact" on the grounds that tourist is lighter than cold air and will normally rise. So, some dehydrators that don't have fans have vents in the base for outside air and vents at the top for warm air to exit.

What Should and Shouldn't Be Dehydrated

Fruits and vegetables are the easiest and most forgiving foods to process. Dried fruit can be eaten without rehydrating. It's a nutrient-dense food that makes an ideal snack. It can be added to oatmeal, muffins, and hot cereal to improve the nutritional quality of simple meals.

Dried vegetables are convenient for soups, stews, sauces, and dips where they can be rehydrated in the cooking process. Aromatic vegetables like onions, garlic, carrots, celery, and peppers can be used as ingredients in meals on their own or combined into spice blends to add flavor to other dishes.

Lean meat, poultry, and fish can also be dehydrated, provided a few precautions are taken with these high-protein foods. When dehydrating, temperatures should reach 165°F (74°C) to kill any spoilage organisms. If your dehydrator doesn't go this high, place the food in the dehydrator at 145°F for at least 4 hrs, till it is done. Then put it in a preheated oven at 275°F for 10 minutes so that it reaches an internal temperature of 165 deg. F or 74 deg. C.

Cured ham can be successfully dehydrated, but pork should never be dehydrated at home or used for jerky. The temperatures used in a home dehydrator cannot destroy the trichinella parasite or other harmful bacteria that are commonly found in pork.

Raw eggs and milk products do not dehydrate well. They are prone to bacterial contamination at dehydrating temperatures.

Fatty and oily foods cannot be dried adequately in a home dehydrator. The fat won't dry properly and as a result, the food spoils quickly. This includes high-fat foods such as avocados and olives.

When dehydrating meat, you should remove all visible fat. Only lean meat, poultry, or fish should be used for dehydrating. Ground meat should be no more than 10 percent fat. Fish like salmon and mackerel have too high a fat content to make them good candidates for dehydrating; they can be dried for short-term storage, but they should not be used for long-term storage due to the increased risk of spoilage.

Benefits Of Dehydrating

Dehydrated Food Tastes Great

Although there are many benefits to consuming fresh ingredients, some dehydrated food like bacon and ham taste good on their own. Dried fish and shrimp are both briny and succulent, which makes them excellent for use in soups and stews.

Dehydrated fruits like apples, bananas, and mangoes make tasty, low-fat, gluten-free snacks. Dried cinnamon bark and desiccated coconut make versatile ingredients in baked goods and beverages. Dehydrated flowers and petals (e.g., hibiscus and lavender) can be used in herbal teas.

Many people love these ingredients because of their intense flavors. When properly reconstituted, using small amounts in dishes brings out a depth of flavor that fresh ingredients can't provide.

Saves Space

Saving space is another reason to start dehydrating. Removing moisture from food shrinks it dramatically, so you can now fit 20+ pounds of dried food in a cupboard easily. For maximum space-saving, using freezer bags is better than glass jars or containers because you can lay them flat. They can also be vacuum-sealed and shrunk even further. For small kitchens and pantries, storage won't be a problem anymore when you dehydrate what you can.

It's Cost-Effective

The primary benefit of dehydrated food is its cost-effectiveness. The longer shelf life results in saving money from not throwing out food because it has gone bad. Dehydrated foods can last for years without electricity to keep the food cool, thus it saves energy too.

Retained Nutritional Values

As compared to other preservation methods like freezing or canning, dehydration retains maximum dietary benefits. Dehydrated food is more calorie-dense, meaning there is a big difference between 1 ounce of dried kiwis and 1 ounce of fresh kiwis.

A Snack In A Snap

Dehydrated foods can serve as healthy snacks that you can have any time a need arises. Moreover, you can add dried fruits and vegetables to a plethora of meals and dishes to give them a creative touch and amaze your family and guests at the same time.

Easy To Carry Around

There aren't a lot of truly portable snacks, and the ones that are, like fruits and vegetables, are easily squished and bruised. When they're dry, they're hardened and much more durable. They also don't take up much space in a bag and they don't squirt juice everywhere when you're trying to eat them. Dehydrated food is the way to go if you're always on the run. Dehydrating food at home saves money and space, makes clean and tasty snacks, and reduces food waste.

Reduces Waste

We throw away a ton of food. In the US, we waste over $160 billion in food every year. While a lot of that comes from restaurants and grocery stores, the average person wastes a lot of the food they buy. It's basically like throwing away money. By dehydrating foods that don't stay fresh for very long, you're doing your part to reduce waste while getting the most bang for your buck.

Dehydrated Food Is Easy To Store

When moisture is removed from food, it can be condensed and stored in smaller containers. These consume less space in the cupboard, fridge, or pantry.

Store dried fruits, meat, and vegetables in small food-grade containers, like freezer-safe bags, resealable pockets, or vacuum pouches. Slip these into lunch boxes, picnic bags, or even coat pockets. It's highly portable.

It's Natural

Drying is one of the few methods of food storage that maintains almost all the organic characteristics and nutrients. Dried food does not go through any chemical or mechanical intervention, nor are any preservatives or other artificial substances added. The process of eliminating water deprives the microorganisms of the fundamental element for their action and, ultimately, blocks their activity. A Lack of liquids inhibits the development of microbes and prevents the oxidation of foods.

For Food Preservation

Food dehydration helps preserve your food until it's needed in the future. Perhaps you need to take a long journey. Food dehydration will sustain you through the journey and save you from the stress of cooking all the time.

Keeps Food Fresh

This is another important reason people dehydrate their food. Dehydration will help you keep your food fresh for a long period of time. For example, if you buy excess meat or fish, sun-drying will help you get that good taste at any time.

Saves Resources

Practicing food dehydration helps save money and food that would have been wasted out of ignorance. Knowing how to dehydrate your nuts, fish, meat, fruits, vegetables, and so on, will allow you to buy them in bulk and save money you would have spent buying food every day in a lower quantity. Or you might sometimes buy more food than you needed. Learning the simple steps of food preservation will help you to keep the remaining raw food. Food dehydration is an effective way to be economical.

Food Availability

This could be your best reason to dehydrate your foods. You'll have access to food at home any time you want it. Food dehydration prevents you from eating just anything you see outside. You'll save time by preparing enough food at home that will last until you feel it is needed.

For Emergency Purposes

One of the many ways to sustain life is to prepare for the unforeseen. There may be times you are broke and falling back on your dehydrated food will be of great help. Or if there is a sudden increase in food prices, your dehydrated foods will also save you from unnecessary spending. Food dehydration could be your savings for the dry season.

There are many benefits to dehydrating food. Generally, it will help you keep fresh food, as it retains the vitamins and other nutrients. Keep reading to learn more about dehydrated food!

It's Cheap

A dried product can be stored without the need for cold storage and without the cost of storing it in oil, vinegar, or salt. And the benefits of a pantry full of typically summery products that can be consumed in the middle of winter are obvious. No need to buy gold vegetables and fruits to taste the flavors of summer in December. It'll be enough to open a jar and prepare tomatoes, eggplant, figs, or mushrooms in the way you prefer.

It's Easy

Drying is a simple and intuitive method that everyone can take advantage of. You'll just need a little hand with thicknesses and drying times, but any product can be stored at its best. Drying does not require any special skills and does not require reading long and complex instruction manuals. Anyone who knows how to use a knife will find drying an easy and fun way to simplify food preparation without sacrificing a natural diet.

Dehydrating Methods

Oven Dehydration

The electric or gas oven in your home can help you dehydrate food, though not on a large scale. There is always the problem of controlling temperature, as the temperature must be preferably around 150F.

When drying food in the oven, leave the oven door open by 2 to 3 inches, and if your oven lacks a built-in fan system, place a small fan outside the oven door to blow out the moist air.

Occasional drying of tomatoes, bananas, apples, sweet potatoes, mixed nuts for snacking, or even meat jerky will prove successful if the proper temperature is maintained throughout.

Always remember to slice your vegetables, fruits, or meat evenly and of the same size. Place your food on cookie sheets on cake cooling racks on oven trays. The trays should be rotated in between for even drying.

Do not dry your fruits and vegetables together, as they require different amounts of time for drying.

Be careful when drying food in the oven as you can easily get burned if you do not pay enough attention, or especially if you have small children around.

Sun Drying

This process is best done with fruits, which have high acid and sugar content, unlike meats and vegetables (except vine-dried beans). Meats contain high amounts of protein, which make them vulnerable to microbial growth when exposed to uncontrollable humidity and heat.

It is best to dry fruits at high temperatures, which should not go lower than 85 degrees Celsius. Sun dry them when the weather is breezy, hot, and dry. Cover the fruits or bring them under shelter at night. The air at night is cool and condenses, returning moisture to the food. Place screens or racks on blocks to keep the right flow of the air. Since the materials will come into contact with the food, use plastic, stainless steel or Teflon-coated fiberglass. Food that is dried using this process will finish dehydrating after a week or longer.

Solar Drying

In this process, the sun's rays are collected in a box that is specifically created for this purpose. This gives more about 30 degrees higher in temperature than when your dry food is in open sunlight. This makes the process faster, then but still not as efficient as with the use of a commercial dehydrator. In these first two processes, you need the weather to stay dry all throughout, or else, your food will absorb moisture and might spoil.

Vine Drying

This method is typically used to dry beans, such as kidney beans and navy beans. Leave the bean pods on the vine and allow nature to take its course. The beans can be picked when they are rattling inside. The process is also ideal for drying raisins.

Air Drying

Air drying can be done indoors if you have sufficient ventilation inside your home. This is a much gentler way to dry your food, especially herbs. This process requires no activity from our side, but it takes a long time for the food to dry as it depends on the air to dry rather than heat.

Dehydrator-Drying

Dehydrating with a food dehydrator is the best method these days. You have control over temperature, time, and airflow. You place food on a tray, close the lid, and heat it at the appropriate temperature with an electrical heating element for the given time. Times vary depending on what you're drying and how much. A fan circulates heat around the food, while vents allow the moist air to escape.

How To Rehydrating: Methods

Rehydrating restores the moisture to dried food, returning it to its original size, form, and appearance. Rehydrated food retains its aroma, flavor, and texture as well as its nutritional content. There are several methods for rehydrating dried food, but in their simplest form, they all add moisture back into the food using either cold or hot liquids.

As a general rule, 1 cup of liquid reconstitutes 1 cup of dehydrated food. If the food hasn't softened enough after an hour, add more liquid. The liquid can be plain water, broth, juice, or milk. Fruit can also be reconstituted in liqueur or brandy.

Most fruit and vegetables reconstitute in one to two hours. However, larger pieces of food may take longer to reconstitute than powders or finely diced pieces. Generally, food that took longer to dehydrate also takes longer to rehydrate. Use only enough liquid as the food will absorb. Using too much liquid makes the food soggy and unappetizing.

Soaking does not take the place of cooking. Food still needs to be cooked after it is reconstituted by soaking.

Save the soaking liquid to add to soups, stews, or cereals. It contains the water-soluble vitamins and minerals leached from the dehydrated food.

Methods

Quick soak: Some things can be rehydrated with a quick dip in boiling water. For instance, the Dehydrated Apple-Potato Cakes require dipping in boiling water for less than 10 seconds before being placed in a hot frying pan to crisp. This also applies to greens such as spinach and collard greens.

15-minute soak: The majority of dried fruits and vegetables can be rehydrated in 15 minutes or less by soaking them in a basin of hot water that has been covered before their use in a recipe. This can be done while preparing other ingredients in order to save time.

Rehydration by refrigeration: This approach is ideal for rehydrating dehydrated items so that they are ready to use when you return home from work. Place 1½ cups of sliced dehydrated items such as; beets, apples, peaches, or zucchini into a 24-ounce canning jar. (If using small or diced ingredients like peas, corn kernels, or onions, use approximately 2/3 cup of the dehydrated ingredient.) For dehydrated vegetables, fill the jar to the brim with boiling water. For dehydrated fruits, fill containers to the brim with lukewarm water, fruit juice, or flavored water. For vegetables, after the water has cooled, keep the jar in the refrigerator for 24 hours (put fruit immediately into the fridge). The rehydrated foods offer a tasty snack straight from the jar. If you rehydrate cucumber spears, chips, or other veggies in brine in this manner, you will have the easiest pickles ever—they will be crunchy, cool, and ready to eat the next day!

Pros And Cons Of Dehydration

Pros

Dehydration is healthy for consumption because of the following reasons:

- Retains Nutrients: When we dehydrate foods, the nutrients in the food are one of our primary concerns. Unlike other methods of preservation, dehydration saves the nutrients in the dehydrated food, when it is carried out effectively.
- Bactcria Free: Dehydrated foods are germ-free. When we keep these foods for a long period of time, they still maintain their healthy state.
- No Addition of External Chemicals: The heat used to dehydrate food is the only external requirement for the process. This heat contains no chemicals or acids that may be dangerous

to the food. Unlike some preservative methods which engage the addition of preservative chemicals, dehydration is a healthy choice for storing food.

- Safe Handling: Since dehydration has nothing to do with handling dangerous chemicals or intense equipment, it is safe for the user to dehydrate easily. Dehydration can be done with the simplest household mechanical devices like an oven, microwave, or dehydrator. The smoke or steam that escapes from dehydrating food is not unhealthy to the environment, unlike the regular burning of waste products. This makes the process healthy.

Cons

- Time Consumption: Dehydrating food requires a lot of time in order to achieve perfect results. Some foods have a large amount of water content and reducing the water will require a lot of time and meticulous observation. Taking so much time may be inconvenient for some individuals.

- Unwanted Weight Gain: Dehydrated food might be rich in calories. Since it has shrunken in size, it may appear small; a small quantity consumed may seem insufficient, while a large quantity consumed implies large nutrient consumption. The excess calories in the dehydrated food may lead to weight gain. People should be aware of it when consuming dried food.

- Loss of Nutrients: Although, when done correctly, dehydrating food can preserve nutrients when done incorrectly it may lead to loss of nutrients in the food. Some nutrients can't stand high levels of heat. The degree of heat applied therefore determines the survival of the nutrients in food. If the dehydrated food is not stored properly too, the nutrient can be lost due to excessive heat and poor storage conditions.

- Change in Taste and Look: With high heat, the appetizing appearances of common meals change. In most cases, people are easily turned off when foods don't wear the expected looks. When foods are dehydrated, the loss of water makes them shrink and their looks drastically change.

- Technical Knowledge: Since not all foods are dehydrated in the same way or following the same pattern, dehydration requires technical knowledge in order to be carried out well. There is also the place of experience that gradually makes a person perfect in the art.

Why Dehydration Is Healthy?

Fresh fruits and vegetables are the best sources to get vitamins, minerals, sugars, proteins, and other healthy nutrients essential to good health. How important it is, then, that we do everything we can to conserve these nutrients. Even after being picked or gathered, fruits and vegetables are still living things that can go on with their own life's 'processes.' After the product is taken away from its source of life, if these 'processes' aren't stopped, they destroy the quality of the product because they include the oxidization of valuable parts of the product.

"The Chemical changes that hurt the quality of a product and attacks by organisms that cause decay can be slowed down by putting it in the fridge until it's processed, however, this storage should be as short as possible; last no more than two days."

Only products that are in prime conditions should be dried. This means that they are at their best for drying when they are fully grown and fresh from the garden or orchard.

Dehydrated fruits and vegetables that have been rehydrated and cooked have about the same amount of carbs, fats, proteins, minerals, and bulk as the original fresh fruits and vegetables that have been prepared in the same way. The proteins and minerals in dehydrated foods after reconstituting are not different from those of the original foods if dehydrated as long as they were dehydrated at the right temperature. Since steaming vegetables helps to keep more of their nutrients than scalding does, you should follow the steps on dehydrating vegetables.

Fruits and vegetables not only provide important nutrients, but they also help the body work properly in other ways. Fruits, except for cranberries, plums, prunes, and most vegetables, except for rhubarb, spinach, and chard, make the body more alkaline when they are broken down. The free acids and acid salts of Fruits and vegetables are oxidized into carbonic acid which is taken out by breathing. Salts of the metals calcium, magnesium, potassium, and sodium are found in vegetables. These salts are available for the purpose of neutralizing acid by-products that come as a result of the breakdown (metabolism) of proteins, meat, eggs, milk, and cereals. This is just one reason why fruits and vegetables should be part of a healthy diet.

Fruits are a great place to get Vitamins A and C, but are not rich in Vitamin B-1 (Thiamin). While sulfuring kills Vitamin B-1 in fruits, it tends to maintain the potency of vitamins A and C. It is always better to keep the most vitamins possible.

Steamed vegetables retain Thiamin very well, and steaming helps in preserving some of the Vitamin C of vegetables, which is easily destroyed. Vitamin B-2 (Riboflavin), found in a few fruits and a lot of vegetables, is resistant to oxidation, heat, or sulfur fumes, but it is affected by light. Niacin occurs in only a few vegetables. It doesn't break down when exposed to oxidation or by heating to boiling temperature, so there shouldn't be much loss of Niacin in the process of dehydration.

It is clear that fruits and vegetables that have been dehydrated still have almost all of the nutrients they had when they were fresh.

Commons Problems and How to Solve Them

When drying food at home, you have to take care to avoid the following common mistakes:

Not reading the dehydrator manual – Your dehydrator manual will contain several guidelines that must be followed. Ignoring this might lead to improper use of the dryer.

Storing food together – You must never store all the dried food in one container. Instead, divide it between small containers in small quantities so that you can use one container at a time.

Not drying the food completely – The food must be completely dry before it is stored.

Not using your storage – Yes, you have successfully dried food, and it is stored safely. Now what? Do you use them? Or are they just hiding in their storage space? Keep some recipes that make use of the dried food handy. Use them.

Not having variety – You might have so many dried apples that you get tired of eating them and thus they stay where they are. Try having a variety of dried food so that you can have plenty of flavors in storage. Dry several items rather than one single item.

Precautions: Some precautions must also be taken when dealing with dried food. They are:

Metal and plastic containers must be avoided.

If you see moisture or condensation happening inside a container, make sure that you dry it again.

Check your dried food before you eat them. Discard the food if you see mold on them.

The old batches of dried food should be used first.

FAQs

1 How long will dehydrated food last?

If prepared and stored properly, dehydrated food can last 5 to 10 years. But it is advisable to use your own within four to six months.

2 Does dehydrating food remove (or preserve) nutrients?

Yes, some nutrients may be removed when food is dehydrated but no more than other methods of preservation. Heat and light are responsible for the breakdown of vitamins. By implication, the canning method of preservation tears down more nutrients than the low heat, low moisture dehydrating method. The amount of thiamin and vitamin A & C that diminishes from your vegetables can be reduced through blanching.

3 *Does dehydrating food kill bacteria?*

Provided that you dehydrate your vegetables and fruits until their moisture levels are anywhere between five and twenty percent, you have removed the bacteria that can cause food to decay. If you are concerned about bacteria on meat, it is recommended by the USDA that you first heat your raw meat to 160°F temperature and then dehydrate it at a steady temperature of 145°F.

4 *Does Dehydrate Food Increase Sugar*

In most cases, yes, because when you dehydrate food at a higher temperate, it will cause the death of enzymes. More dense foods may withstand higher temperatures without the enzymes being killed. But most enzymes will ultimately become dormant when the temperature rises between 140° to 160°F.

5 *Can Cooked Food Be Dehydrated?*

Yes. Meals can even be dehydrated, but some cooked food dehydrates better than others. If you are drying food for long-term storage, camping, or backpacking, you can prepare rice dishes, stews, and desserts and dry them by using nonstick sheets on the trays of a dehydrator. And then remove the nonstick sheet when they have reached a moist, crumbly consistency.

6 *How can I store dried food?*

Dehydrated vegetables can last up to ten years and fruit up to five if properly stored. The best way to preserve your dried food for the long term is to vacuum seal using an oxygen absorber and keep it in a cool, dark place. If you are going to eat non-meat dried food within 12 months, store them in reusable storage bags or freezer bags with the air squeezed out.

If you consume seafood and meat within a month, you can store in freezer bags and keep them in a cool, dark place; otherwise, the best thing is to vacuum seal and freeze them. Meat can last for up to a year if properly stored in the freezer.

7 *How to Store Herbs?*

When completely dry, separate the leaves from the stems, and store the leaves (either whole or gently crumbled) in light-proof containers.

In terms of oven-drying, allow the dried herbs to cool and gently crush the leaves. Store the dried herbs in light-proof containers.

Store all your dried herbs in a cool dark place, in airtight containers.

Never store your herb vinegar in the sun or on a lighted counter if you intend to use them, no matter how pretty they look. They should always be stored in the refrigerator.

RECIPES

Bread And Chips

1. Green Crackers

Preparation time: 20 minutes
Cooking time: 8 hours
Servings: 4
Ingredients:

- 1 cup green juice pulp
- ¼ cup ground flax seeds
- ¼ cup chia seeds
- ¼ cup nutritional yeast
- 2 tablespoons sesame seeds
- 1 tablespoon tamari
- ½ teaspoon salt
- ¼ cup water

Directions:

1. Combine all the ingredients in a bowl.
2. Transfer to a food processor.
3. Pulse until fully combined.
4. Spread a thin layer of the mixture in the food dehydrator.
5. Score the crackers.
6. Process at 115 degrees fahrenheit for 5 hours.
7. Flip the crackers.
8. Dry for another 3 hours.
9. Storage suggestions: store in a sealable plastic bag for up to 7 days.

Tip: the mixture layer should be 1/8 inch thick only.

Per serving: Calories: 122kcal; Fat: 7.4g; Carbs: 10.8g; Protein: 3.9g

2. Seaweed & Tamari Crackers

Preparation time: 15 minutes
Cooking time: 24 hours
Servings: 15
Ingredients:

- 1 cup flax seeds
- 2 nori sheets, broken
- 2 tablespoons tamari
- 1 ½ cups water

Directions:

1. Mix all the ingredients in a bowl.
2. Spread a layer in the food dehydrator.
3. Set it at 110 degrees f.
4. Process for 24 hours.
5. Break into crackers.
6. Storage suggestions: store in a glass jar with a lid for up to 5 days.

Tip: soak flaxseeds in water for 1 hour before processing.

Per serving: Calories: 122kcal; Fat: 7.4g; Carbs: 10.8g; Protein: 3.9g

3. Garlic Zucchini Chips

Preparation time: 15 minutes
Cooking time: 4 hours
Servings: 4
Ingredients:

- 3 zucchinis, sliced into thin rounds
- 2 tablespoons olive oil
- 2 tablespoons sesame seeds
- 2 tablespoons dried thyme, crushed
- 2 cloves garlic, grated
- Salt to taste

Directions:

1. Coat the zucchini with olive oil.
2. Sprinkle with the sesame seeds, thyme, garlic, and salt.
3. Add these to the food dehydrator.
4. Dehydrate at 158 degrees f for 2 hours.
5. Flip and dry for another 2 hours.
6. Storage suggestions: store in a sealable plastic bag.

Tip: before dehydrating, press the zucchini rounds with a paper towel to remove excess moisture.

Per serving: Calories: 70kcal; Fat: 4g; Carbs: 30g; Protein: 2g

4. Pear Chips

Preparation time: 10 minutes
Cooking time: 6 hours
Servings: 10
Ingredients:

- 10 pears, cored and sliced thinly

Directions:

1. Arrange the pear slices in the food dehydrator.
2. Dehydrate at 145 degrees f for 8 hours.
3. Storage suggestions: store in a sealed food container for up to 7 days.

Tip: make sure the pear slices do not overlap to ensure even crispiness.

Per serving: Calories: 70kcal; Fat: 4g; Carbs: 30g; Protein: 2g

5. Banana Chips

Preparation time: 15 minutes
Cooking time: 12 hours
Servings: 4
Ingredients:

- 4 bananas, sliced thinly
- 1 teaspoon lemon juice

Directions:

1. Drizzle the banana slices with lemon juice.
2. Add these to the food dehydrator.
3. Process at 135 degrees f for 12 hours.
4. Storage suggestions: store in a vacuum sealed plastic for up to 3 months.

Tip: drizzling bananas with lemon juice prevents browning.

Per serving: Calories: 70kcal; Fat: 4g; Carbs: 30g; Protein: 2g

6. Sesame & Carrot Crackers

Preparation time: 45 minutes

Cooking time: 24 hours
Servings: 15
Ingredients:

- 1 ½ cups of golden flaxseeds
- ¼ cup sesame seeds
- 2 cups carrot pulp
- 1 teaspoon of garlic powder
- ½ teaspoon of ground coriander
- 3 tablespoons tamari
- 1 cup water

Directions:

1. Grind the flaxseeds in the spice grinder.
2. Add to a bowl along with the remaining ingredients.
3. Mix well.
4. Let sit for 30 minutes.
5. Spread the mixture in the food dehydrator.
6. Process at 110 degrees f for 24 hours.
7. Storage suggestions: store in an airtight jar for up to 7 days.

Tip: make your own garlic powder.

Per serving: Calories: 122kcal; Fat: 7.4g; Carbs: 10.8g; Protein: 3.9g

7. Peanut Butter & Banana Crackers

Preparation time: 4 hours and 20 minutes
Cooking time: 6 hours
Servings: 12
Ingredients:

- 3 bananas, sliced
- ½ cup peanut butter
- ½ teaspoon cinnamon powder
- 1 cup ground peanuts
- 3 cups graham cracker crumbs

Directions:

1. Mash the bananas and peanut butter in a bowl.
2. Stir in the rest of the ingredients.

3. Roll the dough into a large ball.
4. Flatten the ball to form a long rectangle.
5. Wrap the dough with wax paper and refrigerate for 4 hours.
6. Roll out the dough and slice.
7. Add the slices to the food dehydrator.
8. Process at 145 degrees f for 6 hours.
9. Storage suggestions: store in a glass jar with a lid for up to 5 days.

Tip: do not skip refrigerating the dough before the dehydration process.

Per serving: Calories: 178kcal; Fat: 13.3g; Carbs: 10.7g; Protein: 4.4g

8. Zucchini Chips

Preparation time: 20 minutes
Cooking time: 12 hours 10 minutes
Servings: 6
Ingredients:

- 4 zucchinis, sliced thin
- Juice from 2 lemons
- 1 teaspoon salt

Directions:

1. Combine the zucchini strips, lemon juice, and salt, and stir to coat.
2. Place the zucchini strips on the racks of your Food Dehydrator in a single layer.
3. Set the food dehydrator to 115F and dehydrate for 12 hours or until the zucchini strips are crispy.

Per serving: Calories: 25kcal; Fat: 0.3g; Carbs: 5.8g; Protein: 1.7g

9. Pumpkin Chips

Preparation time: 15 minutes
Cooking time: 18 hours 10 minutes
Servings: 6
Ingredients:

- 1 pumpkin
- 2 tablespoons coconut oil, melted
- 1 teaspoon cinnamon
- 1 teaspoon nutmeg

Directions:

1. Remove the seeds, pulp, and skin from the pumpkin, and slice the pumpkin flesh into thin slices.
2. Try to make the slices no more than 1/8 inch thick.
3. In a large bowl, combine the pumpkin slices, coconut oil, cinnamon, nutmeg, and salt. Stir well to coat.
4. Place the pumpkin slices on the racks of your food dehydrator and set them to 125F. Dehydrated for 18 hours or until the slices are crispy.

Per serving: Calories: 140kcal; Fat: 8g; Carbs: 16g; Protein: 2g

10. Eggplant Chips

Preparation time: 30 minutes
Cooking time: 6 hours 15 minutes
Servings: 6
Ingredients:

- 4 baby eggplants, sliced thin
- 3 tablespoons olive oil
- 1/2 teaspoon smoked paprika
- 1/2 teaspoon oregano
- 1/4 teaspoon cayenne pepper
- 2 tablespoons salt

Directions:

1. In a huge bowl, combine the eggplant slices, olive oil, paprika, oregano, cayenne pepper, and salt.
2. Place the eggplant slices on the racks of your food dehydrator and set them to 135F.
3. Dehydrate for 5- 6 hours or until eggplant slices are entirely dried and crispy.

Per serving: Calories: 35kcal; Fat: 1g; Carbs: 8g; Protein: 1g

11. Crunch Green Bean Chips

Preparation time: 15 minutes
Cooking time: 12 hours 10 minutes
Servings: 12
Ingredients:

- 3 lbs. Fresh green beans
- 1/4 cup coconut oil, melted
- 1 tablespoon salt

Directions:

1. Combine your green beans and oil and stir well to coat. Season with salt and stir again.
2. Place the green beans on the racks of your food dehydrator and set them to 125F.
3. Dehydrate for 12 hours or until the beans are dehydrated and crispy.
4. Remove the green beans from the racks and store them in a cool dry place.

Per serving: Calories: 130kcal; Fat: 5g; Carbs: 20g; Protein: 2g

12. Sweet Potato Chips

Preparation time: 15 minutes
Cooking time: 14 hours
Servings: 6
Ingredients:

- 2 large sweet potatoes
- 2 teaspoons coconut oil, melted
- 2 teaspoons salt

Directions:

1. Slice the potatoes into thin rounds. Combine your potato slices, salt, and coconut oil and toss to coat.
2. Place ParaFlexx Screens on the racks of your Food Dehydrator and place your potato on the screens in a single layer.
3. Set your food dehydrator to 125F and dehydrate for 12 to 14 hours or until

crisp. Transfer to a tray and store in a cool dry place if not used immediately.

Per serving: Calories: 125kcal; Fat: 10g; Carbs: 9g; Protein: 1g

13. Pickle Chips

Preparation time: 5 minutes
Cooking time: 12 hours
Servings: 12
Ingredients:

- 1 jar of large dill pickles

Directions:

1. Remove pickles from the jar then pat dry with paper towels. Slice the pickles length-wise into long, thin slabs about 1/4 inch thick.
2. Lay the pickle slices on the racks of your dehydrator and set them to 125F. Dehydrate for 12 hours or until the pickles are completely dried.
3. Remove from the racks and eat like chips or store and rehydrate when needed. To rehydrate, place the dried pickle slices in a bowl of lukewarm water and wait for 5 to 10 minutes.

Per serving: Calories: 1kcal; Fat: 0g; Carbs: 0.3g; Protein: 0.1g

14. Beet Chips

Preparation time: 12 hours
Cooking time: 12 hours
Servings: 10
Ingredients:

- 4 large beets sliced into thin rounds
- 1 cup apple cider vinegar

Directions:

1. In a wide shallow bowl or tray, pour the vinegar and arrange the beet slices in a single layer. Allow the beet slices to soak for 12 hours.
2. Remove the beets from the vinegar and pat dry with paper towels.

3. Lay the beet slices on the racks of your food dehydrator and set them to 125F. Dehydrate for 12 hours or until beet slices are completely dried. Store in zip-lock bags until ready to use.

Per serving: Calories: 23kcal; Fat: 0.1g; Carbs: 4.2g; Protein: 0.7g

15. Potato Chips

Preparation time: 10 minutes
Cooking time: 6 hours
Servings: 6
Ingredients:

- 2 russet potatoes, peeled
- Vegetable oil spray
- Salt

Directions:

1. Rinse and peel the potatoes and slice them into thin rounds using a mandolin. Lay the rounds on a baking sheet and spray with cooking oil on both sides.
2. Sprinkle the rounds with salt and place them on the racks of your food dehydrator. Set to 110F and dehydrate for 6 hours or until the chips are dried and crispy.
3. Store in a large zip-lock bag until ready to use.

Per serving: Calories: 49kcal; Fat: 0.1g; Carbs: 11.2g; Protein: 1.2g

16. Dehydrated Banana Chips

Preparation time: 10 minutes
Cooking time: 20 hours
Servings: 6
Ingredients:

- 2 – 4 ripe bananas

Directions:

1. Cut the bananas into 1/8-inch-thick slices.

2. Prepare the dehydrator as per the manufacturer's instructions and line it with parchment paper.
3. Spread the banana slices on the parchment paper and dry them for 18 – 20 hours or until they are completely dry.

Per serving: Calories: 60kcal; Fat: 0g; Carbs: 15g; Protein: 1g

17. Cinnamon Apple Chips

Preparation time: 15 minutes
Cooking time: 12 hours
Servings: 4
Ingredients:

- 4 apples, cored, sliced 1/8 inch thick
- 1 teaspoon ground cinnamon
- 2 cups water
- 1 tablespoon lemon juice
- 1 tablespoon vinegar

Directions:

1. Add water, lemon juice, and vinegar in a bowl and mix well.
2. Add apple slices to the water and let sit for 5 minutes.
3. Remove apple slices from the water then pat dry with a paper towel.
4. Arrange apple slices on a dehydrator tray, sprinkle with cinnamon and dehydrate at 135 F/ 58 C for 12 hours.

Per serving: Calories: 119kcal; Fat: 0.4g; Carbs: 31.4g; Protein: 0.7g

18. Green Apple Chips

Preparation time: 10 minutes
Cooking time: 8 hours
Servings: 4
Ingredients:

- 4 green apples, cored and sliced 1/8 inch thick
- ½ lime juice

Directions:

5. Add apple slices and lime juice to a bowl, toss well, and set aside for 5 minutes.
6. Arrange apple slices on dehydrator trays and dehydrate at 145 F/ 63 C for 8 hours.
7. Store in an air-tight container.

Per serving: Calories: 117kcal; Fat: 0.4g; Carbs: 31.3g; Protein: 0.6g

19. Raw Zucchini Bread

Preparation time: 20 minutes
Cooking time: 6 hours
Servings: 6
Ingredients:

- 2 cups Walnuts
- 2 teaspoons Cinnamon
- 1 1/2 cup Dates
- 1 teaspoon Vanilla Extract
- 3 cups Grated Zucchini
- 1 cup Shredded Unsweetened Coconut
- 1/2 cup Raisins
- 1/2 cup Psyllium Husk

Directions:

1. Add the walnuts to your food processor then pulse until ground. Add the cinnamon, dates, and vanilla and process until combined.
2. Transfer to a bowl, add the zucchini, coconut, raisins, and psyllium husk and mix well to combine.
3. Use the mixture to make 10 loaves and place them on the dehydrator trays lined with parchment paper.
4. Dehydrate at 150F/65C for an hour, reduce the temperature to 110F/43C and dehydrate for 5 more hours.
5. When done, allow cooling then store in the fridge.

Per serving: Calories: 373.7kcal; Fat: 22.5g; Carbs: 45.9g; Protein: 6.9g

20. Black Bread

Preparation time: 30 minutes
Cooking time: 8 to 12 hours
Servings: 4
Ingredients:

- 2 Garlic Cloves, peeled
- 1/4 cup Water
- 1 teaspoon Lemon Juice
- 1/4 cup Chopped Red Onion
- 1 tablespoon Agave Nectar
- 1 tablespoon Cacao Powder
- 1/4 cup Ground Flax Seeds
- 1 tablespoon Caraway seeds
- 1/4 teaspoon Black Pepper
- 1 cup Raw Walnuts, soaked overnight, rinsed and drained
- 1 cup Buckwheat Groats, soaked overnight, rinsed and drained

Directions:

1. Add the walnuts and buckwheat groats to your blender or food processor and pulse until chopped. Add the garlic, water, lemon juice, onion, and agave nectar and pulse until combined.
2. Transfer to a medium bowl then mix in the cacao, flaxseed meal, caraway seeds, and pepper.
3. Pour the dough onto a dehydrator sheet, spread it until it is ¼-inch thick and score it into squares or rectangles.
4. Dehydrate at 115F / 46C for 8 to 12 depending on the preferred doneness.
5. When done, break into pieces and store in airtight containers.

Per serving: Calories: 324.1kcal; Fat: 18.7g; Carbs: 38.4g; Protein: 9.8g

21. Vegan Bread

Preparation time: 30 minutes
Cooking time: 6 hours
Servings: 6
Ingredients:

- 1 head cauliflower
- 1 teaspoon turmeric
- 2 tablespoons flax seed
- 1/2 cup psyllium hust
- 1/2 cup brewer's yeast
- 4 large zucchinis
- Salt and black pepper

Directions:

1. Place cauliflower and zucchini in a food processor and pulse until they form a paste.
2. Add turmeric, flax seeds, psyllium, yeast, and a pinch of salt and black pepper.
3. Pulse again until all ingredients are thoroughly combined.
4. Place ParaFlexx Screens on the racks of your Food Dehydrator.
5. Form the mixture into slices about 1/2-inch-thick and place them on the screens.
6. Set your food dehydrator to 150F and dehydrate for 6 hours.
7. The bread should not be dehydrated. One side should be slightly soft.

Per Serving: Calories: 219kcal; Fat: 1.9g; Carbs: 61.6g; Protein: 10.1g

22. Carrot Crackers

Preparation time: 20 minutes
Cooking time: 12 hours
Servings: 12
Ingredients:

- 6 large carrots, peeled
- 1/2 cup ground flax seeds
- 1 tomato, diced
- Juice from 1 lemon
- 1/2 cup sesame seeds
- 1/2 cup chia seeds
- 3/4 cups water

Directions:

1. In a food processor, combine the carrots, flax seeds, tomato, lemon juice, and water, and pulse until paste forms. Add the chia seeds and sesame seeds and stir to combine.
2. Place paraflexx screens on the racks of your food dehydrator. Spread the paste evenly on the screens about 1/4 inch thick.
3. Set your food dehydrator to 105f and dehydrate for 12 hours. Remove the crackers from the food dehydrator and allow cooling completely. The crackers will become crispy as they cool.

Per serving: Calories: 122kcal; Fat: 7.4g; Carbs: 10.8g; Protein: 3.9g

23. Mexican Crackers

Preparation time: 30 minutes
Cooking time: 6 hours
Servings: 15
Ingredients:

- ½ cup chia seeds
- 1 cup golden flaxseeds
- ½ cup pumpkin seeds
- ½ cup sunflower seeds
- 1 red bell pepper, chopped
- ¼ onion, chopped
- 1 cup carrot pulp
- 1 ½ teaspoon chipotle powder
- 1 teaspoon garlic powder
- Salt to taste
- ½ teaspoon cayenne pepper

Directions:

1. In a blender process all the seeds until powdery.
2. Stir in the bell pepper and onion.
3. Pulse until smooth.
4. Stir in the rest of the ingredients.
5. Pulse until fully combined.
6. Spread the mixture in the food dehydrator.
7. Score the crackers.
8. Dry at 115 degrees f for 6 hours.
9. Storage suggestions: store in a sealed food container for up to 5 days.

Tip: soak the seeds in separate bowls of water for 6 hours before processing.

Per serving: Calories: 122kcal; Fat: 7.4g; Carbs: 10.8g; Protein: 3.9gVegetables

24. **Dried Cilantro**

Preparation time: 10 minutes
Cooking time: 3 hours 10 minutes
Servings: 12
Ingredients:

- 2 bunches of fresh cilantro

Directions:
1. You can dehydrate your cilantro with or without the stems; it's totally up to you. Rinse and dry the cilantro and place it in a single layer on the racks of your Food Dehydrator.
2. Set your food dehydrator to 110F and dehydrate for 3 hours. Remove the dried cilantro from the racks and store in jars or zipper-lock bags until ready to use.

Per serving: Calories: 3.68kcal; Fat: 0.083g; Carbs: 0.587g; Protein: 0.341g

25. **Plum Fruit Leather**

Preparation time: 30 minutes
Cooking time: 8 hours 20 minutes
Servings: 12

Ingredients:

- 6 purple or red plums split and pitted
- 2 tablespoons lemon juice
- 2 teaspoons ground cinnamon
- 1/4 cup water

Directions:
3. Place the plums and water in a pot and simmer until the plums begin to break down, about 10 to 15 minutes.
4. When the plums are soft, pour into a blender and blend until smooth. Add the lemon juice and cinnamon and blend.
5. Place ParaFlexx Screens on the racks of your dehydrator and set it to 140F.
6. Pour the puree onto the screens and use a spatula to spread the puree evenly, about 1/8 inch thick.
7. Dehydrate for 8 hours. Make sure the leather is entirely dehydrated and not sticky before removing it from the screens.

Per serving: Calories: 31kcal; Fat: 0g; Carbs: 7g; Protein: 0g

26. **Strawberry Passion Fruit Leather**

Preparation time: 20 minutes
Cooking time: 6 hours 10 minutes
Servings: 6
Ingredients:

- 2 cups fresh strawberries, stems removed
- 2 tablespoons passion fruit syrup
- 1 cup applesauce

Directions:
1. Place the strawberries, passion fruit syrup, and applesauce into a blender and puree until smooth.

2. Place ParaFlexx Screens on the racks of your Food Dehydrator and pour the puree onto the screens.
3. Use a spatula to distribute the puree so it is about 1/8-inch thick evenly.
4. Set your food dehydrator to 140F and dehydrate for 6 hours.
5. Make sure your leather is wholly dehydrated and not sticky before removing it from the screens.

Per serving: Calories: 45kcal; Fat: 0g; Carbs: 12g; Protein: 0g

27. Citrus Potpourri

Preparation time: 20 minutes
Cooking time: 12 hours 15 minutes
Servings: 5
Ingredients:

- 2 lemons
- 2 oranges
- 6 cinnamon sticks
- 3 tablespoons dried cloves

Directions:

1. Slice the lemons and oranges between 1/8 and 1/4-inch-thick and place them on the racks of your Food Dehydrator in a single layer so the slices are not touching.
2. Set your food dehydrator to 150F and dehydrate for 12 hours. The citrus should be dry and firm to the touch and not sticky.
3. Remove the slices from the racks and divide among bowls or jars with equal amounts of cinnamon sticks and dried cloves.

Per serving: Calories: 190kcal; Fat: 0g; Carbs: 41g; Protein: 7g

28. Carrot Cake

Preparation time: 30 minutes
Cooking time: 9 hours

Servings: 6
Ingredients:

- 3 cups carrots, grated
- 1 teaspoon cinnamon
- 1/2 teaspoon nutmeg
- 1/4 teaspoon ground cloves
- 1 cup pecans, crushed
- 1/2 cup shredded coconut
- 1/4 cup water
- 1/2 teaspoon salt

Directions:

1. In a food processor, mix the pecans and coconut and pulse.
2. In a large bowl, combine the carrots, pecans, coconut, cinnamon, nutmeg, cloves, water, and salt.
3. Place ParaFlexx Screens on the racks of your Food Dehydrator.
4. Form the dough into individual cakes about 4 inches across. Place the cakes onto the screens and set your Food dehydrator to 165F. Dehydrate for one hour, then lower the temperature to 125F and dehydrate for another 8 hours.

Per serving: Calories: 211kcal; Fat: 19g; Carbs: 10.2g; Protein: 3.2g

29. Lemon Cookies

Preparation time: 20 minutes
Cooking time: 8 hours
Servings: 15
Ingredients:

- Juice from 2 lemons
- 2 cups cashews
- 1 banana
- 1/2 cups honey
- 2 cups shredded coconut
- 1 teaspoon vanilla

Directions:

1. In a food processor, mix the lemon juice, cashews, banana, honey, coconut, and vanilla. Pulse until smooth.
2. Use a spoon to place dough onto the racks of your Food dehydrator and use the back of the spoon to flatten them. Set your Food dehydrator to 115F and dehydrate for 8 hours.

Per serving: Calories: 187kcal; Fat: 12.1g; Carbs: 19.3g; Protein: 3.3g

30. Maple Carrot Straws

Preparation time: 15 minutes
Cooking time: 6 hours
Servings: 4
Ingredients:

- 1 lb. Carrots, sliced into long strips
- 1 tablespoon maple syrup
- 1 tablespoon olive oil
- Salt to taste

Directions:

1. Combine all the ingredients in a bowl.
2. Arrange the strips in the food dehydrator.
3. Process at 135 degrees f for 6 hours.
4. Storage suggestions: store in a food container.

Tip: use a peeler to slice the carrots.

Per serving: Calories: 214kcal; Fat: 3g; Carbs: 41.4g; Protein: 4.3g

31. Dehydrated Asparagus

Preparation time: 10 minutes
Cooking time: 6 hours
Servings: 2
Ingredients:

- 4 cups asparagus, trimmed and sliced

Directions:

1. Arrange the asparagus in the food dehydrator.
2. Process at 125 degrees f for 6 hours.

3. Storage suggestions: store in a sealable plastic bag.

Tip: you can also season the asparagus with salt or garlic powder.

Per serving: Calories: 434kcal; Fat: 39.4g; Carbs: 20.9g; Protein: 5.8g

32. Fall Carrot Chips

Preparation time: 15 minutes
Cooking time: 6 hours
Servings: 4
Ingredients:

- 1 pound of carrots, peeled
- 3 tbsp. Melted coconut oil
- ¾ tsp. Salt
- 2 tsp. Allspice (or combination of cinnamon, allspice or nutmeg)

Directions:

1. Wash, dry and slice carrots into uniform disks.
2. Mix together carrots, oil, salt and allspice.
3. Place carrots onto dehydrator trays and dry for 6-6 hours at 125 degrees or until crisp.

Per serving: Calories: 11kcal; Fat: 0g; Carbs: 2.7g; Protein: 0.2g

33. Herbed Sweet Potato Chips

Preparation time: 15 minutes
Cooking time: 6 hours
Servings: 4
Ingredients:

- 3 medium to large sweet potatoes
- 4 tbsp. Olive oil
- 2 tbsp. Fresh lemon juice
- 2 tsp. Dried thyme
- 1 ½ tsp. Salt
- ¼ tsp. Pepper

Directions:

1. Slice sweet potatoes into thin, uniform slices.
2. In a bowl combine sweet potato slices, oil, lemon juice, thyme, salt and pepper. Toss until well coated.
3. Place slices on dehydrator trays.
4. Set the temperature to 140 degrees. Dehydrate for 6-6 hours, or until crisp to touch.

Per serving: Calories: 35kcal; Fat: 0.2g; Carbs: 8.3g; Protein: 0.6g

34. Dried Cauliflower Popcorn

Preparation time: 15 minutes
Cooking time: 8 hours
Servings: 1
Ingredients:

- 2 cups cauliflower florets
- 4 tablespoons hot sauce
- 3 tablespoons coconut oil
- 1 teaspoon smoked cayenne
- ½ teaspoon ground cumin
- 1 tablespoon paprika

Directions:

5. Toss the cauliflower florets in hot sauce and coconut oil.
6. Sprinkle with the smoked cayenne, cumin and paprika.
7. Add the seasoned cauliflower to the food dehydrator.
8. Dry at 130 deg. F for 8 hours.
9. Store in an airtight plastic bag.

Tip: add more cayenne pepper for spicier cauliflower popcorn.

Per serving: Calories: 9kcal; Fat: 0g; Carbs: 2.1g; Protein: 0.2g

35. Zucchini Snacks

Preparation time: 45 minutes
Cooking time: 12 hours
Servings: 4

Ingredients:

- 8 zucchinis, sliced into rounds and seeds removed
- 1 cup grape juice concentrate
- 1 cup water

Directions:

1. Place all the ingredients in a pot over medium heat.
2. Bring to a boil.
3. Reduce heat and simmer for 30 minutes.
4. Drain the zucchini and let cool.
5. Add the zucchinis to the food dehydrator.
6. Process at 135 degrees f for 12 hours.
7. Storage suggestions: store in the refrigerator for up to 1 week.

Tip: do not overcook the zucchinis.

Per serving: Calories: 9kcal; Fat: 0g; Carbs: 2.1g; Protein: 0.2g

36. Cucumber Chips

Preparation time: 15 minutes
Cooking time: 6 hours
Servings: 4
Ingredients:

- 3 cucumber, sliced into rounds
- 1 tablespoon avocado oil
- 2 teaspoons apple cider vinegar
- Salt to taste

Directions:

1. Toss the cucumber slices in avocado oil and vinegar.
2. Season with salt.
3. Add the cucumber slices to the food dehydrator.
4. Dehydrate at 135 degrees f for 6 hours.
5. Storage suggestions: store in an airtight container.

Tip: you can use a mandolin slicer to slice the cucumbers thinly. Dry the cucumber slices with a paper towel before processing.

Per serving: Calories: 9kcal; Fat: 0g; Carbs: 2.1g; Protein: 0.2g

37. Dehydrated Okra

Preparation time: 15 minutes
Cooking time: 12 hours
Servings: 4
Ingredients:

- 12 okra, sliced

Directions:

1. Add the okra to the food dehydrator.
2. Dry at 130 degrees f for 12 hours.
3. Storage suggestions: store in an airtight container.

Tip: sprinkle with powdered herb or spice for added flavor.

Per serving: Calories: 70kcal; Fat: 4g; Carbs: 30g; Protein: 2g

38. Dried Sweet Potato

Preparation time: 10 minutes
Cooking time: 12 hours
Servings: 4
Ingredients:

- 2 sweet potatoes
- 1 teaspoon onion powder

Directions:

1. Season the sweet potato slices with onion powder.
2. Arrange in a single layer in the food dehydrator.
3. Set at 115 degrees f.
4. Process for 12 hours.
5. Storage suggestions: store in a sealable plastic bag.

Tip: use a mandolin slicer to prepare the sweet potatoes.

Per serving: Calories: 70kcal; Fat: 4g; Carbs: 30g; Protein: 2g

39. Dehydrated Beets

Preparation time: 20 minutes
Cooking time: 12 hours
Servings: 4
Ingredients:

- 3 beets, sliced thinly
- ¼ cup water
- ¼ cup vinegar
- 1 tablespoon olive oil
- Salt to taste

Directions:

1. Combine all the ingredients in a bowl.
2. Marinate for 10 minutes.
3. Arrange the beet slices in the food dehydrator.
4. Dehydrate at 135 degrees f for 12 hours.
5. Storage suggestions: store in a sealable plastic bag.

Tip: use a mandoliner slicer to slice the beets thinly.

Per serving: Calories: 70kcal; Fat: 4g; Carbs: 30g; Protein: 2g

40. Dehydrated Tomatoes

Preparation time: 20 minutes
Cooking time: 8 hours
Servings: 2
Ingredients:

- 2 tomatoes, sliced into quarters
- Salt to taste

Directions:

1. Add the tomatoes to the food dehydrator.
2. Sprinkle with salt.
3. Set to 135 degrees f.
4. Process for 8 hours.

5. Storage suggestions: store in a sealable plastic bag. Squeeze out the air. Store for up to 2 months in a cool dry place.
6. Freeze then store for up to 6 months.

Tip: don't forget to scrape the seeds before drying.

Per serving: Calories: 250kcal; Fat: 7.6g; Carbs: 41.8g; Protein: 4.5g

41. Spiced Cucumbers

Preparation time: 20 hours
Cooking time: 4 hours
Servings: 2
Ingredients:

- 2 cucumbers, sliced into rounds
- 2 teaspoons olive oil
- 2 teaspoons vinegar
- 1 tablespoon paprika
- 2 teaspoons onion powder
- 2 teaspoons garlic powder
- 2 teaspoons sugar
- Pinch chili powder

Directions:

1. Toss the cucumbers in oil and vinegar.
2. Sprinkle with sugar and spices.
3. Put the cucumber slices in the food dehydrator.
4. Process at 135 degrees f for 6 hours.
5. Storage suggestions: store in an airtight container.

Tip: dehydrate longer if you want your cucumber crispier.

Per serving: Calories: 250kcal; Fat: 7.6g; Carbs: 41.8g; Protein: 4.5g

42. Dehydrated Corn

Preparation time: 10 minutes
Cooking time: 12 hours
Servings: 4
Ingredients:

- 8 cups corn kernels

Directions:

1. Spread the corn kernels in the food dehydrator.
2. Process at 125 degrees f for 12 hours.
3. Storage suggestions: store in a glass jar with a lid.

Tip: you can also drizzle the corn kernels in olive oil before dehydrating.

Per serving: Calories: 214kcal; Fat: 3g; Carbs: 41.4g; Protein: 4.3g

43. Spinach Balls

Preparation time: 15 minutes
Cooking time: 6 hours
Servings: 4
Ingredients:

3 cups cashews

- 3 cups blanched spinach
- 4 tbsp. Olive oil
- ¼ cup dehydrated onion flakes
- 3 cloves of garlic
- ¼ tsp. Nutmeg
- Pinch of cayenne pepper

Directions:

1. Process the cashews until they are finely ground. Add all the remaining ingredients and pulse several times until well combined and paste-like in consistency.
2. Pour mixture into a bowl and form into small, bite-size balls.
3. Place spinach balls on dehydrator sheets and dehydrate at 120 degrees for 5 hours.

Per serving: Calories: 137kcal; Fat: 10.5g; Carbs: 9.2g; Protein: 3.7g

44. Moroccan Carrot Crunch

Preparation time: 15 minutes
Cooking time: 6 hours

Servings: 4

Ingredients:

- 1 pound of carrots, peeled
- 4 tbsp. Olive oil
- 1 tbsp. Honey
- 1/8 tsp. Cayenne pepper
- 2 tsp. Cumin
- 1 tsp. Dried parsley flakes
- ½ tsp. Salt

Directions:

1. Wash, dry and thinly slice carrots.
2. Mix together oil, honey, and seasonings.
3. Place carrots onto dehydrator trays. Using a pastry brush, dab the mixture onto the carrot rounds.
4. Dehydrate for 6-6 hours at 125 degrees or until crisp.

Per serving: Calories: 26kcal; Fat: 0.3g; Carbs: 6g; Protein: 0.5g

45. Ranch Brussels Sprout Skins

Preparation time: 15 minutes

Cooking time: 6 hours

Servings: 4

Ingredients:

- 4 cups brussels sprouts, coarsely chopped, tough centers discarded
- 1 cup buttermilk
- 1 tsp. Mustard
- 3 tbsp. Oil
- ½ tsp. Salt
- 1 tsp. Onion powder
- 1 tsp. Minced garlic flakes
- 1 tsp. Dried dill
- 1 tsp. Dried parsley
- 1 tsp. Celery salt

Directions:

1. Place sliced brussels sprouts in a bowl. Blend the seasonings in another small bowl.
2. Whisk together buttermilk, mustard and oil. Pour over brussels sprouts.
3. Spray the dehydrator tray with nonstick spray and place brussels sprouts on the tray. Sprinkle with seasonings. Set the dehydrator to 110 degrees and dehydrate for 8-6 hours.

Per serving: Calories: 16kcal; Fat: 0.2g; Carbs: 3g; Protein: 1.1g

46. Root Vegetable Medley

Preparation time: 15 minutes

Cooking time: 6 hours

Servings: 4

Ingredients:

- 2 medium beets
- 1 sweet potato
- 2 medium parsnips
- 1 medium celery root
- 3 tbsp. Olive oil
- 1 ½ tsp. Salt
- 1 tsp. Garlic powder
- ½ tsp. Oregano
- Pinch of black pepper

Directions:

1. Wash, peel and slice vegetables as thinly as possible, preferably with a mandolin.
2. Place vegetables in a bowl. Mix olive oil with seasonings and pour over vegetables. Toss to coat.
3. Lay vegetables on trays using different trays for different vegetables. Dehydrate at 105 degrees for at least 8 hours.

Per serving: Calories: 48kcal; Fat: 0.2g; Carbs: 11g; Protein: 1.3g

47. Sweet Kale Chips

Preparation time: 15 minutes
Cooking time: 6 hours
Servings: 4
Ingredients:

- 1 bunch curly kale, washed, tough stems removed and leaves roughly torn
- ½ cup pine nuts
- 1/8-1/4 cup white sugar
- ½ tbsp. Cinnamon
- 1/3 cup water
- 1/8 cup apple cider vinegar

Directions:

1. Place pine nuts, sugar and cinnamon in a food processor.
2. Blend water and vinegar and add slowly to the food processor.
3. Pour mixture over kale and mix until coated.
4. Place on dehydrating trays for 2-4 hours at 140 degrees.

Per serving: Calories: 108kcal; Fat: 7.9g; Carbs: 9.4g; Protein: 1.9g

48. Sweet And Savory Beet Rounds

Preparation time: 15 minutes
Cooking time: 6 hours
Servings: 4
Ingredients:

- 4 large beets, washed
- 2 tbsp. Olive oil
- 1 tsp. Fresh rosemary, finely chopped
- ½ tsp. Sea salt
- ¼ tsp. Pepper

Directions:

1. Cut tops of beets. Slice beets about 1/8-1/4 inch wide. Use a mandolin if possible.
2. Toss beets, olive oil, rosemary, salt and pepper in a bowl until evenly coated.
3. Set the dehydrator to 145 degrees. Place trays in the dehydrator for 10-12 hours.

Per serving: Calories: 21kcal; Fat: 0.5g; Carbs: 4.6g; Protein: 0.6g

49. Tex-Mex Green Beans

Preparation time: 15 minutes
Cooking time: 6 hours
Servings: 4
Ingredients:

- 5 pounds of green beans
- 1/3 cup melted coconut oil
- 1 tsp. Chili powder
- 1 tsp. Cumin
- ½ tsp. Each paprika, onion powder, garlic powder, salt, and pepper

Directions:

1. Blanch green beans in boiling water for several minutes. Dry beans.
2. Melt coconut oil in the microwave. Mix oil and seasonings in a bowl.
3. Coast green beans in oil mixture.
4. Place green beans onto dehydrator and dry for 8-6 hours at 125 degrees.

Per serving: Calories: 12kcal; Fat: 0.2g; Carbs: 2.4g; Protein: 0.6g

50. Vegan Broccoli Crisps

Preparation time: 15 minutes
Cooking time: 6 hours
Servings: 4
Ingredients:

- 2 heads of broccoli, washed and cut into bite-size florets
- ½ cup cashews, soaked for at least 1 hour and drained
- 4 tbsp. Nutritional yeast
- 1 tsp. Curry powder

- ½ tsp. red pepper flakes

Directions:

5. Blend the cashews, nutritional yeast and spices in a food processor. Add water to achieve a smooth texture. Nuts should be fully blended.

Side Dishes

51. BBQ Jerky Strips

Preparation time: 15 minutes
Cooking time: 6 hours
Servings: 4
Ingredients:

- 2 ½ pounds lean ground beef
- 2 tsp. Salt
- ½ tsp. Garlic powder
- ½ tsp. Onion powder
- 1 ½ tbsp. Brown sugar
- ¼ cup Worcestershire sauce
- ½ cup barbecue sauce, slightly diluted with water

Directions:

1. Mix ground beef with dry ingredients until incorporated.
2. Combine liquids and coat beef strips with sauce.
3. Press strips into the jerky gun. Squeeze onto dehydrator trays and dry at 145-155 degrees for 6-12 hours.

Per serving: Calories: 54kcal; Fat: 1.2g; Carbs: 4.6g; Protein: 5.8g

52. Salmon Jerky

Preparation time: 15 minutes
Cooking time: 6 hours
Servings: 4
Ingredients:

- 1 ½ pounds salmon, bones removed

6. Pour dressing into a bowl and add broccoli. Coat the florets evenly.
7. Place florets onto dehydrator sheets and dehydrate at 110 degrees for 18 hours.

Per serving: Calories: 104kcal; Fat: 6.8g; Carbs: 8g; Protein: 5.1g

- ¼ cup soy sauce
- ¼ cup teriyaki sauce
- 1 tbsp. Dijon mustard
- 1 tbsp. Maple syrup
- 1 freshly squeezed lime
- ½ tsp. Black pepper

Directions:

1. Freeze salmon for 45 minutes to 1 hour prior to slicing.
2. Place remaining ingredients in a bowl and whisk together.
3. Slice salmon into thin strips and add them to the liquid. Marinate for 3 hours.
4. Remove salmon strips, pat dry and place on dehydrator sheets.
5. Dehydrate for 10-12 hours at 155 degrees.

Per serving: Calories: 36kcal; Fat: 1.4g; Carbs: 1.3g; Protein: 4.7g

53. Spiced "Hamburger" Jerky

Preparation time: 15 minutes
Cooking time: 6 hours
Servings: 4
Ingredients:

- 2 ½ pounds lean ground beef
- 1 tsp. Adobo seasoning
- 2 tsp. Salt
- ½ tsp. Garlic powder
- ½ tsp. Onion powder
- 1 tbsp. Meat tenderizer
- ½ tsp. Cayenne pepper

- ¼ cup tomato sauce
- 1 ½ tbsp. Brown sugar
- ¼ cup Worcestershire sauce
- ¼ cup liquid smoke

Directions:

1. Mix ground beef with dry ingredients until seasonings are well distributed.
2. Combine liquids and coat beef strips with sauce.
3. Press strips into the jerky gun. Squeeze onto dehydrator trays and dry at 145-155 degrees for 6-12 hours.

Per serving: Calories: 52kcal; Fat: 1.3g; Carbs: 3.5g; Protein: 6.2g

54. Dried Bell Peppers

Preparation time: 10 minutes
Cooking time: 24 hours
Servings: 4
Ingredients:

- 4 bell peppers cut in half and de-seed

Directions:

1. Cut bell peppers into strips then cut each strip into ½-inch pieces.
2. Arrange bell peppers strips on dehydrator racks and dehydrate at 135 f/ 58 c for 12-24 hours or until crisp.
3. Store in an air-tight container.

Per serving: Calories: 38kcal; Fat: 0.3g; Carbs: 9g; Protein: 1.2g

55. Avocado Chips

Preparation time: 15 minutes
Cooking time: 6 hours
Servings: 4
Ingredients:

- 4 avocados, halved and pitted
- ¼ tsp. Sea salt
- ¼ tsp. Cayenne pepper
- ¼ cup fresh cilantro, chopped

- ½ lemon juice

Directions:

1. Cut avocado into slices.
2. Drizzle lemon juice over avocado slices.
3. Arrange avocado slices on dehydrator trays and sprinkle with cayenne pepper, salt and cilantro. Dehydrate at 160 f/ 71 c for 6 hours.

Per serving: Calories: 62kcal; Fat: 5.1g; Carbs: 3.2g; Protein: 1.1g

56. Healthy Squash Chips

Preparation time: 10 minutes
Cooking time: 12 hours
Servings: 8
Ingredients:

- 1 yellow squash, cut into 1/8-inch-thick slices
- 2 tbsp. Apple cider vinegar
- 2 tsp. Olive oil
- Salt

Directions:

1. Add all ingredients into the bowl and toss well.
2. Arrange squash slices on dehydrator trays and dehydrate at 115 f/ 46 c for 12 hours or until crispy.
3. Store in an air-tight container.

Per serving: Calories: 15kcal; Fat: 1.2g; Carbs: 0.9g; Protein: 0.3g

57. Broccoli Chips

Preparation time: 15 minutes
Cooking time: 12 hours
Servings: 4
Ingredients:

- 1 lb. Broccoli, cut into florets
- 1 tsp. Onion powder
- 1 garlic clove
- ½ cup vegetable broth

- ¼ cup hemp seeds
- 2 tbsp. Nutritional yeast

Directions:

1. Add broccoli florets to a large mixing bowl and set aside.
2. Add remaining ingredients into the blender and blend until smooth.
3. Pour blended mixture over broccoli florets and toss well.
4. Arrange broccoli florets on dehydrator trays and dehydrate at 115 f/ 46 c for 10-12 hours.

Per serving: Calories: 106kcal; Fat: 4.3g; Carbs: 11.2g; Protein: 8.7g

58. Brussels Sprout Chips

Preparation time: 15 minutes
Cooking time: 6 hours
Servings: 4
Ingredients:

- 2 lbs. Brussels sprouts, wash, dry, cut the root and separate leaves
- 2 fresh lemon juice
- ½ cup water
- ¼ cup nutritional yeast
- 1 jalapeno pepper halved and remove seeds
- 1 cup cashews
- 2 bell peppers
- 1 tsp. Sea salt

Directions:

1. Add brussels sprouts leaves to the large bowl and set aside.
2. Add bell peppers, water, lemon juice, nutritional yeast, jalapeno, cashews, and salt to the blender and blend until smooth.
3. Pour blended mixture over brussels sprouts leaves and toss until well coated.

4. Arrange brussels sprouts on dehydrator trays and dehydrate at 125 f/ 52 c for 6 hours.
5. Allow cooling completely then store in an air-tight container.

Per serving: Calories: 237kcal; Fat: 11.7g; Carbs: 27.7g; Protein: 12.3g

59. Smokey Mexican Jerky

Preparation time: 15 minutes
Cooking time: 6 hours
Servings: 4
Ingredients:

- 2 pounds beef top round or bottom round, fat trimmed, sliced into ¼ inch thick slices
- ½ cup soy sauce
- 1 cup fresh lime juice
- 1-2 canned chipotle peppers in adobo sauce
- 1 tsp. Chili powder
- 1 cup Mexican beer

Directions:

1. Place all the ingredients, excluding the beef, into a blender and process until smooth.
2. Pour marinade over meat and refrigerate for 6-8 hours.
3. Remove from the refrigerator and place the meat on dehydrator sheets in a single layer.
4. Dehydrate at 145-160 degrees for 6-6 hours.

Per serving: Calories: 59kcal; Fat: 1.7g; Carbs: 2.7g; Protein: 8.2g

60. Sweet And Spicy Venison Or Beef Jerky

Preparation time: 15 minutes
Cooking time: 6 hours
Servings: 4

Ingredients:

- 2 pounds venison or beef
- ½ cup brown sugar
- ¼ cup pineapple juice
- 1 tbsp. Black pepper
- 1 tbsp. Lemon juice
- 1 tbsp. Minced garlic
- 1 tbsp. Paprika
- ¼ cup Worcestershire sauce
- ½ cup soy sauce
- 1 tsp. Sriracha sauce

Directions:

1. Cut pre-frozen venison or beef into ¼-inch thick slices.
2. Mix all ingredients and coat strips in the sauce.
3. Cover and refrigerate overnight.
4. Place beef or venison slices on dehydrator trays and dry at 145-155 degrees for about 6-6 hours.

Per serving: Calories: 53kcal; Fat: 0.4g; Carbs: 9.5g; Protein: 3.5g Thai Sweet Chili Jerky

Preparation time: 15 minutes

Meat

61. Beef Jerky

Preparation time: 30 minutes
Cooking time: 4 hours
Servings: 4
Ingredients:

- 2 lbs. London broil, sliced thinly
- 1 tsp sesame oil
- 3/4 tsp garlic powder
- 1 tsp onion powder
- 3 tbsps. Brown sugar
- 3 tbsps. Soy sauce

Directions:

Cooking time: 6 hours
Servings: 4
Ingredients:

- 2 pounds beef top or bottom round, trimmed, cut into ¼-inch slices
- 3 tbsp. Soy sauce
- 1 tbsp. Worcestershire sauce
- 1 tbsp. Teriyaki sauce
- ½ cup water
- 1 cup sweet chili sauce
- 1 tsp. Ground ginger

Directions:

1. Combine the marinade ingredients in a huge bowl. Place meat in a Ziplock bag and pour marinade over the meat.
2. Marinate meat in the refrigerator overnight.
3. Place meat on dehydrator sheets in a single layer.
4. Dehydrate at 155 degrees for 6-8 hours.

Per serving: Calories: 59kcal; Fat: 1.1g; Carbs: 5g; Protein: 5.6g

62. Chicken Jerky

Preparation time: 10 minutes
Cooking time: 7 hours
Servings: 4
Ingredients:

- 1 ½ lb. chicken tenders, boneless, skinless and cut into ¼-inch strips
- ¼ tsp ground ginger
- ¼ tsp black pepper
- ½ tsp garlic powder
- 1 tsp lemon juice
- ½ cup soy sauce

Directions:

5. Mix all ingredients except chicken into the zip-lock bag.

6. Add chicken and seal bag and mix until chicken is well coated. Place in refrigerator for 30 minutes.

7. Arrange marinated meat slices on dehydrator trays and dehydrate at 145 F/ 63 C for 6-7 hours.

Per serving: Calories: 342kcal; Fat: 12.6g; Carbs: 2.9g; Protein: 51.3g

63. Ranch Beef Jerky

Preparation time: 15 minutes
Cooking time: 8 hours
Servings: 6
Ingredients:

- 2 lbs. flank steak that is cut into thin slices
- ¼ tsp cayenne pepper
- 1 ½ tsp liquid smoke
- 2 tbsps. red pepper flakes
- 3 tbsps. ranch seasoning
- ¾ cup Worcestershire sauce
- ¾ cup soy sauce

Directions:

1. Add all ingredients into the huge mixing bowl and mix well. Cover bowl and place in refrigerator overnight.

2. Arrange marinated meat slices on dehydrator racks and dehydrate at 145 F/ 63 C for 7-8 hours.

Per serving: Calories: 346kcal; Fat: 12.9g; Carbs: 9.5g; Protein: 44.3g

64. Turkey Jerky

Preparation time: 15 minutes
Cooking time: 5 hours
Servings: 4
Ingredients:

- 1 lb. turkey meat, cut into thin slices
- 1 tsp salt
- 2 tsp garlic powder

- 1 tbsp. onion powder
- 2 tsp brown sugar
- 1/3 cup Worcestershire sauce
- ¼ tsp Tabasco sauce
- 2 tbsps. soy sauce
- 1 tbsp. liquid smoke

Directions:

1. Add all ingredients except meat to the large zip-lock bag and mix until well combined.

2. Add meat to the bag. Seal the bag and massage gently to cover the meat with marinade. Place in refrigerator overnight.

3. Arrange marinated meat slices on the dehydrator racks and dehydrate at 160 F/ 71 C for 5 hours.

Per serving: Calories: 233.kcal; Fat: 5.7g; Carbs: 8.5g; Protein: 34.1g

65. Asian Pork Jerky

Preparation time: 15 minutes
Cooking time: 4 hours 30 minutes
Servings: 5
Ingredients:

- 1 lb. pork loin, cut into thin slices
- ¼ tsp salt
- 1 tsp black pepper
- ½ tsp onion powder
- ½ tsp garlic powder
- 1 tsp sesame oil
- 1 tbsp. chili garlic sauce
- 1 tbsp. brown sugar
- 1 tbsp. Worcestershire sauce
- 1/3 cup soy sauce

Directions:

1. Add all ingredients except meat slices into the large bowl and mix well.

2. Add sliced meat to the bowl and mix until well coated. Cover bowl and place in refrigerator overnight.

3. Arrange marinated meat slices on the dehydrator racks and dehydrate at 160 F/ 71 C for 4 1/2 hours.

Per serving: Calories: 249kcal; Fat: 13.6g; Carbs: 4.3g; Protein: 26g

66. Tofu Jerky

Preparation time: 10 minutes
Cooking time: 4 hours
Servings: 4
Ingredients:

- 1 block tofu, pressed
- 4 drops of liquid smoke
- 2 tbsps. Worcestershire sauce
- 2 tbsps. sriracha

Directions:

1. Cut tofu in half then cut into slices.

2. In a bowl, mix together liquid smoke, Worcestershire sauce, and sriracha.

3. Add tofu slices to a bowl and mix until well coated with the marinade. Cover bowl tightly and place in refrigerator overnight.

4. Place marinated tofu slices on the dehydrator trays and dehydrate at 145 F/ 63 C for 4 hours.

Per serving: Calories: 44kcal; Fat: 1.8g; Carbs: 3.9g; Protein: 3.2g

67. Sweet & Spicy Beef Jerky

Preparation time: 15 minutes
Cooking time: 6 hours
Servings: 8
Ingredients:

- 2 lbs. flank steak, trimmed the fat and sliced into thin strips
- 1 tsp red pepper flakes
- 1 tsp liquid smoke

- 1 tsp garlic powder
- 1 tsp onion powder
- 2 tsp black pepper
- 1 tbsp. brown sugar
- 2/3 cup soy sauce
- 2/3 cup Worcestershire sauce

Directions:

1. Add red pepper flakes, liquid smoke, garlic powder, onion powder, black pepper, brown sugar, soy sauce, and Worcestershire sauce in a large zip-lock bag and mix well.

2. Add sliced meat to the zip-lock bag. Seal the bag well and shake until meat is well coated. Place in refrigerator overnight.

3. Arrange marinated meat slices on a dehydrator rack and dehydrate at 160 F/ 71 C for 5-6 hours.

4. Store in an air-tight container.

Per serving: Calories: 260kcal; Fat: 9.5g; Carbs: 7.7g; Protein: 33.1g

68. Sweet & Smoky Salmon Jerky

Preparation time: 15 minutes
Cooking time: 5 hours
Servings: 6
Ingredients:

- 2 lbs. salmon, sliced into strips
- 3 tsp black pepper
- 3 tbsps. smoked sea salt
- ¼ cup liquid smoke
- 2 tbsps. black pepper
- 1 cup brown sugar
- 1 cup soy sauce
- 1 orange juice

Directions:

1. Add all ingredients except salmon slices into the large bowl and mix well.

2. Add sliced salmon to the bowl and mix until well coated. Cover bowl and place in refrigerator overnight.

3. Arrange marinated salmon slices in a single layer on the dehydrator racks and dehydrate at 160 F/ 71 C for 5 hours.

Per serving: Calories: 329kcal; Fat: 9.5g; Carbs: 30.5g; Protein: 32.5g

69. Lemon Salmon Jerky

Preparation time: 15 minutes
Cooking time: 4 hours
Servings: 6
Ingredients:

- 1 ¼ lbs. salmon, cut into ¼-inch slices
- 1/2 tsp liquid smoke
- 1 ¼ tsp black pepper
- 1 ½ tbsps. fresh lemon juice
- 1 tbsp. molasses
- ½ cup soy sauce, low sodium

Directions:

1. In a bowl, mix together liquid smoke, black pepper, lemon juice, molasses, and soy sauce.

2. Add sliced salmon into the bowl and mix until well coated. Cover bowl and place in refrigerator overnight.

3. Strain sliced salmon in a colander and pat dry with a paper towel.

4. Arrange sliced salmon on a dehydrator tray and dehydrate at 145 F/ 63 C for 3-4 hours.

Per serving: Calories: 148kcal; Fat: 5.9g; Carbs: 4.5g; Protein: 19.7g

70. Easy Mexican Jerky

Preparation time: 15 minutes
Cooking time: 5 hours
Servings: 4
Ingredients:

- 1 lb. pork lean meat, sliced thinly
- 1 tsp paprika
- ½ tsp oregano
- ½ tsp garlic powder
- 1 tsp chili powder
- ¼ tsp black pepper
- 1 tsp salt

Directions:

1. Add paprika, oregano, garlic powder, chili powder, black pepper, and salt in a bowl and mix well.

2. Add sliced meat in a bowl and mix until well coated. Cover bowl and place in refrigerator for overnight.

3. Arrange marinated meat slices on dehydrator rack and dehydrate at 160 F/ 71 C for 5 hours.

Per serving: Calories: 168kcal; Fat: 4.2g; Carbs: 1.1g; Protein: 29.9g

71. Perfect Lamb Jerky

Preparation time: 10 minutes
Cooking time: 6 hours
Servings: 6
Ingredients:

- 2 ½ lbs. boneless lamb, trimmed fat and sliced into thin strips
- ½ tsp black pepper
- 1 tbsp. oregano
- 1 tsp garlic powder
- 1 ½ tsp onion powder
- 3 tbsps. Worcestershire sauce
- 1/3 cup soy sauce

Directions:

1. Add soy sauce, Worcestershire sauce, onion powder, garlic powder, oregano, and black pepper in the large bowl and mix well.

2. Add meat slices in the bowl and mix until well coated. Cover bowl tightly and place in refrigerator for overnight.
3. Arrange marinated meat slices on dehydrator racks and dehydrate to 145 F/ 63 C for 5-6 hours.

Per serving: Calories: 373kcal; Fat: 14g; Carbs: 4g; Protein: 54.2g

72. Flavorful Teriyaki Jerky

Preparation time: 15 minutes
Cooking time: 6 hours
Servings: 6
Ingredients:

- 1 ½ lbs. beef bottom round thin meat
- 1 tsp onion powder
- 1 tsp garlic, minced
- 1 tsp red pepper flakes
- 1/3 cup soy sauce
- 1/3 cup Worcestershire sauce
- 1 tsp liquid smoke
- ½ cup teriyaki sauce

Directions:

1. Cut meat into thin slices.
2. Add teriyaki sauce, onion powder, garlic, red pepper flakes, soy sauce, Worcestershire sauce, and liquid smoke in the large bowl.
3. Add meat slices in the bowl and mix until well coated. Cover bowl tightly and place in refrigerator for overnight.
4. Place marinated meat slices on dehydrator trays and dehydrate at 160 F/ 71 C for 5-6 hours.
5. Store in an air-tight container.

Per serving: Calories: 246kcal; Fat: 7.4g; Carbs: 8.1g; Protein: 33.9g

73. Flavorful Turkey Jerky

Preparation time: 15 minutes
Cooking time: 6 hours

Servings: 4
Ingredients:

- 1 lb. turkey tenderloins, trimmed fat and sliced ¼ inch thick
- ½ tsp liquid smoke
- 1 tsp black pepper
- 2 tbsp. brown sugar
- 2 tsp Worcestershire sauce
- ¼ cup soy sauce
- ½ cup water
- ¼ tsp garlic powder
- ¼ tsp onion powder

Directions:

1. In a large mixing bowl, combine together onion powder, liquid smoke, pepper, sugar, Worcestershire sauce, soy sauce, water, and garlic powder. Stir until seasoning dissolve.
2. Add meat slices and mix until well coated. Cover bowl tightly and refrigerate for overnight.
3. Spray dehydrator racks with cooking spray.
4. Remove marinated meat slices from the marinade and shake off excess liquid. Arrange meat slices on dehydrator racks.
5. Arrange dehydrator tray according to the manufacturer's instructions and dry at 145 F/ 63 C for 5-6 hours.
6. Let cool jerky for 5-10 minutes then store in a container.

Per serving: Calories: 151kcal; Fat: 1.5g; Carbs: 6.7g; Protein: 29.2g

74. Mushroom Crusted Beef Tenderloin

Preparation time: 20 minutes
Cooking time: 40 minutes
Servings: 8
Ingredients:

- 4 lbs. beef tenderloin
- 1/2 cup dehydrated porcini mushrooms
- 4 tablespoons olive oil
- Salt and black pepper

Directions:

1. Season the beef with salt and pepper then set your oven to 350F. Place the beef on a rack in a roasting pan and place in the oven for 10 minutes.
2. While the beef is cooking, place the dehydrated mushrooms in a blender and blend into a powder.
3. Remove the beef from the oven and rub it on all sides with the mushroom powder. Place back in the oven for approximately 30 to 40 minutes, or until an instant-read thermometer registers 125F.
4. Remove from the oven and rest for 10 minutes before serving.

Per serving: Calories: 438kcal; Fat: 22.5g; Carbs: 3.8g; Protein: 51.1g

75. Fish Teriyaki Jerky

Preparation time: 4 hours and 10 minutes
Cooking time: 8 hours
Servings: 2
Ingredients:

- 1 lb. Salmon, sliced
- ¼ teaspoon ginger, grated
- ¼ cup sugar
- ½ cup soy sauce
- ¼ cup orange juice
- 1 clove of garlic, minced

Directions:

1. Combine all the ingredients in a bowl.
2. Mix well.
3. Transfer to a sealable plastic bag.
4. Seal and refrigerate for 4 hours.
5. Drain the marinade.

6. Add the salmon to the food dehydrator.
7. Process at 145 degrees f for 8 hours.
8. Storage suggestions: store the salmon jerky in a glass jar with a lid.

Tip: you can process longer in the dehydrator if you want the fish slices crispier and dryer.

Per serving: Calories: 389kcal; Fat: 6.4g; Carbs: 22.9g; Protein: 49.3g

76. Cajun Fish Jerky

Preparation time: 4 hours and 10 minutes
Cooking time: 8 hours
Servings: 2
Ingredients:

- 1 teaspoon garlic powder
- 1 teaspoon paprika
- 1 teaspoon onion powder
- ¼ teaspoon cayenne pepper
- 1 tablespoon lemon juice
- Salt and pepper to taste
- 1 lb. Cod fillet, sliced

Directions:

1. Mix the spices, lemon juice, salt and pepper in a bowl.
2. Season the fish with this mixture.
3. Transfer the seasoned fish and marinade in a sealable plastic bag.
4. Marinate in the refrigerator for 4 hours.
5. Drain the marinade.
6. Arrange the salmon slices on the food dehydrator.
7. Process at 145 degrees f for 8 hours.
8. Storage suggestions: store in a vacuum-sealed plastic bag or glass jar with a lid.

Tip: you can use another white fish fillet for this recipe.

Per serving: Calories: 389kcal; Fat: 6.4g; Carbs: 22.9g; Protein: 49.3g

77. Venison Jerky

Preparation time: 1 day and 30 minutes
Cooking time: 4 hours
Servings: 2
Ingredients:

- 1 lb. Venison roast, silver skin trimmed and sliced thinly
- 4 tablespoons coconut amino
- ¼ teaspoon onion powder
- ¼ teaspoon garlic powder
- ¼ teaspoon red pepper flakes
- 1 tablespoon honey
- 4 tablespoons Worcestershire sauce
- Salt and pepper to taste

Directions:

1. Place the roast venison slices in a bowl.
2. In another mixing bowl, mix the rest of the ingredients.
3. Pour this mixture into the first bowl.
4. Stir to coat meat evenly with the mixture.
5. Cover the bowl.
6. Chill in the refrigerator for 1 day, stirring every 3 or 4 hours.
7. Drain the marinade.
8. Place the venison slices in the food dehydrator.
9. Process at 160 degrees f for 4 hours.
10. Storage suggestions: store in vacuum sealed bags for up to 3 months or in Ziplock bags for up to 2 weeks.

Tip: freeze the venison meat for 1 hour before slicing.
Per serving: Calories: 389kcal; Fat: 6.4g; Carbs: 22.9g; Protein: 49.3g

78. Hickory Smoked Jerky

Preparation time: 12 hours and 10 minutes
Cooking time: 4 hours
Servings: 4

Ingredients:

- 1 lb. Beef round, sliced
- ½ cup hickory smoked marinade
- ¼ cup barbecue sauce
- 2 tablespoons brown sugar
- 1 teaspoon onion powder
- Pinch cayenne pepper
- Salt and pepper to taste

Directions:

1. Place the beef slices in a sealable plastic bag.
2. In a bowl, combine the marinade, barbecue sauce, sugar, onion powder, cayenne, salt and pepper.
3. Pour the mixture into the bag.
4. Seal and marinate in the refrigerator for twelve hours.
5. Discard the marinade and add the beef to the food dehydrator.
6. Process at 180 degrees f for 4 hours, flipping halfway through.
7. Storage suggestions: store in a glass jar with a lid for up to 2 weeks.

Tip: arrange the meat in a single layer without overlapping.
Per serving: Calories: 389kcal; Fat: 6.4g; Carbs: 22.9g; Protein: 49.3g

79. Beer Beef Jerky

Preparation time: 6 hours and 10 minutes
Cooking time: 5 hours
Servings: 2
Ingredients:

- 1 lb. Beef round, sliced
- ½ cup soy sauce
- 2 cloves garlic, minced
- 2 cups beer
- 1 tablespoon liquid smoke
- 1 tablespoon honey
- Pepper to taste

Directions:

1. Add the beef to a sealable plastic bag.
2. Combine the rest of the ingredients in a bowl.
3. Pour the mixture into the bag.
4. Seal and refrigerate for 6 hours.
5. Drain the marinade.
6. Place the beef in the food dehydrator.
7. Dehydrate at 160 degrees f for 1 hour.
8. Reduce temperature to 150 degrees f and process for additional 4 hours.
9. Storage suggestions: store in a food container with a lid for up to 2 weeks.

Tip: make sure beef is trimmed of fat before dehydrating.

Per serving: Calories: 389kcal; Fat: 6.4g; Carbs: 22.9g; Protein: 49.3g

Fruit

80. Tasty Pineapple Chunks

Preparation time: 10 minutes
Cooking time: 12 hours
Servings: 4
Ingredients:

- 1 ripe pineapple

Directions:

1. Peel and cut pineapple. Cut in 1/2 then cut each half into ¼-inch thick chunks.
2. Place pineapple chunks on dehydrator racks and dehydrate at 135 F/ 58 C for 12 hours.

Per serving: Calories: 62kcal; Fat: 0.2g; Carbs: 16.2g; Protein: 0.7g

81.Asian Pear and Ginger Treats

Preparation time: 20 minutes
Cooking time: 9 to 12 hours
Servings: 6 to 8
Ingredients:

- 6 medium-sized Asian pears, peeled, pitted and cored
- 1 ½ teaspoon honey
- 4 tablespoons warm water
- 1 small knob of ginger, finely grated

Directions:

1. In a bowl, mix honey and ginger. Add the water and mix well.
2. Slice Asian pears into uniform slices, around ¼ inch thick. Arrange pear slices onto a dehydrator tray and brush with a thin layer of ginger-honey mixture.
3. Dehydrate for 9-12 hours at 135 degrees.

Per serving: Calories: 18kcal; Fat: 0g; Carbs: 4.9g; Protein: 0.1g

82. Banana Cocoa Leather

Preparation time: 30 minutes
Cooking time: 8 to 10 hours
Servings: 6
Ingredients:

- 4 bananas
- 2 tablespoons cocoa powder
- 1-2 tablespoons. corn syrup
- 1 teaspoon lemon juice

Directions:

1. Puree all ingredients until smooth.
2. Pour mixture onto dehydrator trays and spread to ¼ inch thickness. Dehydrate at 130 degrees for 8-10 hours. About halfway through, flip leather to the other side.

Per serving: Calories: 42kcal; Fat: 0.8g; Carbs: 11g; Protein: 1.1g

83. Fruit Sprinkles

Preparation time: 20 minutes
Cooking time: 6 to 8 hours
Servings: 6 to 8

Ingredients:

- 1 cup raspberries or strawberries, hulled
- 1 tablespoon sugar
- 1 tablespoon orange juice
- Zest of 2 lemons
- Zest of 2 oranges

Directions:

1. Dice strawberries and raspberries into small pieces.
2. Combine with sugar, juice and lemon and orange zest.
3. Spread mixture on dehydrator sheets.
4. Dehydrate for 6-8 hours at 118 degrees. At this point, the fruit should be thoroughly dried.
5. Place all the mixture in a spice grinder and pulse several times until you have sprinkles. Top your favorite treats with fruit sprinkles for added flavor and color.

Per serving: Calories: 25kcal; Fat: 0g; Carbs: 6.5g; Protein: 0.1g

84. Goji Berry Leather

Preparation time: 1 hour 15 minutes
Cooking time: 7 hours
Servings: 2
Ingredients:

- 1 cup dried goji berries
- 2 cups unsweetened applesauce
- 2 tablespoons honey

Directions:

1. Place goji berries in 1 cup of water and let soak until they are rehydrated, about 1 hour.
2. Pour berries, soaking water, applesauce and honey into the blender and blend until smooth. Add more water if necessary.

3. Spread onto dehydrator sheets and dry at 135 degrees for 6-7 hours.

Per serving: Calories: 64kcal; Fat: 0.8g; Carbs: 14g; Protein: 0.5g

85. Nothing But Fruit Bars

Preparation time: 30 minutes
Cooking time: 18 hours
Servings: 8
Ingredients:

- 2 cups sprouted buckwheat or quinoa
- 1 cup dates
- 1 cup dried apricots
- 1 tablespoon cinnamon
- 1/8 teaspoon cardamom
- 1 pear or apple, peeled, cored and diced

Directions:

1. Place all ingredients in a blender. Blend until smooth.
2. Spread the mixture onto dehydrator trays. Use a spatula to smooth. Dehydrate for 18 hours at 130 degrees.

Per serving: Calories: 98kcal; Fat: 1.6g; Carbs: 17.6g; Protein: 3.6g

86. Candied Ginger

Preparation time: 20 minutes
Cooking time: 4 hours
Servings: 6 to 8
Ingredients:

- Fresh ginger roots
- Water, as needed
- Granulated sugar, as needed

Directions:

1. Peel the ginger then cut it into thin slices or chunks.
2. Place the ginger in a medium saucepan and pour in enough water to cover it.
3. Add an equal amount of sugar then bring to a boil.

4. Reduce the heat and simmer for about 45 minutes, then drain off the syrup, reserving it.

5. Measure out the ginger then add it back to the saucepan.

6. Add an equal amount of sugar along with two tablespoons of the reserved syrup for every cup of prepared ginger.

7. Bring the ginger to boil over medium heat then reduce heat slightly and simmer until all of the liquid cooks off.

8. Stir the ginger frequently, boiling it until the sugar separates and dries.

9. Remove the pan from the heat then spread the ginger slices on your dehydrator trays. Let the ginger cool then store in glass jars, sealed tightly with the lids.

Per serving: Calories: 8kcal; Fat: 0g; Carbs: 2g; Protein: 0g

87. Soy Marinated Salmon Jerky

Preparation time: 40 minutes
Cooking time: 16 hours
Servings: 12
Ingredients:

- 1 lbs. boneless salmon fillet
- Salt and pepper to taste
- ½ cup apple cider vinegar
- 2 tablespoons low-sodium soy sauce
- 1 tablespoon fresh lemon juice
- 2 teaspoons paprika
- ½ teaspoon garlic powder

Directions:

1. Freeze the salmon for about 30 minutes until it is firm.

2. Meanwhile, whisk together the apple cider vinegar, soy sauce, and lemon juice in a mixing bowl.

3. Add the paprika and garlic powder then stir well. Season the salmon with salt and pepper to taste then remove the skin.

4. Slice the salmon into ¼-inch thick strips then place them in a bowl or glass dish.

5. Pour in the marinade, turning to coat, then cover with plastic and chill for 12 hours.

6. Drain the salmon slices and place them on paper towels to soak up the extra liquid.

7. Spread the salmon slices on your dehydrator trays in a single layer.

8. Dry for 3 to 4 hours at 145°F (63°C) until it is dried but still tender and chewy.

9. Cool the salmon jerky completely then store in airtight containers in a cool, dark location.

Per serving: Calories: 40kcal; Fat: 1g; Carbs: 5g; Protein: 4g

88. Peach Cobbler

Preparation time: 10 minutes
Cooking time: 8 hours
Servings: 4
Ingredients:

- 2 peaches, sliced into 1/4 inch slices
- 1/3 cup bread crumbs
- 1 tablespoon sugar
- 1/2 teaspoon cinnamon
- 1/2 teaspoon nutmeg
- 1/2 cup water

Directions:

1. Place the peach slices on the rack of your Food dehydrator and set to 125F. Dehydrate for 8 hours.

2. Remove peach slices from the racks and combine with the breadcrumbs, sugar, cinnamon, and nutmeg. Store in a zip-lock bag until ready to use.

3. To rehydrate, simply combine the contents of the bag with 1/2 cup boiling water and stir.

Per serving: Calories: 78kcal; Fat: 0.8g; Carbs: 16.9g; Protein: 1.9g

89. Banana Bread Pudding

Preparation time: 10 minutes
Cooking time: 8 hours
Servings: 4
Ingredients:

- 2 bananas, sliced into rounds
- 1/4 cup cashews, chopped
- 1/2 cup white bread, cut into large chunks
- 1 tablespoon brown sugar

Directions:

1. Place the banana slices on the racks of your Food Dehydrator and set them to 125F. Dehydrate for 8 hours or until completely dried.
2. In a zipper-lock bag, combine the bananas and brown sugar. In another zipper-lock bag combine the bread chunks and cashews.
3. To rehydrate, combine all ingredients with 1/2 cup warm water and allow to sit for 5 minutes before stirring and serving.

Per serving: Calories: 122kcal; Fat: 4.3g; Carbs: 20.7g; Protein: 2.3g

90. Apple Fig Fruit Leather

Preparation time: 30 minutes
Cooking time: 8 hours
Servings: 6
Ingredients:

- 10 figs, ripe and washed
- 2 apples, cored and peeled
- 1 cup orange juice

Directions:

1. Boil all ingredients in a covered pot.
2. Simmer fruits for 30 minutes.
3. Mix all ingredients using a blender.
4. Place the mixture in the dehydrator.
5. Dry for 8 hours at 125 F.

Per serving: Calories: 104kcal; Fat: 0g; Carbs: 27g; Protein: 1g

91. Peach & Raspberry

Preparation time: 15 minutes
Cooking time: 8-10 hours
Servings: 6
Ingredients:

- 10 Peaches, sliced
- 3 cup Raspberries
- Honey, to taste

Directions:

1. Puree the peaches in your blender, add honey and transfer to a bowl.
2. Spread the mixture over dehydrator trays lined with parchment paper.
3. Add the raspberries to the blender then blend until smooth. Pour this mixture over and swirl into the peach mixture.
4. Dehydrate at 120F / 48C for 8-10 hours.
5. When done, remove from the parchment paper, cut into strips, roll them up in parchment paper and store in airtight containers.

Per serving: Calories: 100.4kcal; Fat: 0.8g; Carbs: 25.2g; Protein: 1.7g

92. Mango Lime Fruit Leather

Preparation time: 15 minutes
Cooking time: 6-9 hours or more
Servings: 6
Ingredients:

- 8 Mangos, peeled and diced
- 2 Limes, juiced and zested

- Honey, to taste

Directions:

1. Add the mangoes, lime juice and zest to your blender and blend until pureed. Mix in honey and set aside.
2. Line dehydrator trays with parchment paper then spread the fruit mixture onto them.
3. Dehydrate at 120F / 48C for 6-9 hours. When done, cut into strips, roll up in parchment paper and store in airtight containers Fruit Leather

Per serving: Calories: 141.3kcal; Fat: 0.6g; Carbs: 37.5g; Protein: 1.2g

93. **Banana Cocoa Leather**

Preparation time: 15 minutes
Cooking time: 15 hours
Servings: 4
Ingredients:

- 4 bananas
- 2 Tbsp cocoa powder
- 1-2 Tbsp corn syrup
- 1 tsp lemon juice

Directions:

1. Puree all ingredients until smooth.
2. Pour mixture onto dehydrator trays and spread to ¼ inch thickness. Dehydrate at 130 degrees for 8-10 hours. About halfway through, flip leather to the other side.

Per serving: Calories: 42kcal; Fat: 0.8g; Carbs: 11g; Protein: 1.1g Grain, Nuts And Seeds

94. **Almond Cranberry Cookies**

Preparation time: 15 minutes
Cooking time: 6 hours
Servings: 4
Ingredients:

- Wet pulp from almond milk
- 1 banana

- 2 tbsp. Coconut oil
- ¾ cup shredded coconut flakes
- ½ cup dried cranberries
- 1 tbsp. Honey
- ½ cup almonds, coarsely chopped

Directions:

1. Place almond pulp, banana and coconut oil in a food processor.
2. Mix the remainder of the ingredients and add to the almond pulp mixture.
3. Place a small scoop of dough on dehydrator sheets and flatten it into a cookie.
4. Set the temperature to 105 degrees and dehydrate for 6 hours.

Per serving: Calories: 91kcal; Fat: 7.6g; Carbs: 4.8g; Protein: 2g

95. **Apple Cinnamon Graham Cookies**

Preparation time: 15 minutes
Cooking time: 6 hours
Servings: 4
Ingredients:

- 1 cup cashews, soaked for 1 hour
- 1 cup pecans, soaked for 1 hour
- 6 cups ground almonds
- 2 apples, peeled, cored and chopped
- 1 pear, peeled, cored and chopped
- 1 cup almond butter
- 1 ½ cups flax seed
- ½ cup honey
- 1 tbsp. Cinnamon
- ½ tsp. Nutmeg
- Pinch of salt

Directions:

1. After nuts have been soaked, drain and rinse them.
2. Pulse cashews and pecans in a food processor until small crumbs form. Add

the ground almonds and place them in a bowl.

3. In the food processor, combine apples, pear, almond butter, flax seed, honey, cinnamon, nutmeg and salt. Add the ground nuts.
4. Spread mixture on dehydrator trays, about ¼ inch thick, to the edges.
5. Dehydrate for 6-8 hours at 115 degrees. Flip over and cut into squares. Continue dehydrating for 6-8 hours or until crunchy.

Per serving: Calories: 160kcal; Fat: 13.3g; Carbs: 6.8g; Protein: 5.1g

96. Banana Breakfast Crepes

Preparation time: 15 minutes
Cooking time: 6 hours
Servings: 4
Ingredients:

- 2 medium size ripe bananas
- 1 tsp. Ground flax seed
- 1 tsp. Almond meal
- 1 tsp. Almond milk
- Dash of cinnamon

Directions:

1. Put all ingredients in a food processor then blend into a liquid.
2. Line 2 dehydrator sheets and pour the mixture onto them. The liquid should only be about 1/8 inches in thickness. Spread with a spatula.
3. Dehydrate at 115 degrees for 3 hours. Crepes should be smooth. Do not remove crepes early or they will not hold their shape. Cut into crepe-sized circles.

Per serving: Calories: 48kcal; Fat: 2g; Carbs: 6.6g; Protein: 1.2g

97. Flax Seed Crackers

Preparation time: 15 minutes

Cooking time: 6 hours
Servings: 4
Ingredients:

- 2 cups flaxseeds
- 2 cups water
- ¼ cup low sodium soy sauce
- 2 tbsp. Sesame seeds
- Sea salt and black pepper, to taste
- 1 ½ tbsp. Fresh lime juice

Directions:

1. Cover flax seeds with water and soak for 1-2 hours. The mixture should be gooey, but not too thin. Add more water to achieve this texture.
2. Stir in the remainder of the ingredients.
3. Spread the mixture about 1/8 inch thick on dehydrator sheets.
4. Set the temperature to 105-115 degrees and dehydrate for 4-6 hours. Flip over mixture and dehydrate another 4-6 hours. Break crackers into large pieces after dehydrating.

Per serving: Calories: 133kcal; Fat: 8.2g; Carbs: 7.1g; Protein: 4.6g

98. Fruit N' Nut Balls

Preparation time: 15 minutes
Cooking time: 6 hours
Servings: 4
Ingredients:

- ½ cup dried dates
- ½ cup figs
- ½ cup dried cherries
- ½ cup dried apricots
- ½ cup dried cranberries
- 1 cup crushed pecans
- 1 cup crushed almonds
- 3 tsp. Coconut oil, melted
- 1 cup flaked coconut

Directions:

1. Finely process dates, figs, cherries, apricots and cranberries in a food processor. Mix with nuts and coconut oil in a bowl.
2. Shape into 1" balls and roll balls in coconut.
3. Place in dehydrator at 135 degrees for 6 hours.

Per serving: Calories: 102kcal; Fat: 8.4g; Carbs: 6.9g; Protein: 2g

99. Mint-Scented Chocolate Chip Cookies

Preparation time: 15 minutes
Cooking time: 6 hours
Servings: 4
Ingredients:

- 1 ½ cups almond meal
- 1 ½ cups ground pecans
- 1 cup cocoa powder
- ¼ cup cacao nibs
- ½ cup maple syrup
- 3 tbsp. Coconut oil
- 1 tsp. Peppermint extract
- 1 tsp. Vanilla extract
- 1 tbsp. Almond milk
- ½ tsp. Salt

Directions:

1. Put all ingredients in a food processor then pulse until combined. Ingredients should form a cohesive dough.
2. Roll out dough to about ¼ inch thickness.
3. Cut out circles using a small glass. Alternatively, skip this process, roll dough into balls and flatten it into disks.
4. Dehydrate for 24 hours at 115 degrees.

Per serving: Calories: 140kcal; Fat: 12.1g; Carbs: 8.8g; Protein: 4.3g

100. Sesame Seed Crisps

Preparation time: 15 minutes
Cooking time: 6 hours
Servings: 4
Ingredients:

- ½ cup flax seeds
- 1 cup water
- ½ cup sesame seeds, toasted
- ½ cup black sesame seeds
- ½ tsp. Sea salt
- ½ tsp. Dried thyme
- ½ tsp. Garlic powder

Directions:

1. In a bowl, mix seeds and seasonings with water. Stir till the mixture is well incorporated then leave for 10-15 minutes to allow seeds to become pudding-like.
2. Spread onto dehydrator trays. The batter should be less than ¼ inch thick. Dehydrate at 110 degrees for 8-12 hours. Flip them over and dehydrate for another 8 hours.

Per serving: Calories: 147kcal; Fat: 11.4g; Carbs: 6.8g; Protein: 4.8g

101. Sweet Cocoa Chia Bars

Preparation time: 15 minutes
Cooking time: 6 hours
Servings: 4
Ingredients:

- 1 cup chia seeds
- 2 cups water
- ¼ cup cocoa powder
- 6 figs, chopped
- 1 apple, peeled, cored and chopped
- 1 cup walnuts, chopped
- 3 tbsp. Honey
- 3 tbsp. Cacao nibs

Directions:

1. Soak chia seeds in ½ cup of water for 30 minutes. Drain.
2. Blend all remaining ingredients in a blender, except for cacao nibs. Add a little amount of water to achieve the right consistency.
3. Stir together chia seeds, blended mixture and cacao nibs.
4. Allow to rest for 20-25 minutes.
5. Spread the mixture onto a dehydrator tray. Dehydrate for 1 hour at 135 degrees. Cut into bars.
6. Lower temperature to 110 degrees and dehydrate another 8 hours. Flip bars and dehydrate for another 8 hours.

Per serving: Calories: 125kcal; Fat: 9.6g; Carbs: 5.6g; Protein: 5.2g

102. Graham Crackers

Preparation time: 15 minutes
Cooking time: 6 hours
Servings: 4
Ingredients:

- 4 cups almond flour
- 1 cup oat flour
- ½ cup flax seeds
- ½ cup almond milk
- 1 cup maple syrup
- 1 tbsp. Vanilla
- 1 tbsp. Cinnamon

Directions:

1. Mix all the ingredients into the food processor.
2. Spread onto dehydrator trays. Make sure the graham cracker mixture is about 1/8" thick. Dehydrate at 115 deg. F for 4 hrs.
3. Cut into squares then flip and dehydrate for 6 more hours.

Per serving: Calories: 142kcal; Fat: 10.2g; Carbs: 9.6g; Protein: 5g

103. Hazelnut Lemon Crackers

Preparation time: 15 minutes
Cooking time: 7 hours
Servings: 4
Ingredients:

- ½ cup chia seeds
- 1 cup water
- 3 cups hazelnuts, soaked overnight, skins removed
- 1 ½ tbsp. Lemon zest
- 1 tbsp. Maple syrup
- ½ tsp. Sea salt
- Black pepper to taste

Directions:

1. Mix chia seeds in 1 cup of water then let soften.
2. Remove soaked hazelnuts then drain them. Place hazelnuts in a food processor then grind until fine.
3. Pour ground nuts into a bowl then combine with chia seeds, lemon zest, maple syrup, salt and pepper.
4. Spread onto dehydrator trays. Use a spatula to flatten the dough to approximately ¼ inch thick. Dehydrate at 145 degrees for 1 hour. Decrease the heat to 115 and continue to dehydrate for 8 hours.

Per serving: Calories: 169kcal; Fat: 15.6g; Carbs: 5.5g; Protein: 4.4g

104. Macadamia-Sage Crackers

Preparation time: 15 minutes
Cooking time: 6 hours
Servings: 4
Ingredients:

- 2 cups macadamia nuts

- 2 cups chia or flax seeds
- 1 ½ tbsp. Fresh sage, crushed
- Sea salt and white pepper to taste
- 3 cups water
- ½ cup olive oil

Directions:

1. Put macadamia nuts and flax seeds into a food processor then grind into flour. Add sage, salt and pepper. Process until you have a fine texture.
2. Add water to nut and seed mix in a huge bowl, then stir until thick. Don't pour all the water at once. Add little amounts until a soft dough forms.
3. Spread onto dehydrator sheets. Sprinkle with olive oil then sprinkle additional sea salt.
4. Dehydrate at 110 deg. F for 4 hrs. Score the crackers, flip them over then dehydrate another 8 hours.

Per serving: Calories: 176kcal; Fat: 15.1g; Carbs: 7.2g; Protein: 4.2gHerbs And Powder

105. Dried Basil Powder

Preparation time: 10 minutes
Cooking time: 15 hours
Servings: 5
Ingredients:

- 3 cups basil leaves

Directions:

1. Add the basil leaves to the food dehydrator.
2. Dry at 105 degrees for 15 hours.
3. Grind the dried basil in a spice grinder or food processor.
4. Storage suggestions: store in an empty spice jar.

Tip: use only fresh basil leaves.

Per serving: Calories: 198kcal; Fat: 12g; Carbs: 16g; Protein: 8g

106. Dried Herb Mix

Preparation time: 15 minutes
Cooking time: 8 hours
Servings: 5
Ingredients:

- ½ cup thyme leaves
- ½ cup rosemary leaves
- 2 teaspoons lemon zest
- 6 cloves garlic, peeled

Directions:

1. Mix all the ingredients into a food processor.
2. Pulse until smooth.
3. Spread the mixture in the food dehydrator.
4. Dehydrate at 135 deg. F for 8 hours.
5. Storage suggestions: store in an empty spice bottle.

Tip: you can also add other herbs such as oregano or thyme.

Per serving: Calories: 98kcal; Fat: 12g; Carbs: 16 g; Protein: 8g

107. Onion Powder

Preparation time: 10 minutes
Cooking time: 8 hours
Servings: 5
Ingredients:

- 5 onions, sliced

Directions:

1. Arrange the onion slices in one layer in the food dehydrator.
2. Dehydrate at 145 degrees f for 8 hours.
3. Transfer the dried onion to a food processor.
4. Pulse until powdery.
5. Storage suggestions: store the onion powder in a mason jar.

Per serving: Calories: 76kcal; Fat: 5g; Carbs: 5 g; Protein: 3g

108. Tomato Powder

Preparation time: 15 minutes
Cooking time: 12 hours
Servings: 5
Ingredients:

- Skins from 10 tomatoes

Directions:

1. Add the tomato skins to a food dehydrator.
2. Dry at 135 degrees f for 12 hours.
3. Transfer the dried tomatoes to a coffee grinder.
4. Grind until the mixture turns to powder.
5. Storage suggestions: store in a glass jar with a lid.

Tip: you can also make tomato flakes from this recipe.

Per serving: Calories: 243kcal; Fat: 14g; Carbs: 25g; Protein: 14g

109. Leek Powder

Preparation time: 5 minutes
Cooking time: 12 hours
Servings: 5
Ingredients:

- 4 cups leeks, sliced

Directions:

1. Place the leeks in the food dehydrator.
2. Dehydrate at 135 degrees f for 4 hours.
3. Put the dried leeks in a spice grinder.
4. Grind until powdery.
5. Storage suggestions: store in a tightly sealed food or spice container.

Tip: do not use any browned parts of leeks.

Per serving: Calories: 23kcal; Fat: 14g; Carbs: 2g; Protein: 4g

110. Dried Parsley, Basil & Oregano Powder

Preparation time: 15 minutes
Cooking time: 8 hours
Servings: 5
Ingredients:

- 2 tablespoons parsley leaves
- 2 tablespoons basil leaves
- 2 tablespoons oregano leaves
- 2 tablespoons brown sugar
- 2 tablespoons salt

Directions:

1. Add the herb leaves to the food dehydrator.
2. Dehydrate at 135 deg. F for 8 hours.
3. Transfer the dried leaves to a food processor.
4. Stir in the sugar and salt.
5. Storage suggestions: store in a mason jar with a lid.

Tip: you can also skip the sugar and salt and simply mix the dried herbs.

Per serving: Calories: 98kcal; Fat: 12g; Carbs: 16g; Protein: 8g

111. Garlic Powder

Preparation time: 15 minutes
Cooking time: 12 hours
Servings: 2
Ingredients:

- 6 heads of garlic, cloves separated, peeled and sliced

Directions:

1. Spread the garlic slices in the food dehydrator.
2. Dry at 125 degrees f for 12 hours.
3. Transfer the dried garlic into a blender or spice grinder.
4. Storage suggestions: sift the mixture before storing. Store the garlic powder

in an airtight spice jar. Keep it in a cool and dry area.

Per serving: Calories: 98kcal; Fat: 2g; Carbs: 16g; Protein: 8g

112. Powdered Ginger

Preparation time: 15 minutes
Cooking time: 8 hours
Servings: 5
Ingredients:

- 5 pieces ginger, sliced

Directions:

1. Put the ginger in the food dehydrator.
2. Dry at 95 degrees f for 8 hours.
3. Transfer the dried ginger to a food processor or spice grinder.
4. Grind the dried ginger into powder.
5. Storage suggestions: store in a mason jar.

Tip: use a mandoline slicer to slice the ginger.

Per serving: Calories: 75kcal; Fat: 3g; Carbs: 5g; Protein: 10g

113. Onion & Garlic Powder Mix

Preparation time: 20 minutes
Cooking time: 12 hours
Servings:
Ingredients:

- 5 cloves garlic, peeled and sliced
- 1 onion, sliced

Directions:

1. Place the garlic and onion slices in the food dehydrator.
2. Dehydrate at 135 degrees f for 12 hours.
3. Transfer to a spice grinder.
4. Grind until powdery.
5. Storage suggestions: store in a mason jar.

Tip: slice the onion and garlic thinly before dehydrating.

Per serving: Calories: 75kcal; Fat: 3g; Carbs: 5g; Protein: 10g

114. Kimchi Powder

Preparation time: 5 minutes
Cooking time: 12 hours
Servings: 5
Ingredients:

- 2 cups kimchi

Directions:

1. Add the kimchi to the food dehydrator.
2. Dehydrate at 155 degrees f for 12 hours.
3. Add the dried kimchi to a spice grinder, blender or food processor.
4. Process until powdery.
5. Storage suggestions: store the powder in an empty spice jar.

Tip: dehydrate longer if there is still moisture after 12 hours.

Per serving: Calories: 76kcal; Fat: 5g; Carbs: 5g; Protein: 3g

115. Thyme, Garlic, Rosemary & Lemon Herb Mix

Preparation time: 15 minutes
Cooking time: 8 hours
Servings: 5
Ingredients:

- ½ cup thyme leaves
- 6 cloves garlic, peeled
- ½ cup rosemary leaves
- 2 teaspoons lemon zest

Directions:

1. Put all the ingredients in a food processor.
2. Pulse until well mixed.
3. Add the mixture to the food dehydrator.
4. Dry at 135 degrees f for 8 hours.

5. Storage suggestions: store in a mason jar.

Tip: This recipe can also use garlic powder instead of garlic slices.

Per serving: Calories: 43kcal; Fat: 14g; Carbs: 5g; Protein: 14g

116. Parsley, Oregano, Basil, Thyme & Red Pepper Herb Mix

Preparation time: 15 minutes
Cooking time: 8 hours
Servings: 5
Ingredients:

- 2 tablespoons fresh oregano leaves
- 2 tablespoons fresh parsley leaves
- 2 tablespoons fresh basil leaves
- 1 tablespoon fresh thyme leaves
- 1 teaspoon lemon zest
- 1 teaspoon red pepper, sliced

Directions:

1. Combine all the ingredients in a bowl.
2. Add to the food dehydrator.
3. Dehydrate at 135 deg. F for 8 hours.
4. After dehydrating the herbs and spices, transfer them to a food processor.
5. Pulse until powdery.
6. Storage suggestions: store in a glass jar with a lid.

Tip: you can also use red pepper flakes for this recipe.

Per serving: calories15kcal; Fat: 13g; Carbs: 2g; Protein: 1g

117. Lemon Powder

Preparation time: 30 minutes
Cooking time: 12 hours
Servings: 5
Ingredients:

- Peel from 6 lemons

Directions:

1. Add the lemon peels to the food dehydrator.
2. Dehydrate at 95 degrees f for 12 hours.
3. Transfer to a food processor.
4. Pulse until powdered.
5. Storage suggestions: store in sealable plastic bags.

Tip: you can stir in garlic powder for lemon garlic mix.

Per serving: Calories: 85kcal; Fat: 13g; Carbs: 32g; Protein: 11g

118. Green Onion Powder

Preparation time: 10 minutes

Cooking time: 12 hours

Servings: 12

Ingredients:

- 1/2 lb. green onions

Directions:

1. Wash the green onions, cut off the white bottoms and slice the green parts into 1/2-inch pieces.
2. Place ParaFlexx Screens on the racks of your Food dehydrator and set it to 115F. Evenly distribute the chopped green onion on the screens forming a single layer.
3. Dehydrate for 12 hours or until all the onions are completely dried. Transfer the contents to a blender and pulse until you have a fine powder. Store in jars or a zipper-lock bag.

Per serving: Calories: 6kcal; Fat: 0g; Carbs: 1.4g; Protein: 0.4g

119. Homemade Chili Powder

Preparation time: 15 minutes

Cooking time: 5 to 6 hours

Servings: 24

Ingredients:

- 12 red chili peppers

Directions:

1. Place ParaFlexx Screens on the racks of your Food Dehydrator.

2. Carefully slice the chili peppers into thin strips. Note: The heat in your chili powder will depend on how much pith and seed you allow staying with the peppers. Suppose you want super-hot powder to keep the seeds and pith. For less spicy powder discard most of the seeds and pith.

3. Lay the peppers (and seeds and pith if desired) on the screens and set your Food dehydrator to 115F.

4. Dehydrate for 5-6 hours or until the peppers are completely dried. Transfer the contents of your Food dehydrator to a blender and pulse until a rough powder forms. Store in jars or zipper-lock bags.

Per serving: Calories: 1kcal; Fat: 0g; Carbs: 0.2g; Protein: 1g

Conclusion

Food drying is one of the oldest known methods of preserving food. Before there were grocery stores in every town and refrigerators in almost every home in the Western world, people had to come up with ways to make the harvest last into the winter months.

Our not-so-distant ancestors didn't have the convenience of grocery stores packed full of food imported from all over the world. If they wanted something, they had to grow it, buy it or trade for it, and they were largely at the mercy of Mother Nature. Fruits and vegetables weren't available year-round like they are now, so if people wanted to eat healthy food during the winter, they had to figure out ways to preserve the harvest to make it last year-round.

Back then, learning to dry and otherwise preserve food was something people had to know to survive, especially in harsh winter climates where it was impossible to grow to produce during the winter. Once the first frost set in, the ground would soon freeze solid. Intense cold and heavy snow made working the fields impossible. Food for the winter meant the difference between going to bed with a full stomach and slowly starving to death.

Now, take some time to sit down and think about preserving and storing food through dehydration, and have a particle understanding of the steps, tools, and techniques required for it. It will prove to be a significant change in your kitchen habits and lifestyles.

I believe that once you get a handle on the basic techniques, you can start growing and branching out into all kinds of other creative and novel endeavors of dehydrating foods. Just keep it simple at the start to gain enough experience. Once you become a grand maestro of dehydration and have a bunch of successful batches for the season, you can start playing with your creative ideas.

Remember, different foods have different timings and pre-treatments, so you must follow each step accordingly. Thoroughly drying the food is the key to successful dehydration. The presence of liquid in the dehydrated food turns it smelly and prone to many harmful bacteria such as E. coli. Also, selecting the best quality food ensures healthy and perfect dried food. Always prefer farmer's market for selecting fruits and vegetables as they provide the freshest food.

When you start with your creative ideas for dehydration, try limiting it to one or two new ingredients. Occasionally what appears to be a great idea, can muddle the flavors or emphasize the taste of the original fruit, vegetable or meat. Limiting the ingredients to one or two possible suspects will enable you to distinguish the culprit quickly.

Storing dried food is crucial to ensure the most extended shelf life. If not stored well, moisture, heat and oxygen decrease the shelf life and turn them bad sooner than expected. Store your dehydrated bounties in a cool and dry place, or in zip lock bags in the freezer to ensure longer shelf life. You can increase it by vacuum-sealing the bags and storing them in the freezer.

Before you get too enthusiastic about dehydrating batches upon batches of dried foods and pilling your pantry up with all your favorite foods, you need to look and practice all the rules of dehydration and have an idea for the space you have for storing; it will be of no use if you are drying more than the available space unless you intend to sell or gift them.

Finally, I wish you a happy dehydrating journey. Enjoy the process of drying your bounty and remember to follow safe practices while drying your food.

Let's promote organic food preservation.

Wish you success!

Made in United States
Troutdale, OR
07/30/2024

21647014R10133